"An excellent study; insightful, scholarly, sensible and written in a style that is a joy to read. Erudite and full of wisdom, the connections it makes between scripture and today's world offer much for careful reflection."

*Bishop Laurie Green*

—

"A real achievement. Written with a relaxed ease, it is a delight to read. I warmed to the way that the themes are teased out with an impressive range of theological, economic, biblical and literary reference. This is a book for Christians to get their teeth into without feeling hampered by a lack of theological or biblical education."

*Dr Bridget Nichols*

—

"This thoughtful and challenging book is a treasure trove. Hope is central to the Christian faith and these meditations on it contain much to nourish that hope. It deserves to be widely read."

*Dr John Inge, Bishop of Worcester*

—

"These thoughtful and prayerful reflections offer an admirable way of reflecting on the place of faith and hope in today's world."

*Professor Canon Robin Gill*

**Also by Peter Sills**

www.peter-sills.co.uk

*The Life Hidden with Christ in God*

*The Time Has Come: A Lenten Journey with St Mark*

*Ely Cathedral*

*Theonomics: Reconnecting Economics with Virtue & Integrity*
(co-edited with Andrew Lightbown)

*Médard's Journey: Following the Pilgrim Way to Santiago de Compostela*

# Light in the Darkness

*Exploring the Path of Christian Hope*

— PETER SILLS —

Sacristy
Press

**Sacristy Press**
PO Box 612, Durham, DH1 9HT

www.sacristy.co.uk

First published in 2020 by Sacristy Press, Durham



Sacristy Limited, registered in England & Wales, number 7565667

**British Library Cataloguing-in-Publication Data**
A catalogue record for the book is available from the British Library

ISBN 978-1-78959-100-2

# Contents

*The light shines in the darkness,*
*and the darkness has never overcome it.*

*John 1:5*

# Preface

To be human is to hope, and what we hope for shapes our lives. Saint Paul said hope is one of the things that last for ever, and the most poetic and prayerful expression of the Christian hope is to be found in the Advent Antiphons, the praises of Jesus sung on the seven days before Christmas. They have been described as some of the most beautiful prayers ever written, and they inspired this exploration. The antiphons are familiar to Christians in a versified form through the hymn "O come, O come, Emmanuel!", and I had sung the hymn for many years before I came across the antiphons themselves. The images they use to speak of Jesus resonated with me, and so I decided to explore them. I had in mind an Advent book, a devotional preparation for Christmas, but I found that these prayers led me on a different journey, and central to that journey was the realization that the antiphons are prayers of hope, and that their message reaches beyond Advent, just as the message of the Incarnation reaches beyond Christmas.

The antiphons provide a good structure for the exploration of hope: they express a sustained and hopeful longing. Speaking of a hope that is both personal and social, they reflect the hopes of people in every age and of every faith: for truth, for justice, for freedom, for a new beginning, for light, for peace, and for love—seven hopes that are brought together in the one, great hope for God. My exploration led me to link them with the ten I AM sayings of Jesus in the Gospel of John and the Book of Revelation. These sayings affirm that in Jesus the hopes expressed in the antiphons are fulfilled. Explored together they help us to enter more deeply into the meaning of the Incarnation, to see more clearly how Jesus fulfils our hopes, and the difference it makes to our lives if we put our hope in him.

While much seems dark and discouraging in today's world, there is also much that points to the light, much that is both encouraging and hopeful, and this exploration of hope is written out of my conviction that the Christian understanding of both the human person and human society offers the best way forward out of our present confusions. At a time when Christianity is often portrayed in negative terms, it is important to stress the positive vision that it offers, and its potential to shape hopeful lives. While Christians do not have all the answers, and indeed have been shamed by the all-too-human failings that have led to deeply grievous and shocking abuses of power and authority, we remain the guardians of a treasure that offers hope both to individuals and to the world. When we transcend the temptation to reduce religion to no more than a badge of identity, or to treat it as a source of power, and allow the love of God proclaimed by Jesus to shape our values and our perspectives, we find, I believe, a deep source of hope. And now, in the midst of the coronavirus pandemic (as this book goes to press), we find ourselves living in a time when we need to draw on that deep source of hope. It is a time unique in our history; a time of profound re-evaluation of the way we live; a time of rediscovery within ourselves of virtues like solidarity, that many have thought outmoded. I have been able to add a few references to the effect of the pandemic, but its relevance to an exploration of hope hardly needs stressing.

My thanks to Dr Matthew and Dr Hilary Lavis, who read the first draft and offered many helpful comments; also to my former colleague at Ely, Bishop John Inge, and to Professor Robin Gill, Bishop Laurie Green, Dr Bridget Nichols, the Revd Nicol Kinrade, and the Revd Dr Caroline Currer for reading and commenting on later drafts as the book took shape. I owe a special debt of gratitude to my friend the Revd Dr Dan Stevick, sadly no longer with us, and to the many other scholars whose work has led me to new insights and understandings. Above all, my thanks to my wife Helen for her unfailing support and encouragement.

**Peter Sills**

# The Advent Antiphons

The praises of Jesus known as the Advent Antiphons are sung at Evening Prayer in the second half of Advent, as refrains before and after the Magnificat, the Song of Mary. These are the days of "The Great Os", beginning with *O Sapientia* on 17 December and ending with *O Emmanuel* on 23 December. Although the antiphons have an ancient pedigree, it is not known who composed them. They are referred to by Boethius, a Roman senator and philosopher (*c.*AD 480–542), in the sixth century, so clearly they had been written by then, and probably many years earlier. I imagine that a monk of the Early Church composed them originally for the Advent liturgy of his monastery; other monasteries would have copied them, and in time they were taken up more widely, since by the eighth century they were used at Vespers in Rome. Over the centuries other hands have contributed, and the number of antiphons has varied: there were once as many as twelve, but they have now settled at seven. Composed in Latin, the texts vary a little in translation; the version used in this book follows the general consensus:

*O Wisdom, from the mouth of the Most High;*
*you reign over all things to the ends of the earth*
*and dispose them by the power of your love;*
*come and teach us the way of truth.*

*O Adonai, and Head of the House of Israel;*
*you appeared to Moses in the fire of the burning bush*
*and you gave him the law on Sinai;*
*come with outstretched arm and ransom us.*

*O Scion of Jesse, standing as a sign among the nations;*
*before you kings will keep silence,*
*and peoples will summon you to their aid;*
*come and set us free and delay no more.*

*O Key of David and Sceptre of the House of Israel;*
*you open and none can shut, you shut and none can open;*
*come and free the captive from prison.*

*O Morning Star,*
*Splendour of the Light eternal and bright Sun of Justice;*
*come and enlighten all who dwell in darkness*
*and in the shadow of death.*

*O King of the Nations;*
*you alone can fulfil their desires;*
*Cornerstone, you make opposing nations one;*
*come and save us, whom you formed from clay.*

*O Emmanuel,*
*Hope of the nations and their Saviour;*
*come and save us, Lord our God.*

# Prologue

*Hope is a thing given,*
*so that a more lovely thing can be.*
*— John Masefield —*

## The Praises of Hope

The practice of counting the years from the date of Jesus' birth took time to become established. It was devised in AD 525 by the Scythian monk Dionysius Exiguus, who wished to move away from the secular system then in use, but it did not become widespread until the eighth century. The coming of Jesus was an event utterly without precedent, so profound in its meaning, and so fundamental in its nature, that it was eventually acknowledged that the only adequate way to mark it was to restart the calendar; time had indeed begun again. The apostle Paul described the world into which Jesus was born as "without God and without hope", and basic to the sense of a new beginning was a rekindling of hope. At Christmas Jesus is hailed as the Christ, the One anointed of God, the Light of the world. In his life and teaching, his death and resurrection, Christians have found a source of hope that is life-changing. What it means to hope in Christ is beautifully expressed in the Advent Antiphons which hail Jesus as the Saviour and pray for the fulfilment of the hope that his coming makes real. We may think of them as the praises of hope.

The hopes that the antiphons express have an eternal quality; the seven hopes are those of people in every age: for truth, justice, freedom, a new beginning, light, peace, and love. Those who composed them drew on some significant Old Testament images, particularly from the Book of Isaiah, the work of several hands stretching over more than two centuries.[1] The three principal authors spoke respectively at times of crisis, suffering, and opportunity in the story of Israel—each, in a different way, a time of hope. What we see in their prophecies, and in those of other prophets like Hosea, Amos, and Jeremiah, is not a narrow, personalized faith, but one that informs all aspects of life, public as well as private, political as well as personal. It is to these prophecies that the first Christians turned in order to understand the meaning of the coming of Jesus, and the authors of the antiphons did the same. They recognized the picture of God portrayed in the prophetic images as having been fulfilled in Jesus. He was none other than the human face of the eternal God of hope.

Reflecting on these Old Testament images, the extent to which the antiphons express a *public* hope becomes apparent. They are so much more than beautiful personal prayers for wisdom, light, and love; they are also a sustained cry for justice, freedom, and peace, uniting the witness of the prophets of the Old Testament with the good news of the New Testament, and giving voice to our hope for a better world. They connect the Christian hope in Christ to its Jewish roots, reminding us of the extent to which we Christians have made our faith a private thing, losing contact with its bearing on social, political, economic, and business life—though for many years now the Church has striven to regain that connection. They focus the basic question of the faith revealed in both Testaments: Who comes first, God or me? The common good or our individual wants and ambitions? Too often we let our personal desires and our moral and political preferences shape our faith, but if we really want God to come first, then our faith should shape our lives, our ethics, our relationships, and our politics; and it is in our political and business affairs that this challenge is most demanding. In all areas of life, but with particular urgency today in our public and business life, faith poses deeper questions than those with which we generally feel comfortable, questions about purpose and destiny. So, for example, in *Faith in the Public Square*, Rowan Williams argues that in the economic sphere faith obliges us to question the "nostrums" of recent decades, asking persistently the awkward question of what we need growth *for*. What model of wellbeing do we actually assume in our economics? As he says, "Without an answer to that, we enter just the 'virtual reality' atmosphere that has created (and maintained) financial disaster in the last few years."[2] If we are going to be realistic about our hopes, then these questions cannot be avoided and, as I show in this exploration, the

Christian faith offers answers that are distinctively deeper than those of the secular world, answers which derive from the truth of God revealed in Jesus. Wherever we place ourselves on the moral and political spectrum, this is the standard by which we are judged, and—this is the hard part—if we do not see things as God sees them, it is for us to adjust our outlook. It has always been a huge challenge, and it is particularly challenging in today's world where powerful forces are ranged against it, even among Christians.[3]

The way in which faith has become a private matter would make no sense to Isaiah or the other prophets whose words inspired the antiphons. Their call is for a faith active in the public square, and not simply in our private lives, and their hope for the coming of the Messiah was a universal hope—not just for the salvation of Israel but for all nations. Familiarity has dulled the meaning of the first petition of the Lord's Prayer: "Your kingdom come, your will be done, *on earth as it is in heaven*." The coming of heaven on earth *is* the good news that Jesus proclaimed, and this is the heart of the Christian hope. For too long we have kept private virtue separate from public values. If we wonder why our hopes are not fulfilled, it is, I believe, largely because we live our lives in separate compartments; if our hopes are to be fulfilled, we need to live a more integrated life. Faith is one, and hope is one; what we do and believe in the marketplace cannot be separated from what we do and believe in the holy place.

## The Context of Hope

Hope does not exist in a vacuum, and the ideas that shape today's world and its hopes date from the Enlightenment of the eighteenth century. The separation between the sacred and secular which it brought about gave rise to the way in which life is now lived in separate compartments. It was, in its own way, a new beginning, and it led to new hopes of freedom, equality, and a fairer world. Those hopes have only been partially fulfilled, and for many remain unfulfilled. Pankaj Mishra has described the two centuries that have followed as the "Age of Anger".[4] This should come as no surprise because the aim of the Enlightenment was not fairness and social justice, but a change in those who exercised power: from royalty, aristocracy, and the Church to the newly rising entrepreneurial and intellectual classes. Voltaire, perhaps the foremost Enlightenment thinker, notably did not argue for social justice or universal suffrage; the hope he offered was for the few, not for the many. With the notable exception of Rousseau, Enlightenment thinkers were not interested in social equality or representative democracy; the liberty they proclaimed meant freedom and social mobility for the man of talent. As Voltaire pointedly remarked, "We have never claimed to enlighten shoemakers and servant girls." He believed that a powerful ruler was still needed, not only to check ecclesiastical, aristocratic, and corporate power, but also to repress the ignorant and superstitious who threatened enlightened civilization. Voltaire himself rose from a humble background to a position of great influence, advising—among others—the Russian Empress Catherine the Great; he also became successful in business, and died a very wealthy man. His life epitomizes both his own philosophy and modern dreams and ambitions for wealth and power; but these dreams and ambitions, by their very nature, will only ever be realized by the few, an outcome that flows ineluctably from the economic system on which they rest, shaped by the Enlightenment principles of individual autonomy and utilitarian ethics.

Mishra traces the events since the eighteenth century through which the anger caused by the frustration of the hope for a fairer world has been manifested. Anarchists, nationalists, communists, fascists, and Nazis have all played a part in that explosion of anger, and in recent years we have seen it explode in events as diverse as the feminist movement, the Arab Spring, and the growth of Al-Qaeda and ISIS. We have seen it also in atrocities committed by individuals like Timothy McVeigh and Anders Breivik, in the election of populist leaders in the USA, India, Turkey, Hungary, Brazil, and elsewhere, and in the vote for Brexit in the UK. These events are a continuation in our own age of the unrest that has marked European society for over two hundred years, and which has now become global. Since the 1990s "a democratic revolution of aspiration" has swept across the world, but this aspiration remains unfulfilled. While it is true that under liberal regimes living standards have risen and the quality of life has dramatically improved (halving, for example, the number of people living in poverty), the benefits have been distributed in a way that is grossly unequal, particularly between the developed nations and the rest of the world. In 2014, *The Economist* said that on the basis of IMF data, emerging economies—in other words, most of the world's population—might have to wait three centuries in order to catch up with the West. No wonder the anger is global. The paradox of liberalism is that while it has brought about the greatest escape from deprivation, it has at the same time created the greatest sense of alienation. While the anger of some is about unfulfilled dreams of wealth, power, and status, for most people it is simply about wanting to live a decent life with a sense of personal worth and dignity, access to good housing, education, employment, and healthcare, being able to provide adequately for your family, and feeling that your opinion counts. What the last two decades have shown is that the sense of alienation is not confined to the developing world; increasingly in "Western" countries the same angry feelings are being expressed, often violently, as the gap between the rich and the rest, and between men and women, is not addressed.

### *Ressentiment*

Any exploration of hope has to take the Age of Anger seriously and seek to understand its nature. It is best conveyed by the French term *ressentiment*, which conveys something more complex than simple resentment or envy, though these play their part. More particularly, *ressentiment* describes the sense of hostility directed towards the cause of a person's frustration. It arises out of being placed unfairly in an inferior position and the inability to do anything to improve it, coupled with a justified sense of personal worth and dignity that is being wrongly denied. *Ressentiment* leads to a denial of the values of those who are the cause of the sense of hopelessness, and to the adoption of a morally superior position which is used to justify any action taken in revenge. This intense mix of envy, humiliation, and powerlessness is seen clearly in the actions of groups like al-Qaeda, and so-called "domestic terrorists" like McVeigh and Breivik. The resort to violent action is justified by a superior moral or theological position based on religious, nationalistic, and racist grounds.

Globalization feeds *ressentiment*, as people with very different pasts are herded into a common present where cultural differences are obliterated. For example, the Islamic idea of the *umma*, the worldwide community of Muslims, which engenders a sense of solidarity that transcends nationalism and speaks of the duty of all Muslims to support one another in need, struggles to survive in a global economic system that places individual and corporate interests above the common good. As Rowan Williams observed in a lecture given in 2001, "We have to acknowledge that areas of our world feel that they have been invaded by our culture, conscripted into enterprises they have not chosen, and had their values disregarded, sometimes casually and unthinkingly, sometimes, they believe, with active hostility or contempt . . . The insecurity that globalization exports to so many weaker countries has come home to roost with a vengeance."[5]

The result, to use philosopher Hannah Arendt's phrase, is "negative solidarity", seen particularly among educated young men who have abandoned the most traditional sectors of their societies and succumbed to the fantasies of consumerism—mediated through films, television, and social media—without being able to satisfy them. Their consumerist ambitions have foundered because predictions of growth from left, right, and centre alike have routinely failed to take into account limiting factors like finite geographical space and natural resources, and fragile ecosystems. Globalization has produced a unified economic system but has not brought about a united society: unification is a technical matter, while unity is a moral matter. Mishra comments: "The modern religions of secular salvation have undermined their own main assumption: that the future would be materially better than the present. Nothing less than this sense of expectation, central to modern political and economic thinking, has gone missing today, especially among those who have themselves never had it so good."[6] The longer the cry of the people for a unity in which all are respected goes unheard, a unity where there is mutual support rather than the exploitation of the weak by the strong, the more the dark side of *ressentiment* will force itself upon us in violent action and protest.[7]

**Spiritual vacuum**

The conclusion to which we are drawn is that for too long we have placed our hopes on the wrong things, and in the wrong people and ideas. It is not only religious commentators who take this view; secular thinkers like

John Gray also point to the inadequacy of Enlightenment humanism and rationalism when it comes to explaining today's world.[8] For very many people, and no longer in the non-Western world alone, the future is dark, but we rightly reject the idea that some alleviation of the darkness is all that we can hope for; there must be a path to the light.

Although Mishra does not offer a solution to the crisis that he analyses, it is notable that he ends by drawing attention to the *spiritual* diminishment of the society built upon Enlightenment ideas. The advent of the self-affirming individual who, opening up new possibilities of human mastery, paved the way to a world free from superstition and belief in God, to the new age of reason, science, and commerce, has cut society adrift from its spiritual roots. Almost a century ago, Eric Voegelin argued that the spiritual substance of Western society had diminished to vanishing point, and that the vacuum did not show any signs of refilling from new sources.[9] I would put it differently: it is not that society gave up on religion, it is rather that it adopted a new religion, based on the belief that continuous material progress would usher in the new age; but this new religion, lacking theological foundations and any notion of transcendent authority, has foundered. Nevertheless, people routinely say they are spiritual rather than religious, indicating that while they have a sense of a reality beyond the material, they no longer look for it in any of the established faiths. We humans are unable to live in a spiritual vacuum, and if the new religion has foundered, then another must be sought. The economic stress on autonomy and choice has shaped this search; the result in the so-called millennial generation is a pick-and-mix approach fed by the resources available on the internet. For this generation, their religion (though they would not use that word) is a reflection of their own self.

If we want to regain some kind of spiritual rootedness, we have to be clear about what we are seeking. The idea of the spiritual has to be rescued from its general understanding as something added on to life *as it is*, a dimension of life that somehow will provide relief from our feelings of hopelessness and frustration. Similarly, people express an interest in "spirituality" as though it were an entity with some kind of independent existence. I take spirituality to mean something rather different. Our spirituality is the core of our being; it is what shapes the whole of our life, our whole way of being in the world. Spirituality is not just a religious thing confined to "spiritual" people. To be human is to have a spirit, the animating, life-giving part of our being, connecting our beliefs and our behaviour, our character and our motivations. Our spirituality is the way our spirit expresses itself. Tom Jordan OP, a Dominican friar, described it as "a particular way of living and doing things". Spirituality, he says, "derives from the coming together of two things, a person's life and a set of beliefs and practices. Spirituality does not exist on its own apart from the person (or group) who lives and practises it."[10]

There are many kinds of spirituality, religious and secular. The new materialistic religion has its own spirituality, its own "way of living and doing things", its own essence and motivating force. We focus on the wrong task if we talk of the need to *regain* our spirituality; what we need to do is to *transform* it. The prevailing materialistic, human-centred spirituality needs to be transformed into one that is shaped by other values and motivations, one that, above all, reflects the wholeness of life and rejects its compartmentalization. Mishra ends his "history of the present" with a call for "some truly transformative thinking, about both the self and the world".[11] Saint Paul would respond, as he did before the Court of the Areopagus in Athens, "What you seek I now reveal to you." Following him, we may be bold in affirming that it is precisely in transforming our spirituality that the Christian faith has much to offer. The world may seem dark, but as I endeavour to show in this exploration of hope, Christian insights about both the nature of the human person and the nature of human society provide a good map to help us find a path to the light.

## Hope in Christ

Christian hope is usually thought of as a hope for the life to come: for a place in heaven, as it were. This was very much the medieval hope, and it was a consistent strand of Jesus' teaching, but not the only one and arguably not the predominant one. I noted above that in the Lord's Prayer he teaches us to pray for the kingdom to come on earth *as it is in heaven*. This is a different focus for hope: for this life rather than the life to come. The Greek word generally translated as "kingdom" has a more dynamic sense, conveyed better by the phrase "kingly rule", a power that liberates and makes possible a new reality. Under the kingly rule of God, it is God's will that is determinative for all human relationships—political, commercial, social, and personal. The Dutch theologian Edward Schillebeeckx put it like this: "The kingdom of God is a new relationship of human beings to God, with as its tangible and visible side a new type of liberating relationship between men and women, within a peaceful, reconciled society."[12] The kingly rule of God is about transformative relationships; it is what overcomes *ressentiment*; it is what unites the sacred and the secular. It is seen in what Jesus did, particularly in restoring to human society those who were excluded: public sinners, tax collectors, lepers—everyone considered to be "unclean". Jesus, in his own person, embodied this new relationship; as Schillebeeckx says, there is an inner connection between message and proclaimer.[13] We hope above all for the advent of the kingly rule of God here on earth; as the Christian Aid slogan put it, "We believe in life before death." The Christian hope is not just for personal salvation, but also for the salvation of the world. This two-fold hope is reflected in the antiphons: in the world Jesus is hailed as Lord and law-giver, the source of freedom, the one who will reconcile those who are divided, and—at the same time—for each person he is hailed as the source of truth, enlightenment, and forgiveness. Our hopes for justice and peace are one with our hopes for forgiveness and peace of mind. Jesus is the cornerstone upon whom all our hopes rest, revivifying them with his Spirit. In him we find the path that leads to the light.

### Hope and optimism

To be human is to hope. Paul said that hope is one of the three things that last for ever (*1 Corinthians 13:13*), and Alexander Pope said that "hope springs eternal in the human breast", but I do not think they were speaking of quite the same thing. We use the word hope in several senses: at its most superficial, hope is wishing that things will turn out all right, like hoping for a fine day. At another level, hope is the expectation of something desired which, I think, is what Pope had in mind, and it is the frustration of hope in this sense that has produced the Age of Anger, particularly because the frustrated hopes are legitimate expectations that people have a right to be fulfilled. There is, though, a third sense which takes the idea of hope to a yet deeper level, and that is as a motivating force which underlies human striving. This is the hope of which the poet John Masefield spoke towards the end of his life when he said, "Hope is a thing given, so that a more lovely thing can be." Here, hope has a dynamic quality, it is a source of motivation and creativity, akin to the kingly rule of God. It is in this sense that Paul speaks of hope, uniting it with love and faith, two other powerful sources of motivation. Hope understands that the coming of the kingdom is not guaranteed by any doctrine of progress or theory of evolution. God may be "working his purpose out", as the hymn says, but in this "working out" we are his[14] co-creators; called to work with him, embracing that which is difficult but possible to attain, that a more lovely thing can be.

Thus, to hope in Christ is more than being optimistic. Optimism looks on the bright side, entertaining only the possibility of success and refusing to entertain the possibility of failure. Optimism is disinclined to take the world as it is; hope, by contrast, does just that. It accepts that things frequently do not work out for the best; it accepts the failures and defeats familiar in human life, and yet affirms that there are possibilities of good that are worth striving for. In this sense hope is a virtue, an inner strength or disposition of the will, that shapes the way we approach the whole of life. It is hope that kept the peace process going in Northern Ireland despite all the setbacks and disappointments, and still keeps it alive today. It is hope that sustains those who work for effective measures to combat climate change despite the forces ranged against them; it is hope that inspires those who work to find a cure for cancer and other major diseases; and it is hope that keeps love alive in the face of betrayal. In a sceptical world, hope sustains those who live by faith; it keeps us going when optimism fails. John Macquarrie draws out the contrast between hope and optimism: "Optimism is a philosophy that misses the ambiguity of the world and fails to consider seriously its evil and negative features . . . [It] is frequently brash, arrogant, complacent and insensitive." Hope is different; it is vulnerable, tentative, sensitive, and compassionate. In contrast to the optimisms of the world, "true hope lives in the awareness of the world's evils, sufferings and lacks. Hope must remain vulnerable to evidences that count against it, humble in face of the evils that have to be transformed, and, above all, compassionate toward those whose experience has been such that their hopes have grown dim or have even been dissolved in despair."[15] Hope both provides the vision of a better, fairer world and enables us to work for its realization. As Jürgen Moltmann said, hope hears the voice of the one who said, "Behold, I make all things new."[16]

### Hope and faith

"By faith we find the path, through hope we are kept on it."[17] We see this clearly in the biblical story of Israel which is founded on two epic journeys, neither of which, to those who undertook them, can have appeared to have had an assured outcome. Abraham is called to move from his own country, leaving his kin and his father's house, to a new country that the LORD will show him. And he sets out with no more than a promise to keep him going: "I shall make you into a great nation; I shall bless you and make your name so great that it will be used in blessings" (*Genesis 12:1–2*). Moses, likewise, is called to lead the Israelites from slavery in Egypt to freedom in the promised land. Just what it meant to be led on by hope came home to me when I followed the journey of the Exodus from Mount Sinai through Jordan to the Dead Sea on the border with Israel. The Israelites left Egypt believing that they would soon occupy a new homeland; the journey actually took many years, and many were the times when they wished they had never begun and turned against Moses, putting their hope in things of their own devising like the golden calf.[18] But Moses kept going; his hope was on God. He hoped that despite all the setbacks and the suffering, and the rebellion of the people, God would be true to his promise to bring them to their promised land, and his hope was fulfilled. Moses' hope was almost tangible, something real, something to hang on to. It was not simply a personal determination to accomplish his mission; it certainly was not optimism, but something given to him that he could rely on: "Follow my way," says the LORD, "and I will accomplish my purpose through you." In these journeys, faith and hope are seen to be symbiotic: God discloses himself to his people in the form of a promise in which they put their faith, and at the same time the promise contains the hope that motivates them. Promise is future-oriented and, as Moltmann says, gives a dynamic quality to both faith and hope—the promise is not for an old world to be recovered, but for a new world to be discovered: "It is from promise that there arises that element of unrest which allows of no coming to terms with a present that is unfulfilled."[19]

We forget just how much of the history of Israel is the history of a captive people. The individual hope for liberation was one with the national hope for freedom; the story of Israel teaches us that the personal and the political belong together, joined in a single continuum. Hope in the Bible is not confined to individuals; it is also a social hope. A purely individual hope would have made no sense to the Israelites, neither in Moses' day nor in Jesus' day—nor indeed for Israelis in our own day. When Cleopas and his companion walked to Emmaus, not knowing of the resurrection, their hopes dashed, they lamented, "we believed that he was the one who would liberate Israel" (*Luke 24:21*). The hope of Israel was always for a people, for a society where justice and peace would reign, expressed in the Hebrew word *shalom*, where the poor, the orphans, and widows were cared for, and in which each person could grow to his or her full potential. The antiphons express the depth of this communal longing; they hail Jesus not just as a personal saviour, but as the law-giver, judge, and peacemaker. Christian hope, likewise, is a total hope; it touches on all aspects of human life, both individual and social.

**The Sign of hope**

Hope goes before us like a light in the darkness and calls us to follow. Hope calls us to transcend ourselves in striving for the good. Hope is powerful, and because it is powerful, we need to be careful about on what or in whom we place our hopes. The Age of Anger has been marked by false hopes on a grand scale: anarchy, communism, fascism, liberalism and capitalism; the free market, science and technology—all have been offered as the harbingers of the new age, but that age has not dawned. It is not, of course, wrong to hope for material and political progress, nor for scientific and technological advances, but it is not enough to place our hopes in these things alone. It was, I believe, Bishop John V. Taylor who said that science must walk hand in hand with the Spirit, and that technology is safe only in the context of sacrifice. In other words, new ideologies and new technologies need to be offered to God, and their use directed by his Spirit, otherwise they will enslave rather than enhance our humanity, as we are only too aware. In 2003, the author John Le Carré said that he found it impossible to write hopeful fiction in today's world. The utterly inadequate response of national leaders to the challenge of climate change, the erosion of trust, ethical conduct, and good character in banking, in the care of the elderly, in the police and other public services, and the shocking revelations of the extent of child abuse have further weakened our hope. To Christians, indeed to all people of faith, the lesson is obvious. If we take ourselves as the measure of all things, as the Enlightenment taught us, then our hopes will fail; it is only by looking outside ourselves to a greater reality that we get the true measure of things and our hopes have a chance of being realized. Christians see in Jesus of Nazareth that greater reality, clothed in a form suitable to human understanding. As a son is often the image of his father, so the Son is the image of the Father. Jesus is the human face of the eternal God. The most important thing that he revealed was the true nature of God. In him we see the eternal, almighty, and ineffable God expressed in human form: he bears "the imprint of God's very being" (*Hebrews 1:3*). At the last supper, when Philip said to Jesus, "Show us the Father," Jesus replied: "Have I been all this time with you, Philip, and still you do not know me? Anyone who has seen me has seen the Father. Then how can you say, 'Show us the Father'? Do you not believe that I am in the Father, and the Father in me? I am not myself the source of the words I speak to you: it is the Father who dwells in me doing his own work" (*John 14:9–10*). As Bishop Michael Ramsey said, God is Christlike and in him there is no un-Christlikeness at all, a truth that John affirms when he speaks of the advent of Christ:[20]

> In him was life, and that life was the light of mankind. The light shines in the darkness and the darkness has never overcome it.
>
> *John 1:4–5*

To speak of Jesus is to speak of God, and the many references to him in this exploration of hope need to be understood in this way. Taking him as our Lord is to move towards the light, and to resist the temptation to give in to despair. Christian hope accepts the reality of darkness: "Christ has died," and sets against it another reality: "Christ is risen!" Jesus is the sign and symbol of our hope, because he transcends human life; he is the true sign of what we have it in us to become. He personifies our hope; he shows that out of failure and defeat God can bring new life, and to all who believe in him he gives the right to become children of God (*John 1:12*).

## Light in the Darkness

Light and darkness are universal spiritual images, and coming to faith is often described as moving from darkness to light. This is the movement with which the biblical story begins, and the divine command, "Let there be light!" echoes down the ages giving substance to our hopes. The overcoming of darkness by the light of Christ is one of the characteristic themes of the fourth Gospel. John describes Jesus as "the light that was coming into the world" (*John 1:9*), a light that the darkness will never overcome; it is a powerful image of hope. Jesus is the sign of God's new beginning, the fulfilment of the divine promises given to Abraham and Moses—and as the Gospel unfolds, the nature of that new beginning is made plain. John does this particularly in a series of seven signs (or miracles) and in seven sayings, each beginning with the words I AM. These sayings, together with three more in the Book of Revelation, reach back to one of the foundational dialogues of the Old Testament. When Moses asked God his name, the divine reply was elliptical; God answered, "I AM that I AM." So when Moses was asked by the Israelites who had sent him, he had to reply, "I am has sent me to you." (*Exodus 3:13–14*)[21] In the Old Testament the face of God is unknown; the divine name conceals the mystery of God. In the New Testament, however, God's face is known; in Jesus the divine mystery is revealed and made available in a form suitable to human sight and understanding. In the I AM sayings God himself is disclosed:

> I AM the bread of life.
> I AM the light of the world.
> I AM the door of the sheepfold.
> I AM the good shepherd.

I AM the resurrection and the life.
I AM the way, the truth, and the life.
I AM the true vine.
I AM the Alpha and the Omega.
I AM the offspring of David.
I AM the bright star of dawn.[22]

As Daniel Stevick has said, "The divine 'I'—while shrouded in mystery—is self-disclosed. God is met on God's own terms. 'I am' speaks of the self-existent one, the singular one, the one whose purposes come from within and will be carried out in faithfulness. 'I will prove myself to be what I will be.'"[23] These sayings declare that God in Jesus has disclosed himself to be the food that sustains us, and the light that gives life and guidance; he is the door that gives security, and the shepherd who provides protection and care; he both embodies the true human life, and is the agent of its transformation—not just in the transition from this life to the life to come, but also in the way we live our lives on earth. He is the true and living way that sets the standard by which we should live; like the branch of a vine, it is in fellowship with him that we find our true community and are able to bring forth good fruit in abundance. Like the bright star of the dawn, Jesus embodies our hope; he is David's greater son, the one to whom we look forward, no less than the author of time, alpha and omega, the beginning and the end, the Eternal.

Just as it takes time for the rising sun to brighten the sky, so the true significance of what God had done in Jesus took time to dawn. It was only after his death and resurrection that his birth acquired significance, and stories about him began to be told; and it was later still that Christians understood his coming to be the turning point of history, restarting the calendar from the day of his birth. As with all profound truth, the light of God dawns gradually in the human heart, and as it does, our memory reaches back to the events that heralded the dawn but were not noticed at the time, and gives them meaning. Thus, the first Christians went back to the words of Isaiah about a new branch flowering from the root of Jesse, the father of David (*Isaiah 11:1–10*), and understood them to refer to Jesus. In the same way, the Advent Antiphons take us back to the Old Testament and help us to understand the meaning of the Incarnation through its images. As these praises of hope are sung, the coming of Christ is believed, not known—anticipated, rather than celebrated. It may be dark, but in the darkness there are the first signs of light.

**Waiting**

As Israel discovered, those who hope must learn to wait. We, like the Israelites, live in an in-between time; God will not be hurried. Today we have seen his revelation in Christ, but we wait for the fullness of that revelation to be revealed (at the time often referred to as the Second Coming). Rowan Williams describes hope as not simply confidence in the future, but the confidence that past, present and future are held together in one relationship, and this, he says, means that those who hope must be marked by "a profound patience". He adds: "Only a Church that is learning patience can proclaim hope effectively."[24] Learning patience is counter-cultural, and in-between times are not comfortable, particularly in an age when so many of the old certainties have passed away. Life has a fragility which is hard to bear; relationships are tense and tentative, and the temptation is to put our hope in the wrong things, like economic growth, scientific progress, or military power. But economic forecasts turn out not to be dependable; science brings many benefits, but its very progress brings ethical dilemmas which threaten to confound us; terrorists undermine a security based on military power. We long for deliverance from these false gods, but "How long, O Lord, how long?"

T. S. Eliot explores the nature of hope in his poem "East Coker", which he links with the experience of waiting. He describes the in-between time in these words:

> I said to my soul, be still, and let the dark come upon you
> Which shall be the darkness of God. As, in a theatre,
> The lights are extinguished, for the scene to be changed
> With a hollow rumble of wings, with a
>     movement of darkness on darkness,
> And we know that the hills and the trees, the distant panorama
> And the bold imposing façade are all being rolled away . . .[25]

Just as in a play the darkness does not signify nothingness but a change of scene, so the darkness of God does not signify his absence but his unseen and unknowable activity. The mistake is to assume that we can guess what God is doing. But this is what we cannot do. All our time is in-between time, a time of waiting. Hope is not about putting our trust in a specific event or promise, even the promise of a Second Coming; hope is the conviction that God never ceases his work, that his love never fails; hope is walking with God even though we cannot see the way ahead; hope is the willingness to wait until his actions are revealed, as Eliot says:

> I said to my soul, be still, and wait without hope
> For hope would be hope for the wrong thing; wait without love
> For love would be love of the wrong thing; there is yet faith
> But the faith and the love and the hope are all in the waiting.[26]

Waiting, of course, is the one thing that we don't want to do. It is hard to wait in a society where the emphasis is on ever faster communication and instant results; where, like hapless athletes or pressured sales staff, you are measured only by your last performance. As Rowan Williams observes, these days we are short-termist, almost by compulsion; we are encouraged to assume that the solving of the problem immediately in front of us is what matters, and we lose track of the larger questions about the meaning and purpose of life.[27] History has been thinned out, and so the context of our waiting has atrophied. And yet learning to wait is the way of faith: "The faith and the love and the hope are all in the waiting." That's why the Church prescribes a time of waiting before the great festivals of Christmas and Easter; Advent and Lent make us wait and listen. Did not Jesus say, "Heaven and earth will pass away, but my words will not pass away" (*Mark 13:31*)? The things made by God, even heaven and earth, do not last for ever; God and his truth alone are eternal. These seasons give us time to reflect on where our hopes are truly placed. Are they placed on God alone and not on the fulfilment of any particular scheme or promise? Are we prepared to wait, even in the darkness, trusting simply that he is?

> Wait without thought, for you are not ready for thought:
> So the darkness shall be the light and the stillness the dancing.[28]

### Longing

Truth resists being projected into certainty, and paradox often characterizes our experience of life and our search for meaning. As we live from day to day, we have to hold together good and evil, light and darkness, certainty and doubt, joy and sorrow, life and death. Advent, the season of the antiphons, reflects this diurnal paradox: in the dead of winter we celebrate new life; in the darkness we hail the new light; in the one life we see salvation for all; in a particular story we see universal truth. Faith holds together these paradoxical symbols; we too need simply to hold on to them and to resist trying to resolve them, letting the tension between them draw us more deeply into the truth to which they point but do not exhaust.

This is the way of faith, and it needs reaffirming in a world where faith is in decline and hope hard to come by. Faith is not an opiate, but a foundation, a source of energy and strength, the expression of a deep longing within us that good will outlast evil, light will overcome darkness, joy overcome sorrow, and new life vanquish death. John Macquarrie put it well: "Death has not quenched hope. Unclear though the hope may be, there has always been a hope that has stood out against death. Life has seemed stronger than death, and in the face of the total threat of death there has arisen the total hope that even death can be transformed and made to contribute to life."[29]

We know that we have been seduced by the gods of the age, but we should know also that God alone is our true hope. Our hearts beat with his heart when we feel the futility of much of modern life, and when, in spite of it all, we refuse to give in to despair, because there are possibilities of good that are worth striving for. What keeps me going is my conviction that Jesus offers a better hope than the gods of the age. He alone is the fullest expression of what it means to be human; he offers a way of life that enables us to value both individual freedom and collective needs, and the inner strength to keep the one from dominating the other; he offers us the moral resources to contain the operation of the free market so that with justice and generosity it serves the common good; he enables us to connect science with the Spirit so that it works to enhance our humanity and not to destroy it. He is the human expression of the divine passion for the wholeness of creation; he alone can hold our hopes and fulfil them.

Longing is part of the spiritual life; it quickens our hope. The things we long for are the things that motivate us and give shape to our lives. We long to love and to be loved, for depth in our relationships, for a real sense of meaning and purpose in life, for the mess the world is in to be overcome, for justice and peace between the nations. Longing marks the beginning of a spiritual journey. When two of the disciples of John the Baptist asked Jesus where he was staying, he replied, "Come and see" *(John 1:39)*. The journey of hope is about moving to where Jesus is. It is in making that journey that our longings will be fulfilled, and thus the image of the journey is a recurring theme in this exploration.

The Advent Antiphons, these ancient praises and prayers of hope, express our longings, which have also been the longings of people in every age. As prayers they are timeless, and so speak afresh in every year and to everyone. They lead us towards the Life through which our longings are satisfied and our hope is made real. And what we see in that Life, above all, is what it means to love. The love that we see in Jesus of Nazareth is self-giving to the point of self-sacrifice, a bridge that others can cross. Love is the foundation of our hopes:

> Without love wisdom degenerates into mere cleverness; without love justice becomes dry and lifeless; without love roots wither and die; without love liberation is no more than the way into a new bondage; without love light is overcome by darkness; without love reconciliation is refused; without love hope gives way to despair.[30]

To love is to long. The antiphons call us to be longing, so that we may belong to the one in whom our hopes are fulfilled.

*O come Emmanuel,*
*Hope of the nations and their Saviour;*
*come and save us, Lord our God.*

1

# Living Way: The Hope for Truth

*O Wisdom, from the mouth of the Most High*
*you reign over all things to the ends of the earth*
*and dispose them by the power of your love;*
*come and teach us the way of truth.*

*I am the way, the truth, and the life.*

*I am the Alpha and the Omega.*

## Truth, Word and Wisdom

In a world of soundbites, alternative facts, and fake news, truth is in short supply; image and impression take centre stage—but even so, the hope for truth is not extinguished. It is the most fundamental of all our hopes, because without truth, without knowing how things really are, we lack a firm foundation upon which to build our lives and a reliable path to follow. So, appropriately, the first antiphon asks that we be led in the way of truth.

The question that immediately arises is: What is truth? Placed by John on the lips of Pontius Pilate, it is the most famous question in the Bible (*John 18:38*). To put it another way: what did Jesus have in mind when he said it is the truth that sets us free, and prayed that his disciples be consecrated in the truth (*John 8:32; 17:17*)? As I said in the Prologue, along with the other aspects of hope that are explored in this book, the Christian faith offers a distinctively deeper understanding of truth than that of ordinary usage. Generally we think of truth as reliable factual information, or as a firm theoretical foundation. This understanding is reflected in the Bible, especially in the Wisdom books, but more importantly the Bible also offers a deeper understanding of truth: the truth that lies at the heart of Jesus' confrontation with Pontius Pilate.

Pilate was clearly disturbed by the man who stood shackled before him. He tried to discover if Jesus was making a claim to kingship: "So you are the king of the Jews," he said. In response Jesus replied: "'King' is your word. My task is to bear witness to the truth. For this I was born; for this I came into the world, and all who are not deaf to truth listen to my voice." Pilate responded dismissively, "What is truth?" and terminated the interrogation. As so often in the fourth Gospel, two different understandings are juxtaposed: as Jesus is questioned by Pilate, it is clear that truth means very different things to each of them. Pilate's response to Jesus is curt, which James Moffatt brings out in his translation: "Truth!" said Pilate, "what does truth mean?" Pilate's reply is not so much a question as a dismissal. His conception of truth does not go beyond the practical, the facts and realities with which he had to deal, like the angry crowd that faced him and the need to avoid a riot. Had he been an educated Greek, he might have thought of truth in philosophical terms, but when Jesus speaks of truth, he has in mind something different from the conceptions of both Roman governors and Greek philosophers. For him truth is personal, something lived, something given, the source of life and love. As he said to Pilate, he came to bear witness to the truth, and he did so in the way he lived. In his person the truth stood before Pilate, but Pilate could not recognize it.

The truth to which Jesus bore witness is the greater reality in which all of life and the whole of the created universe are enfolded. It is at one and the same time both ineffable and personal; it addresses us through the person of Jesus and through the created world, and it is these two sources of truth that I explore in this chapter. We cannot apprehend this greater reality in its entirety, but we can glimpse it and follow it. Jesus is this greater reality, this foundational truth, expressed in the form of a human life. Truth in this sense is not so much apprehended as experienced, and it was the experience of this truth, in the unity of word and deed, of spirit and being, that characterized Jesus' life, that so impressed all who encountered him, and which confounded Pilate. The hope for truth leads us towards him, the way, the truth, and the life. So, to answer my question: when Jesus prayed that his disciples be consecrated in the truth, he was not asking that they be given solid factual information; he was asking that their lives be caught up in the whole message of God's love and glory that he had taught them. He asks, in effect, that God will gather them to himself and make them like him, drawing them, as a dedicated and compassionate people, into his own holiness and justice.[1] His prayer echoes that of the Psalmist:

> O send forth your light and your truth; let these be my guide.
> Let them bring me to your holy mountain,
> to the place where you dwell.
>
> *Psalm 43:3 (The Grail version)*[2]

It is this movement toward God that lies at the heart of the hope for truth and leads to its fulfilment. Truth as a foundation on which to build one's life is not a free-standing entity that can be discovered by philosophical or empirical enquiry; it is the gift of God. Truth in this deeper biblical understanding is not propositional, but personal; not static, but dynamic, active in the world. In the Second Letter of John, this is the truth of which John the Elder speaks in his opening greeting:

> To the lady chosen by God and to her children, whom I love in the truth, and not I alone but all who know the truth. We love you for the sake of the truth that dwells among us and will be with us for ever.
>
> *2 John 1–2*

The lady and her children were a local Christian congregation for which the Elder had pastoral responsibility. He is not, like an anxious lover, seeking to reassure them that his love is true, rather he is saying that their mutual love exists within a greater reality which sustains them and gives them their identity and their destiny. It is like the love that exists between those who have committed themselves to each other in marriage or companionship. The truth, John says, dwells among them; it has an almost tangible, personal quality, and he urges them to live by it. Truth in this sense is precisely what is denied by the soundbite culture, but for those who hope for truth it is what we have to learn to live by.

**Word of life: Spirit of power**

*O Wisdom, from the mouth of the most high.* The opening line of the antiphon brings together two dynamic and creative images, Wisdom and the Word, that speak of how we are led in the way of truth. The images come from an oracle of Isaiah of Babylon,[3] and were used by Jesus when he prayed that the disciples be consecrated by the truth. He ended his prayer with the affirmation: "your word is truth" (*John 17:17*). Before this he had assured them that the Spirit of truth (i.e. wisdom) would guide them into all the truth (*John 16:13*). The conception of the Word of God as the source of life is familiar to us from the opening words of John's Gospel: "In the beginning the Word already was . . . and through him all things came to be; without him no created thing came into being" (*John 1:1, 3*). This conception is both powerful and personal, and resonates with the opening words of Genesis which depict the Spirit of God brooding over the primal waters: the Spirit that is the source of life and order, the One through whose power the creation that God speaks comes into being. This identification of wisdom with the Holy Spirit is made explicitly in Ecclesiasticus: "I came forth from the Most High; and I covered the earth like a mist" (*Ecclesiasticus/Sirach 24:3, Jerusalem Bible*).

Both the biblical creation stories picture God working with the raw material that he had brought into being but which lacked form, a process beautifully described in the Book of Proverbs:

> The LORD created me the first of his works long ago,
>     before all else that he made.
> I was formed in the earliest times
>     at the beginning, before earth itself.
> I was born when there was as yet no ocean,
>     when there were no springs brimming with water,
>     before the mountains were settled in their place,
>     before the hills I was born, when as yet he had made
>     neither land nor streams nor the mass of the earth's soil.

When he set the heavens in place I was there,
  when he girdled the ocean with the horizon,
  when he fixed the canopy of clouds overhead
  and confined the springs of the deep,
  when he prescribed limits for the sea
  so that the waters do not transgress his command,
  when he made the earth's foundations firm.
Then I was at his side each day, his darling and delight,
  playing in his presence continually,
  playing over his whole world,
  while my delight was in mankind.

*Proverbs 8:22–31*

This poem describes the way a certain pattern and order—everything that is optimal for the emergence of life, as the scientists say—is embedded in creation. As the truth stood before Pilate in the person of Jesus, so the truth also stands before us in creation. The simple device of ascribing creation to the speech of God implies the most profound relationship: just as speech gives expression to will and desire, so the creation is the expression of the will and desire of God. God is the ultimate truth, the source and origin of all that is, the One in whom "we live and move and have our being", as Paul said (*Acts 17:28*). God's Word gives expression to God's Will through the power of God's Spirit, and the majestic opening of John's Gospel identifies Jesus as the living embodiment of the divine, creative wisdom: "So the Word became flesh; he made his home among us, and we saw his glory, such glory as befits the Father's only Son, full of grace and truth" (*John 1:14*).

Word and Spirit are inseparable, and the Bible presents them indivisibly as the Wisdom of God. This is something very different from the everyday conception of wisdom as the capacity to make right and sound judgements. Holy Wisdom is another way of speaking of the creative power of God, the source of all that is, which the antiphon describes metaphorically when it speaks of Wisdom reigning over all things to the ends of the earth, and disposing them (i.e. assigning them their place in the created order) by the power of love. Long before John wrote, the Psalmist rejoiced in the power of the divine Word, uttering a great shout of praise to the "voice of the LORD" which resounded on the waters, full of power and splendour (*Psalm 29*). As a creative power, wisdom is the gift that allows us to grasp the truth, or rather, it is the gift that allows us to be *grasped by* the truth. We read in the Wisdom of Solomon:

> She is the radiance that streams from everlasting light,
> the flawless mirror of God's active power,
> and the image of his goodness.
> . . . age after age she enters into holy souls,
> she makes them friends of God and prophets . . .
>
> *Wisdom 7:26–7*

Here, wisdom is not pictured as an abstract quality of mind, but as an active agent who touches our very being, uniting us with God. Again, we see wisdom as a metaphor for the Holy Spirit, the active power of God in the world. Wisdom, Word, and Spirit merge into one another; they are another way of speaking of the Holy Trinity, aspects of the same reality, and Jesus is their expression in human form; as Paul said, he is "the power of God and the wisdom of God" (*1 Corinthians 1:24*). Wisdom, Word, and Spirit lead us along the path of truth. The importance of this image of movement to the hope for truth cannot be overstated, whether it is described as following a star, walking a path, or growing in relationship, because it is through allowing ourselves to be led that we shall apprehend that truth is a journey and not a proposition, and our hope for truth will be fulfilled.

## True and Living Way

At the last supper, when Jesus sought to allay the disciples' anxiety about what would happen after his death, he used the same image of a journey, and to reassure them he said that they knew the way to where he was going. Thomas did not appreciate that Jesus was speaking metaphorically and responded that, as they did not know where he was going, how could they know the way. In reply Jesus said that he is himself the way, as he is also the truth, and the life (*John 14:6*). In what sense is Jesus the way? How we understand Jesus' reply depends, as Daniel Stevick pointed out, on whether *way*, *truth*, and *life* are three equal items in a list, or whether one of them is the subject which the other two qualify. Given the structure of the sentence, with the weight on the initial term *way* (the word that baffled Thomas), Stevick suggests that the subject is *the way*, and that the emphasis belongs on the start of the series. Jesus is speaking about making a journey for which he is a "reliable and vital way". Thus he is "the true way, as he is the true vine (*15:1*) and the true light (*1:9; 1 John 2:8*). He is the living way, as he is the living water (4:10) and the living bread (*6:48*)."[4] Moffatt's translation of Jesus' reply conveys this sense: "I am the real and living way." I find this reading helpful. The hope for truth will not be fulfilled simply by gaining information or knowledge—not even by knowing the theory of everything, the holy grail of physics. The hope for truth is fulfilled by travelling a way, through a personal relationship with the author of truth. This was one of the last things that Jesus taught the disciples. Through faith in him, he said, those who followed him would receive the gift of the Holy Spirit—the Spirit of truth—who, he promised, would lead them into all truth. The hope for truth is fulfilled by following a way, making a journey; and it is clear that this journey will include the disclosure of new truths:

> "There is much more that I could say to you, but the burden would be too great for you now. However, when the Spirit of truth comes, he will guide you into all the truth . . . "
>
> *John 16:12–13*

Allowing the Spirit to lead us is how we discover that truth is a journey, not a destination.

This understanding means that truth, like God, is ineffable, and our perception of it necessarily has a contingent quality. We see this in our close relationships: we may know someone intimately over many years, able to anticipate their thoughts and feelings, aware of their strengths and weaknesses, but however well we know them, in the depths of their being they remain a mystery. Our knowing does not exhaust their being; in a relationship of love there is always more to experience, more to delight in. Their truth is ineffable. We see the contingent quality of our perception of truth also in our own growth to maturity, as the "certainties" of youth give way to more mature and nuanced understandings; we see it in scientific discoveries, where new knowledge displaces the old, and established theories have to be revised or even abandoned. While we need, for practical purposes, to try to encapsulate truth in formulae, creeds, theories, and philosophies, we need also to appreciate their provisional nature, no more than work in progress, and to reject any claim of inerrancy. No century has been free from these corruptions of truth, and in the twentieth century we had them on a grand scale, from political and economic creeds like fascism, communism, and free-market capitalism to Scientology, Transcendental Meditation, personal growth, and dieting programmes. None have brought us to the promised land, though many have enriched their advocates. Truth resists being projected into the certainty of human propositions.

A contemporary Christian example is the argument in the Catholic Church about admitting those who are divorced to holy communion. At the heart of this dispute are two different conceptions of truth: on the one hand as a store of mysterious, unchanging, supernatural teachings, of which the hierarchy are the guardians and exponents, and on the other hand as a journey to be made, a person to encounter, which is the task of all the people of God. Pope Francis approaches the problem along the lines of the second understanding, incurring the wrath of those "who continue to find solace in the certitudes and clear lines of ecclesiastical authority typical of the neo-scholastic world".[5] There is, of course, more to this, including how to balance the Church's witness to the indissolubility of marriage with the need to reach out in mercy to those who have fallen short of the ideal. No one pretends that resolving these disputes is easy, but at least understanding truth as a journey to be made rather than a dogma to be defended indicates the hopeful direction of travel.

It seems to me that the Church has not learnt fully the lessons of the Reformation. On one of my pilgrimages I followed the last journey of Czech reformer Jan Hus from Prague to Constance. Hus' main concern was moral rather than doctrinal reform; he denounced the immoral lives of the clergy which made them unworthy holders of their offices, and argued that obedience was not due to a pope and prelates who did not conform their lives to the Scriptures. Rather than engage with him, the response was to condemn him, and in a show trial at the Council of Constance in 1415—which was a travesty of justice even by the standards of the time—he was condemned as a heretic and burnt at the stake. Pope John Paul II apologized for his death in 1999, implicitly acknowledging Hus as a martyr. His life held more truth than the lives of those who condemned him. The Reformed Churches have not learned either: protestants still divide and split over small issues of belief and denounce those who disagree. Despite the access of new knowledge that Jesus promised, the tendency is still to defend established power and dogma rather than to engage with criticism and make the journey into truth.

The Church is an easy target, but none of this is unique to Christianity; the same problem is encountered wherever truth is dogmatized and linked to the defence of authority. Islamist militants terrorize and execute those whose faith differs from theirs; scholars in all disciplines are anathematized when they question the academic consensus; political parties silence those who question the policy of the leadership (and not just in authoritarian regimes); business executives are dismissed when they differ in their understanding of corporate goals, and so on . . . Against such attitudes we have to insist that apart from God there is no absolute truth that we can know.

**Alpha and Omega**

Jesus is the true and living way because he was truly *grasped by the truth*, and this is seen in his teaching which showed a marked contrast to the conventional wisdom of the times, characterized by the search for the rational rule, "something permanently valid, something by which one can reckon and on which one can rely".[6] The Bible contains an extensive wisdom literature which reflects this search, but much of the teaching does not progress beyond popular maxims, as, for example:

> A wise son is his father's joy, but a foolish son is sorrow to his mother. No good comes of ill-gotten wealth; uprightness is a safeguard against death. Idle hands make for penury; diligent hands make for riches. A person who

> is wise takes commandments to heart, but the foolish talker comes to grief.
>
> *Proverbs 10:1,2,4,8*

While there is truth in these sayings, it is hardly the stuff that fulfils hope. The poet T. S. Eliot was unimpressed by the claims of wisdom uttered by "quiet-voiced elders, bequeathing us merely a receipt for deceit":

> . . . There is, it seems to us,
> At best, only a limited value
> In the knowledge derived from experience.
> The knowledge imposes a pattern, and falsifies,
> For the pattern is new in every moment
> And every moment is a new and shocking
> Valuation of all we have been.[7]

The patterns that our knowledge imposes (i.e. the way we interpret our experience) are of our own devising. Jesus offers us truth on an altogether different level. His teaching rose above "the knowledge derived from experience". It was not founded on human experience or the rational precepts of human beings, but on the conviction that God was both the beginning and the end of all that exists, a truth often reflected in the psalms, and memorably stated in the opening verses of the Book of Revelation: "'I am the Alpha and the Omega,' says the Lord God, who is, who was, and who is to come, the sovereign Lord of all" (*Revelation 1:8*). God is Alpha, the source and origin of all that is, and at the same time God is Omega, the final horizon of history and the ultimate reality existing at the end of time. In God, beginning and end become one, an eternal present. God is the pattern that does not falsify, the pattern that is new in every moment and which reveals the truth. Before this reality the only appropriate attitude is humility, for "the only wisdom we can hope to acquire is the wisdom of humility".[8]

Humility gives space for God to illuminate our knowing; it is an act of faith. Anselm of Canterbury, rephrasing a saying of Augustine of Hippo, put it memorably: "I believe so that I may understand." When we truly let God illuminate our knowing—when we let the truth grasp us—wisdom becomes the pursuit of Christlikeness. At this level we *know* that truth has an objective existence, bounding all we know and experience. This is something given, not achieved. It is out of this *knowing* that Jesus spoke his words of truth.

Jesus can do this because he is one with God. In the final I AM saying this identity is affirmed: "I am the Alpha and the Omega, the first and the last, the beginning and the end" (*Revelation 22:13*). In Jesus we see the human face of the Eternal One who holds time in his hands, and whose wisdom is the source of truth. His teaching and his acts do not draw on the wisdom tradition, but upon his relationship with God. When called upon to make a judgement in a difficult situation, his decision is born of his understanding of God's purpose for human life, rather than the rational rule of human beings. So, when a woman caught in the very act of adultery is brought to him, and her accusers ask him if he agrees with the law that requires such women to be stoned, he replies, "Let whichever of you is free from sin throw the first stone at her," thus saving her life without condoning her sin (*John 8:7*). In contrast to traditional wisdom, which might have emphasized the importance of upholding the law and the subordinate place of women, Jesus addresses the motivation of the woman's accusers, effectively reminding them that in the eyes of God they are no better than her. In Jesus the truth of God stood before the worldly-wise.

When, on another occasion, he was asked by his opponents if it was lawful to pay taxes to Caesar (*Mark 12:13–17*), he avoided the trap they set for him by raising the matter to a higher level. Coinage was regarded as the property of the ruler whose image it bore; "so," he said, "pay Caesar what belongs to Caesar," and then emphatically declared, "and God what belongs to God!" We do not hear the truth if we read both parts of Jesus' reply with equal emphasis; Jesus would have placed the stress on the second part. This is not a man of the world dissembling, nor an adept politician avoiding a difficult question; it is the Son of God establishing priorities, pointing the questioner to the ultimate standard against which judgements should be made. Jesus, the wisdom of God, discloses the truth of God: it is not their duty to Caesar that should be first in their hearts, but their duty to God.

In Jesus' words we hear the truth that, in the words of the antiphon, comes forth from the mouth of the Most High. The truth stood before those who sought to trap Jesus just as it stood before Pontius Pilate. And what assures us of this is that with Jesus, word and deed were one; there was no equivocation, no gap between precept and action, between principle and policy. God was for him the beginning and the end, the ultimate source of value and truth. Giving to God the things that are God's was his whole being; he gave to God wholeheartedly his worship, his obedience, and his faith. He is the true and living way, and this belief is the foundation of the hope for truth, indeed of all Christian hope.

## Reigning over all things

The antiphon pictures wisdom as reigning over all things, both bringing forth and ordering creation, and this is the second way in which we are led into the truth. The image comes from the Wisdom of Solomon:

> She is more beautiful than the sun, and surpasses every constellation. Compared with the light of day, she is found to excel, for day gives place to night, but against wisdom no evil can prevail. She spans the world in power from end to end, and gently orders all things.
>
> *Wisdom 7:29–8:1*

Creation has its own truth, its own integrity, and if, as we believe, it is the expression of the will of God, then taking to heart the truth and integrity of the created order, absorbing its rhythms and relationships and learning to live by them, is part and parcel of dwelling in the truth, to use John the Elder's phrase. The most fundamental aspect of our hope for truth today is for the truth and integrity of the creation to be safeguarded, and for effective action to reverse the damage done to it through global warming, environmental pollution, and the decline of species. The way in which our ideas about creation and the natural environment have changed over recent decades illustrates well the way that truth is apprehended through making a journey. Empirical research has been an important part of that journey, both occasioning its start and directing its course, but at the heart has been an inner change in perception of the relationship of humanity to the rest of creation. It has been nothing less than a profound spiritual awakening, a consecrating by the truth, although it is not usually described in that way. As it is so basic to the hope for truth, it is helpful to consider it further.

**A new ethic**

That creation has its own truth and integrity is now widely understood. The truth about the planet is the most fundamental of the new truths into which we have been led by the Spirit, and hope is focussed on the need to value and safeguard it. This concern has become progressively less human-centred and more creation-centred, an ethical change to which the Church has contributed. In the early 1980s, the World Council of Churches called for a *Just, Participatory and Sustainable Society (JPSS)*; after only a few years this was replaced by a new call for *Justice, Peace and the Integrity of Creation (JPIC)*.[9] The new call represents a re-direction of hope. The earlier formulation, *JPSS*, placed the emphasis on human society which, it had been generally assumed, the rest of creation existed to serve. The later formulation, *JPIC*, reverses this assumption; it acknowledges the God-given value and unity intrinsic to the whole of creation, of which humanity is simply a part, and which humanity exists to serve and preserve. What we see in this shift of understanding is a move away from the predominance of the first creation story, where men and women are given dominion over the earth, to fill it and subdue it, to the second (and earlier) story where God made a garden in Eden and placed Adam in it "to till it and look after it" (*Genesis 2:15*). The problem is that the later story has been placed first in the biblical narrative, thus giving it prominence and obscuring the original vision of the earlier story. In this earlier story the magisterial conception of the later story is entirely absent; creation originates not in a divine command, but in an act of divine love. God is close to what he makes; Adam is formed from the dust of the earth, and God breathes into his nostrils the breath of life, the very breath, or Spirit, of God himself.[10] God cares for Adam: he plants the garden and makes trees to grow up from the ground, "every kind of tree, pleasing to the eye and good for food".

The two stories not only have a very different tone, they also have a very different ethic. In the earlier story, Adam comes from the very earth which is to sustain him and for which he must care. Here is mutuality, a sense of connectedness between humankind and the rest of creation, the workings of which Charles Darwin and others have made plain. The key concept is not dominion, but humility (from the Latin *humus*, meaning "earth"). This story resonates with our ecological concerns; if only it had taken root in our collective psyche in the way that the later story has done. If only we had been truly earthed! But we have preferred dominion to humility: the world is ours—we can do what we like with it. Truth is seen in the earlier story as God sets a framework for the life of humankind. Two trees in the garden are out of bounds: the tree of life and the tree of the knowledge of good and evil. Thus Adam's life has ethical boundaries and, as the story unfolds, it is when he tries to overstep these boundaries (by eating the forbidden fruit of the tree of knowledge) that he falls from grace. An important part of the hope for truth is that we shall recognize that we are not the centre of our lives; we are not our own moral authority. To be fully human, we need to be earthed, in touch with what is real, and that means accepting a source of authority outside of the self. Not for nothing did Saint Benedict describe humility as the chief virtue. Not for nothing is it said that living in awe of God is the beginning of wisdom.

We tend to look at the two creation stories separately, but in truth they should be held together. The later story is no less true than the earlier one. We *do* have dominion over creation; and within us *is* the divine image, the capacity to relate to God and to live in communion with him. It is because of this—because we are so fearfully and wonderfully made, as the Psalmist said—that God commissions us as his co-creators. The earlier story shows us how that divine commission is to be discharged: with reverence, love, and care, with concern for the common good, and within the divine moral framework. This is the goal of truth towards which we reach out in hope.

### The power of love

Both creation stories show the power of the love of God which the antiphon identifies as the source of order, and so we may hope that it is also by the power of love that disorder will be overcome. The grounds for this hope are seen both in Jesus' miracles and in his encounters. Taking the miracles first, perhaps the most dramatic is the calming of the storm on the Sea of Galilee. It is the divine Word that calms the storm. Jesus speaks to the wind and the waves: "Peace! Be still!" The disciples are awe-struck: "Who can this be?" they ask. "Even the wind and the sea obey him" (*Mark 4:39–41*). Scarcely less dramatic was the healing of Legion, the demoniac who lived among the tombs, crying aloud on the hillsides and gashing himself with stones (*Mark 5:1ff.*). This deeply disturbed man was restored to his right mind also by the divine command; order is restored to a disordered life. Similarly with the woman who suffered from haemorrhages (*Mark 5:25–34*): here no command was needed—her simple act of reaching out to Jesus and touching his robe was enough to restore order to her disordered body. In all three examples we see the power of the love through which the world was made.

That same power is evident in those encounters where Jesus re-orders inner perception. When Nicodemus went to see Jesus one night, he said to him, "Rabbi, we know that you are a teacher sent by God; no one could perform these signs of yours unless God were with him." Jesus "hears" the unspoken need behind the compliment: Nicodemus is really asking, "What do these signs mean?" Jesus replies that only those who have been born again can know their meaning (*John 3:2–3*). "Born again" has acquired a particular meaning these days, describing a particular experience of charismatic renewal; "born from above" (as in the *NRSV*) better conveys the sense of Jesus' reply and avoids confusion. He says to Nicodemus that he needs to open himself to the Spirit of God so that he can see things as God sees them, by allowing God's kingly rule, the gift of the Spirit, to re-order his life—in other words, to be born from above. Similarly, when Jesus meets the Samaritan woman at the well (*John 4:1–30*), he sees beyond her immediate need to satisfy her physical thirst to her deeper need to re-order her life, which he alone can fulfil through his gift of "living water". This, he tells her, will be "a spring of water within her, welling up and bringing eternal life". Her deep thirst is for a living faith, and that comes through the gift of the Spirit; she too must be born from above.

A third example is Jesus' encounter with the rich young man who ran up to him, knelt before him, and asked, "Good teacher, what must I do to win eternal life?" (*Mark 10:17–22*). Jesus asks him if he has kept the law; he says that he has done so faithfully since he was a boy. From his reply, and even more from his behaviour, Jesus can see that the young man is in earnest, but he also sees beyond the young man's question to his real need: it is his attachment to his wealth that is getting in the way of his journey to God, and so, in love—Mark tells us that Jesus' heart "warmed to him"—he speaks the word that will re-order his life: "One thing you lack. Go, sell everything you have and give to the poor, and you will have treasure in heaven; then come and follow me." As with Nicodemus and the Samaritan woman, it is through opening himself to the Spirit that his hope will be fulfilled.

In all three encounters we see the power of love: Jesus hears their hope and shows them the way of truth. The Samaritan woman hurried away and immediately told her neighbours she had met the Messiah; Nicodemus became a secret disciple and, after the crucifixion, helped Joseph of Arimathea to bury Jesus; the young man went away with a heavy heart, and no more is known of him. Jesus offers the same gift of truth to all who place their hope in him; we decide how we shall receive it, and whether our hopes will be fulfilled.

**The groan of creation**

The power of love that characterized Jesus' ministry is also at work on a cosmic scale, and it motivates our hope for the better care of our world. The amazing wildlife television series of recent years, particularly those made by Sir David Attenborough, have shown us how love has disposed the world. As we delight in its wonder and beauty, we share in the delight of God who "saw all that he had made, and it was very good" (*Genesis 1:31*). We see, too, the malign effects of the lack of love. At one and the same time we see the beauty, unity, order, and fragility of the natural world, and the dire effects of the wanton exploitation of its resources, and we are invited to understand that just as the power of love disposed the world and sustains it, so it is by the power of love that its disorder will be healed and its fulfilment accomplished. This was Paul's vision of the world: a single unity, created and sustained by a love that cherishes things as they are, seeks the best for them, desires them to grow, and does not exploit or dominate. In a remarkable passage in his letter to the Romans, he connects the destiny of the planet, indeed of the whole universe, with our own human destiny which he describes in terms of hope:

> The created universe waits with eager expectation for God's sons to be revealed. It was made subject to frustration, not of its own choice but by the will of him who subjected it, yet with the hope that the universe itself is to be freed from the shackles of mortality and enter upon the glorious liberty of the children of God. Up to the present, as we know, the whole created universe in all its parts groans as if in the pangs of childbirth. What is more, we also, to whom the Spirit is given as first fruits of the harvest to come, are groaning inwardly while we look forward eagerly to our adoption, our liberation from mortality.
>
> *Romans 8:19–23*

Paul echoes the understanding of his time that just as the human creation is subject to sin and decay, so is the whole created order; and just as Jesus came to liberate men and women from sin and death so that they might share the glory of Christ, so that too is the destiny of creation. The belief at the time, says C. H. Dodd, was that "the material universe would be transfigured into a substance consisting of pure light or glory, thus returning to its original perfection as created by God".[11] This belief is founded on the notion that the universe, like Jesus, points forward to the new world that is to be when, in N. T. Wright's words, "its beauty and power will be enhanced and its corruptibility and futility will be done away."[12] Paul will have had in mind the prophecy of Isaiah: "See, I am creating a new heavens and a new earth" (*Isaiah 65:17; 66:22*), the fulfilment of which John of Patmos saw in his final vision (*Revelation 21:1*). This strong biblical witness to the truth—the truth that the destiny of humanity and the destiny of the material world are intimately linked—speaks clearly to our time. Both the natural world and humankind are disordered; both groan to be free from all that shackles them, and deliverance will come only when men and women allow the truth to shape their desires and exercise properly their responsibility, both to one another and as stewards of the earth.

**A holistic vision**

As with the creation stories, we do not look to Paul for scientific information, but for an understanding of relationships and of moral value. It is the truth of creation that motivates the hope that the relationship of humankind to its environment will be re-ordered to reflect the divine purpose. Because the process of climate change is slow it has not, until now, presented itself as a dramatic crisis like the banking crisis of 2008, but it is a crisis none the less, and far more serious. Like all crises it is also an opportunity. The hope must be that we seize it properly. Some, like Naomi Klein in her book *This Changes Everything*, argue that effective action requires fundamental changes to the world economic system. There is no doubt that such changes are necessary. An economic system that measures outcomes by exclusively financial criteria has no way of putting a value on things that cannot be traded, like the air we breathe and the ecosystems that are basic to life, a failure potentially catastrophic in its consequences, and made worse by the tendency to pursue short-term economic goals. This is not just a feature of modern capitalism; collective regimes like the Soviet Union and China also have a materialistic outlook, and under them some of the worst environmental disasters of the twentieth century occurred. Seeking economic solutions, like the trade in carbon credits, may present the illusion of progress, but they raise false hopes; they seduce us into believing that the system can fix it, with no change in lifestyle needed. The truth is otherwise: the system can't fix it, and lifestyle changes are essential, as we are now learning. As Pope Francis says, the environment cannot be protected solely on the basis of financial calculations of costs and benefits:

> The environment is one of those goods that cannot be adequately safeguarded or promoted by market forces. . . . Where profits alone count, there can be no thinking about the rhythms of nature, its phases of decay and regeneration, or the complexity of ecosystems which may be gravely upset by human intervention. Moreover, biodiversity is considered at most a deposit of economic resources available for exploitation, with no serious thought for

> the real value of things, their significance for persons and cultures, or the concerns and needs of the poor.[13]

However, more than economic change is needed. Paul points us to the way our hope can be fulfilled when he connects the future of the planet to the moral future of humanity. Just as Jesus said that the things which defile us come from within our hearts (*Mark 7:20–3*), so the systems that govern us are determined by the kind of people we are. As with all major problems today, climate change is at root a spiritual challenge rather than a technological, economic, or political problem—something that journalists and other opinion-formers tend not to address. Notably, Rowan Williams begins his discussion of the climate crisis not with the facts about the crisis, but with what it means to be human, one species in a diverse world disassociated from its environment.[14] This spiritual challenge is akin to the challenge Jesus posed to Nicodemus, the Samaritan woman, and the rich young man: What shapes your life? What motivates you and defines who you are? The answers to these questions determine the structures and values of the society we create and the systems we put in place. Both capitalism and socialism define progress in material terms, and as long as we do so our hope for the right ordering of creation will not be fulfilled. The truth, which in creation stands before us, requires us to redefine our notion of progress. As Pope Francis says, "A technological and economic development which does not leave in its wake a better world and an integrally higher quality of life cannot be considered progress." For many, their quality of life has actually declined in the midst of economic growth, through the deterioration of the environment, low-quality food, the depletion of resources, lack of jobs, and exploitative working practices. Talk of sustainable growth "absorbs the language and values of ecology into the categories of finance and technocracy, and the social and environmental responsibility of business often gets reduced to a series of marketing and image-enhancing measures".[15]

The true basis for hope is the holistic vision of Paul. Hope demands that ecology and society are considered together: that questions of justice shape policy on the environment. At one and the same time we need, as Pope Francis says, to hear "*both the cry of the earth and the cry of the poor*".[16] It was through the power of love that creation was disposed, and it will be only through the power of love that our hope for its re-ordering will be fulfilled. N. T. Wright expresses this eloquently: the wider vista that Paul opens up, he says, is the invitation to live within the horizon of God's new creation, which began with the resurrection of Jesus and will continue until the whole world is transformed under the just and healing rule of God's children. There is nothing passive about this; accepting God's invitation is not to sit back and wait for his salvation to be revealed. Rather, as Paul's call to personal transformation (*Romans 8:12–17*) makes clear, "the Christian is to embody the tension in bringing the new to birth already within the old". This, Wright avers, is the context for all Christian work in the areas of ecology, justice, and aesthetics: "If the creation is to be renewed, not abandoned, and if that work has already begun in the resurrection of Jesus, it will not do simply to consign the present creation to acid rain and global warming and wait for Armageddon to destroy it altogether." Christians must be in the forefront of bringing the signs and foretastes of God's eventual full healing to bear upon the created order, in all its parts and at every level. And this includes dealing effectively with issues of justice, corruption, oppression, and war. If the beauty and grandeur that we see in creation are the foretaste of what is to be revealed, then "it will not do to regard beauty, and its creation and conservation, as a pleasant but irrelevant optional extra within a world manipulated by science, exploited by technology, and bought and sold in the economic marketplace".[17]

The groan of creation has both opened our eyes to the nature of truth, and also opened up new perspectives of hope. The situation may be bad, and worsening, but there are possibilities of good worth striving for; there are many signs that we are learning to love creation as something given, with value in itself, and not just as something instrumental, a means to an end. We are made for communion, not consumption, and protecting God's handiwork is not an optional or secondary aspect of Christian life; it is essential to a life of virtue. It is the power of love that opens our eyes (as it did for Nicodemus), motivates us to change our notion of progress, and enables us to re-order the relationship of humanity and the planet. This is the way of truth.

## Come and teach us

Do we hope for truth? Then we need to understand it as a gift. This goes against the grain of today's Western culture, where the stress is on acquisition, individual achievement, and making one's own way. We need to learn from Solomon. When he became king, he did not ask God for wealth or power, but for "a heart with skill to listen" (*1 Kings 3:9*). "What he, the paradigm of the wise man, wished for himself was not the authoritative reason which reigns supreme over dead natural matter, the reason of modern consciousness, but an 'understanding' reason, a feeling for the truth which emanates from the world and addresses man."[18] Wisdom is the gift of love drawing us towards the eternal truth which lies behind and motivates all other truth, something that the rational mind can approach, but which cannot be known by rational processes of thought alone.

The idea of a "listening heart" is thought to come from Egyptian tradition, where it was believed that the meaning and order of the world was taken in by the heart.[19] We use the word "heart" to signify the whole person, spirit, mind, and body—as, for example, when we describe someone as "big-hearted". Saint Benedict urged his monks to listen with the ears of their heart, that is with their whole being.[20] If we hope, in the words of the antiphon, to be taught the way of truth, or as Jesus prayed, to be consecrated in truth, we need to understand that this means, as I have said, we have to allow ourselves to be led on a journey where we try to open ourselves totally—body, mind, spirit; feelings, reason, and intuition—becoming big-hearted, so that we are wholly receptive to the gift of God. Truth is a gift that we have to *want* to receive, with all our heart, all our soul, all our mind, and all our strength (*Mark 12:28–34*). Truth and wisdom do not come through passivity, but through an active, open receptivity; and in marked contrast to the modern idea that truth is discovered by reason alone, the path of wisdom requires our intuition and our imagination as well as our reason.

Today what we prize is knowledge, know-how, and the power to control, but this is inimical to the receptivity of wisdom. The internet has vastly increased the amount of information available to us, but what it does not do is to provide the skills and the values and the insights that enable us to sift and weigh the knowledge that we gain, and so determine its value. To do that we need wisdom, the ability to discern what is true and valuable, to judge rightly, and choose the right path in life. As E. F. Schumacher said, we are "far too clever to be able to survive without wisdom".[21]

The way of wisdom offers a different approach. As we have seen, the word used for wisdom in the Bible is feminine, as in the Greek *sophia* (which we use as a female forename). King Solomon, when he asked God for the gift of wisdom, said:

> Send her forth from your holy heaven, and from your glorious throne bid her come down, so that she may labour at my side and I may learn what is pleasing to you. She knows and understands all things; she will guide me prudently in whatever I do, and guard me with her glory. So my life's work will be acceptable, and I shall judge your people justly, and be worthy of my father's throne.
>
> *Wisdom 9:10–12*

Not every culture speaks of wisdom as feminine, and in doing so the Bible reflects a particular understanding of wisdom and of how we may make it our own. Raimon Panikkar has pointed out that a *sophos* (someone in whom wisdom dwells) is a "good navigator", thus wisdom is the ability to orient oneself in any given context. The way of wisdom is not about controlling or dominating but orienting oneself, sailing safely into harbour. As Panikkar observes, "the attitude behind this approach is certainly not the typical masculine feature of wanting to grasp, apprehend, dominate, and even know, but rather of being grasped, known, assimilated."[22] Growth in wisdom is about allowing oneself to be taken up into a greater reality, just as the ancient navigator, without sat-nav and other modern aids, had to absorb the rhythms of the winds and tides, the lore of the ocean, if he was to orient himself and guide his ship safely. Growth in wisdom also has much in common with the practice of contemplative prayer, in which the believer seeks to open herself to God's eternal spirit, in the same way that Mary allowed the Holy Spirit to fill her and be fruitful within her. Contemplation is not passivity, but requires effort and concentration, as anyone who has practised contemplative prayer will know. It is essentially the prayer of listening, in which we offer a time of silence to God, seeking to still ourselves and let mind and imagination dwell on the truth of God and, as it were, to tune in to his wavelength.[23] This was the path that Jesus took. He spent much time in solitary prayer seeking to hear God's Word above the words of the world. Paul describes Jesus as emptying himself, so that he might be filled by God (*Philippians 2:6–7*).[24] And in Gethsemane, we see the courageous result as he faced his own death, the inevitable conclusion of his ministry: "Not my will but yours be done" (*Mark 14:36*). If we hope for truth, then his example teaches us the way.

**The endless goal and the endless way**

If truth is a divine gift, then allowing oneself to be led "into all truth" cannot be done by human endeavour alone, as King Solomon acknowledged: "For even if one is perfect among the sons of men, yet without the wisdom that comes from you he will be regarded as nothing" (*Wisdom 9:6*). Solomon had the right ideas, but letting God's spirit form him, as Mary and Jesus did, required humility. This is a particular challenge for an absolute monarch, and one, alas, that Solomon did not meet—despite his early good intentions, in his later life he went seriously off the rails, both morally and spiritually. Humility has much in common with self-emptying. To be humble is to be earthed, to be in touch with what is real, and to let it shape you and the way you live your life, your values, attitudes, opinions, and goals. It means putting aside self-concern and all the other things that fill up our lives, and making space for God, the ultimate reality. Jesus put it beautifully in the first Beatitude: "Blessed are those who know their need of God, the kingdom of heaven is theirs." (*Matthew 5:3*)[25] It is only those who acknowledge their spiritual need whom God can fill with his wisdom.

To hope for truth is to know that we are on the right path. Jesus spoke to this hope in his response to Thomas at the last supper, and it is helpful to look again at their exchange. Thomas interrupted Jesus when he told the disciples that he was going to prepare a place for them in his Father's house; that he would come again and take them to himself, so that where he was going they would be also; and he added, "and you know the way that I am taking." When Thomas objected that they did not know where he was going, so how could they know the way, Jesus replied that he was the true and living way to the Father (*John 14:1–6*). Thomas' question seems reasonable enough: to know the way we must first know the destination, but Thomas has not really understood what Jesus is talking about, and Jesus' response is on an altogether different level. Jesus is not, as Thomas has assumed, talking about a physical destination—his Father's house is not a place—but a spiritual destination, and we arrive there by following the way, the journey of life, that Jesus himself has followed. It is in obedient travelling that we discover the room made ready for us in the Father's house; we need no more directions than the way of obedience that Jesus has shown us. The point is made beautifully in these lines from a poem by Frederick Myers:[26]

> With Love re-rising in the cosmic morn
> The inward ardour yearns to the inmost goal
> The endless goal is one with the endless way

*The endless goal is one with the endless way.* Any journey of love has this quality, where we only discover where we are going by heeding the call of love and following where it leads. God in Christ is both our destination and our way. Our hope is made real in a person and the way he leads, for he is the true and living way. Dwelling in the truth, being consecrated by the truth, is about growing in our relationship with him, and this in turn, as in any relationship of love, means opening ourselves to receive what he has to give, rather than seeking to grasp and appropriate.

The truth that God offers us is not a philosophy or a theory, a manifesto or a textbook, but a relationship, a way to travel. Eternal wisdom comes to us as a person; truth is apprehended as we make the journey of faith. It is personal, not propositional, a realization too often hidden from the worldly-wise, as Paul said:

> Among the mature I do speak words of wisdom, though not a wisdom belonging to this present age or to its governing powers . . . I speak of God's hidden wisdom, his secret purpose framed from the very beginning to bring

> us to our destined glory. None of the powers that rule the world has known that wisdom; if they had they would not have crucified the Lord of glory.
>
> *1 Corinthians 2:6–8*

Jesus is the true and living *way*. If we want our hope for truth to be fulfilled, then we need to walk in companionship with him. It is only in union with the Son that anyone comes to union with the Father: "No one comes to the father except by me . . . I am in the father and the father in me" (*John 14:6b, 11a*). Jesus is the *true* way, and as we walk with him, we shall discover for ourselves that truth is a person, not a philosophy or a creed. The foundation of a just and righteous life is something experienced through the life of another, not something to be read and learnt from a book or a manifesto. Truth is personal, with all the nuances and richness that come from the human heart. The truth "is Jesus himself in his divine-human character, making manifest to men the glory of the invisible God".[27] So Jesus is the *living* way: in him we encounter both the source of our being and the authentic human life. He is the alpha and omega, in him is our beginning and our end, all that we can desire or hope for; in him we find our true selves. John Marsh put it well:

> Jesus becomes himself the substance of the life of those who believe in him . . . the supreme reality in which all true life shares . . . It is not the case that Jesus is 'away' from the Father, and must therefore find and tread the way to him; he is the way himself: it is not the case that there is a truth about the Father which Jesus must learn and then pass on; he is the truth himself: it is not the case that the Father has eternal life which he will give to the Son when the Son reaches his home, so that the Son can then bestow life; he is the life himself.[28]

The path of wisdom is the path along which our most basic hope, the hope for truth, will be fulfilled. The path of wisdom is not an individual journey that we make alone, but a shared journey that we make in the company of those who have already made progress along it, and—above all—in the companionship of Jesus. Truth is apprehended through a relationship, a relationship that is on the move, never still, drawing us forward deeper into the mystery that is the wisdom of God. It is beautifully expressed in a prayer from Malling Abbey:

> Timeless,
> yet ever in time
> the mystery moves
> reshaping, remaking
> never old, ever new
> each day for the each
> he is there in heart's depth
> your cross and your crown
> your Christ.[29]

2

# Law from Sinai: The Hope for Justice

*O Adonai, and Head of the House of Israel;*
*you appeared to Moses in the fire of the burning bush*
*and you gave him the law on Sinai;*
*come with outstretched arm and ransom us.*

*I am the bread of life.*

## Law, Justice and Leadership

If truth is our most basic hope, justice is not far behind. One of the first things that we sense acutely as children is unfairness—how often have we heard the protest, "It's not fair!" on young lips? Arranging things in a way that is fair and just is one of the most basic responsibilities of anyone in authority, from parents to government. In public life, justice is not just a moral requirement, but a political necessity: injustice sows the seeds of dissent and will eventually bring down any society that does not address it. The hope for justice sustains all oppressed peoples, and it has a particular urgency in today's world as the gap between the rich and the poor gets wider and wider—indeed, in the face of gross economic inequality, it is not only the desperately poor but any who have a moral sense who feel the injustice at the heart of modern life. Because our life is not founded on truth, we have lost our way; in a real sense we need God to come, in the words of the antiphon, with outstretched arm to enthrone justice in our world.

Justice is fundamental to human society, but down the centuries philosophers from Plato to John Rawls have differed about what it entails, and the Bible also has a distinctive view which informs the Christian hope. Providing justice is a basic function of law. The law given to Moses on Sinai was designed to shape the nature of Israelite society, and this is equally the role of law in today's more developed societies; in both, the understanding of justice moves beyond settling disputes to ensuring that everyone is protected, able to participate in the society, and that at least their basic needs are met. Justice, in this more developed sense of social justice, was basic to Israel's self-understanding. The Hebrew concept of justice moved beyond the Aristotelian notion of even-handed dealing between contending parties, and this marked Israel out from the other nations of the Ancient Near East, as did her understanding of her origin in an historical event, the Exodus, an act of God which called her into being and led her onward. The relationship between God and his people was expressed in the Covenant, summarized succinctly in the covenantal formula "You shall be my people and I will be your God" (*Jeremiah 7:23; 31:33*). A covenant creates, between those who are unrelated, a relationship akin to a natural blood tie. Today marriage is the most widespread example, but in the ancient world covenants were used to create relationships between tribes, between monarchs, and between a king and his people. The Ten Commandments and the other laws received by Moses at Mount Sinai set out the terms of the Covenant between God and Israel, with the object of establishing a righteous society that acknowledged God as its Lord, and where everyone was dealt with justly.

The hope for justice is rooted in this notion of a righteous society, and Christians look to Jesus as its harbinger. One of the things Jesus teaches us is that righteousness will not be established without self-giving, even to the point of self-sacrifice. This fundamental truth is the subject of the first of the I AM sayings, in which Jesus is identified as the bread of life, the living bread: the true bread from heaven (*John 6:32*), a gift that endures for ever in contrast to the manna given by Moses that perished in a day. Justice depends not simply on the structures and systems we create, but more fundamentally on the kind of people we become. As we shall see, the Law given to Moses imposed on the rich a duty of generosity towards the poor—not the kind of generosity that we associate with charitable donations, but a sacrificial sharing of wealth and goods. The way we deal with our wealth and our goods is the subject of economics, and economic ideas bear powerfully on our hope for justice. Paul warned against letting "the greed that makes an idol of gain" take root in our hearts (*Ephesians 5:5*), but today's economic culture encourages precisely that worship of the idol of gain, implicitly legitimizing greed and avarice, and marginalizing any idea of self-giving. For the few, this may seem like the way of hope; for the multitudes, it is the way of despair. Just as Jesus offered himself as the true and living way, so he offers himself as the living bread, given for the life of the world (*John 6:51*). It is by allowing this gift to shape our lives that the economics of gain will give way to the economics of generosity, and the hope for justice be given new life.

### Justice and leadership

As justice is a function of law, so it is also a function of leadership. A fundamental question facing all leaders is to whom, and to what values, they are accountable. Democratic systems are generally understood as offering the answer that the leaders are accountable to the people, to those who elect them, but that cannot be the whole answer if justice is to be upheld. Even with the rise of populist leaders the demand for justice continues to be heard, whether through appeals to faith or common humanity (e.g. in the treatment of migrants) or the imperatives imposed by climate change (e.g. in the need to reduce the use of fossil fuels). Both these demands insist upon a more basic accountability than that of national leaders to the people. In ancient Israel this more basic accountability was to God.

The tribes of Israel shared a strong sense of unity with one another, arising out of their common calling by God. It was the divine will that bound them together and gave them a strong sense of solidarity, and the whole of national life was subordinated to it. This led to attitudes very different from those current today, as Walther Eichrodt observed:

> It is striking that [Israel] draws no clear line to exclude the stranger, but is continually absorbing outsiders into itself. Moreover, the decisive requirement for admission is not natural kinship but readiness to submit oneself to the will of the divine Lord of the Covenant and to vow oneself to this particular God.[1]

The existence of the nation is not an end in itself, and from the start Israel was founded on a higher purpose, the achievement of her religious destiny. This is the character of the House of Israel and the Lord was her Head. God gave Israel her laws and exercised leadership through figures like Moses: part prophet, part statesman, appointed because of their charismatic authority rather than their dynasty or popular support. Even though this tradition could not be maintained and gave way to a monarchy, the idea of the leader as God's representative was never abandoned. King David is looked to as Israel's greatest king who followed the Lord, but later kings turned away from God, taking the example of the kings of other nations as their model. Israel's fortunes waned; eventually she was conquered, her leading citizens sent into exile,[2] but despite defeat and misfortune, Israel never entirely lost the idea that God was her leader, nor that he would come to them. The prophet Jeremiah expressed the hope thus:

> A ruler shall appear, one of themselves, a governor shall arise from their own number. I myself shall bring him near and so he shall approach me, says the Lord. So you shall be my people and I will be your God.
>
> *Jeremiah 30:21–2*

*O Adonai* celebrates Jesus as that ruler, but not in the mould of the former kings, nor even of Moses, a point that is made clear by the use of the Hebrew word *adonai* in the antiphon. *Adoni*, "my Lord", is the Hebrew form of address for human lords; the plural *adonai* was reserved for God alone. Jesus, we are reminded, is not just divinely appointed like Moses, he is the incarnation of the divine Lord himself, and his leadership is the leadership of God himself; he is the Head of the House of Israel. The following lines of the antiphon press home this identification: in Jesus we see the human face of God who appeared to Moses in the burning bush, who gave Moses the law on Sinai, and who, through Moses, brought his people from slavery in Egypt to freedom in the Promised Land. Moses' repeated request to Pharaoh to let the Israelites go was a righteous demand for justice and freedom, and—echoing this—the second antiphon hails

Jesus as the One who comes to ransom us, the harbinger of the Law of God and the justice that it is intended to establish.

### The leader as servant

Jesus is further differentiated from Moses in nature of the leadership that he incarnated. The experience of exile to Babylon in the sixth century BC caused some in Israel to rethink their ideas about God and how he acted in the world, particularly the prophet Isaiah of Babylon.[3] Central to his thought are the four so-called "Servant Songs",[4] which picture God as one who comes close to his people in love, and who saves them by taking their sins upon himself, movingly described in this extract from the fourth song:

> He grew up before the Lord like a young plant
> whose roots are in parched ground;
> he had no beauty, no majesty to catch our eyes,
> no grace to attract us to him;
> he was despised and shunned by all,
> pain-racked and afflicted by disease;
> we despised him and held him of no account,
> an object from which people turn away their eyes.
> Yet it was our afflictions he was bearing,
> our pain he endured,
> while we thought of him as smitten by God,
> struck down by disease and misery.
> But he was pierced for our transgressions,
> crushed for our iniquities;
> the chastisement he bore restored us to health
> and by his wounds we are healed.
> We had all strayed like sheep,
> each of us going his own way,
> but the Lord laid on him
> the guilt of us all.
>
> *Isaiah 53:2–6*

Not only do we see here a new picture of God, we see also a new understanding of leadership and headship. The Head of the House of Israel suffers for his people; mercy and compassion—essential elements of justice—come before law and judgement; willingly and lovingly he takes the burden of their transgressions and iniquities upon himself. Today, we might call this the servant model of leadership.

The idea that God would come and resume his leadership became focussed in the expectation of the Messiah, the anointed one of God, who would come as God's regent to redeem his people. Jesus generally used the enigmatic title "Son of Man" to refer to himself, an indication that he did not accept the popular understanding of messiahship. He did not view his headship as that of a king, but as that of a servant, and as the bread of life he gave himself for his people in fulfilment of Isaiah's prophecy. Jesus made plain the nature of his leadership when he settled a dispute among the disciples about who was the greatest. Unlike kings, he said, who lord it over their subjects, they must bear themselves like the least among them: the one who rules must be like one who serves (*Luke 22:24–7*). John records a similar saying: after washing the disciples' feet, Jesus said, "You call me Teacher and Lord, and rightly so, for that is what I am. Then if I, your Lord and Teacher, have washed your feet, you also ought to wash one another's feet. I have set you an example: you are to do as I have done for you" (*John 13:12–15*). As Archbishop Justin Welby has said, "When the one to whom all power was given knelt down to wash feet, God reversed the world order."[5]

If we hope for justice, then this is the kind of leadership that is required. Jesus may have been addressing the disciples, but I doubt if this approach to leadership was meant to be confined to them. Consistently with the whole approach of the Law given to Moses, Jesus did not divide life into neat compartments, sacred and secular, public and private. His example sets the pattern for all leadership, whether in the marketplace or in the holy place, but what does washing one another's feet mean in the secular world? Saint Benedict's understanding of leadership in monastic communities provides one answer. He did not set out a developed theory, but in describing the way the abbot and other senior figures of the community should conduct themselves, he enunciated an approach that can be extended to non-monastic organizations where people strive together to achieve a common goal, living and acting by common values. This should include all public institutions and commercial enterprises.[6] In Saint Benedict's approach the leader has three basic tasks: firstly, to be accountable—and this includes acknowledging a source of authority beyond the self; secondly, to be concerned for the whole person—that is, for the personal and moral growth of all personnel, and not just for their technical competence; and thirdly, to create a community—a group bound together by common values and aims, and not merely by material goals and the protection of common interests.[7]

This model of leadership is very different from that prevailing in the world in which Jesus lived, and in the modern world also. It challenges all understandings of leadership based on status or power or personality. With Jesus the Old Covenant came to an end, as did the models of leadership and authority associated with it. The New Covenant made through him was sealed by his self-offering, the authentic sign of his headship. At the Last Supper, as he blessed the cup of wine, he said, "This is my blood of the covenant, shed for many" (*Mark 14:24*).[8] As the old covenant had been sealed in the blood of the Passover lambs, so the new covenant would be sealed in the blood of Jesus, the Lamb of God; and just as his blood was "shed for many", so the new covenant would be with all peoples and not just with Israel.[9] The hope for justice is founded on this new covenant and on the leadership of him who said, "I am among you as one who serves." This is the sign of good leadership, whether in the world, in government, business, or the Church, but it is in short supply—the personal journey that it requires is too challenging—and most of today's problems can be traced to bad or inadequate leadership. All too often those who lead us turn out to be either self-serving with little concern for justice, accountable (if at all) solely to their supporters, or so concerned to retain popularity that justice is sacrificed to expediency. We hope and long for better, and Jesus points the way.

## The Spirit of the Law

The antiphon identifies Jesus with the LORD who spoke to Moses out of the burning bush at Horeb, the mountain of God, where he was shepherding his flock (*Exodus 3:4*). The LORD called him and commissioned him to lead the Israelites from slavery in Egypt to freedom in the Promised Land. This was the occasion of the foundational dialogue referred to in the Prologue, when the LORD revealed the divine name: "I AM that I am" (*Exodus 3:14*). In the I AM sayings John makes it clear that Jesus is the human face of the divine name; but Jesus is also the new Moses: Moses who gave the Israelites the manna prefigures Jesus who gives the living bread to the world, and just as God commanded Pharaoh to listen to Moses, so he commanded the disciples to listen to Jesus (*Mark 9:7*). Jesus, like Moses, will lead his people once again from slavery to freedom—this time from the slavery of sin and mistaken ideas about God to the freedom of those who rejoice in the love of God. He will be the mediator of the New Covenant just as Moses was of the Old Covenant. Those whom God calls he also empowers. The gift of his Spirit to Moses was symbolized by the fire of the bush. This was no ordinary fire; it gave life and energy, but did not destroy; it burned without consuming, and prefigured the gift which God promised, through the prophet Joel, would be poured out on all his people (*Joel 2:28–9*), a promise that was fulfilled at Pentecost. It is the Spirit who fires in our hearts the longing for justice, the courage to work for it, and the virtue to be the servant of all.

God has poured out his Spirit, because without it his covenant would be a lifeless thing, and the justice that it enshrines would likewise be lifeless. Justice is a thing of the spirit as much as it is a thing of the law. If a society is to be just, the laws have to be applied according to their spirit and not simply according to their letter; in other words, the rules have to be applied with morality and righteousness, which are prior to law. This is a fundamental point made by the French jurist Montesquieu in his work *The Spirit of Laws*,[10] where he makes a basic distinction between the nature of government and the principle of government, that is, between the way in which a government is constituted (its particular structure), and the way in which it is made to act, the human passions that set it in motion, which he calls the "spring". In a democracy, he says, that spring is *virtue*, the quality which ensures that those who make the laws accept that they also are subject to them, and which, in turn, implies a willingness to put the interests of the community ahead of purely private interests. (I consider virtue more fully in chapter 5.)

While Montesquieu's approach was secular rather than religious, his notion of virtue is essential if the hope for justice is to be fulfilled. As he said, "When virtue is banished, ambition invades the minds of those who are disposed to receive it, and avarice possesses the whole community." And this is precisely what we saw, for example, in the banking crisis, in the abuse of parliamentary expenses by many MPs, in the mis-selling of insurance, in the way multinationals avoid paying a fair share of tax, and (most serious of all) in the way democracy is subverted through what has been described as "the erosion of norms"—the unspoken rules and conventions that transcend political differences and ensure that power will be exercised according to accepted standards. Contemporary examples include gratuitously insulting opponents and questioning their motives, the unprincipled and clandestine use of social media to influence elections, the unlawful prorogation of Parliament in 2019, and the cynical stratagems employed by authoritarian rulers to extend their power.[11] The spirit of the law and virtue are both vulnerable things, all too easily eclipsed by selfish desires, but the hope for justice demands their preservation.

The spirit of virtue lay at the heart of the covenant. The Law given to Moses was righteous, just, and moral; the divine arbitrariness and caprice all too present in the myths of the Greek gods—who interfered in the affairs of mortals simply for their own pleasure, unrestrained by any notion of morality—are entirely absent. The object of pagan worship was to propitiate the gods, to avert their anger and capricious designs; the object of Israelite worship was to align oneself to the will of the LORD and to learn from him. Jesus' summary of the Law expresses it thus:

> "Hear, O Israel: the Lord our God is the one Lord, and you must love the Lord your God with all your heart, with all your soul, with all your mind, and with all your strength. . . . You must love your neighbour as yourself."
>
> *Mark 12:29–31*

### The spring of action

For Jesus these words were not just a pious sentiment, but the spring of action. We see this clearly if we return to his encounter with the rich young man who asked him what he had to do to gain eternal life (*Mark 10:17–25*). When Jesus says he must keep the commandments the young man protests that he has done so since he was a boy, leaving in the air the unspoken question, "Why isn't that enough?" But Jesus takes the matter deeper: he would not achieve his goal simply by keeping the law; he had to show by his actions that the law had taken root in his heart. "Go," says Jesus, "sell all you have and give to the poor, and you will have treasure in heaven; then come and follow me." The young man was in earnest, but despite his lifelong obedience to the law, his heart was in the wrong place. Hearing Jesus' words his face fell, and he went away with a heavy heart. After he had gone, Jesus said to the disciples, "How hard it will be for the wealthy to enter the kingdom of God. It will be easier for a camel to pass through the eye of a needle than for a rich man to enter the kingdom of God." It would be a mistake to take Jesus' words as condemning wealth. Whether today or in Jesus' day, wealth—in the form of capital and material resources—is essential to fighting the very things that grind people down and defeat the hope of justice: contaminated water, poor health care, poor quality food, and the lack of shelter and work, for example. Jesus seems to have accepted that there will always be disparities in the distribution of wealth; as he said, "The poor will always be with you" (*Mark 14:7*), but this is said against the background of the duty of generosity towards the poor that the Law of Moses placed upon the rich. Wealth comes with responsibilities; Jesus does not condemn the right use of wealth, he condemns the way we come to depend on it as a substitute for God and use it for our own enrichment. It is the place the rich young man's possessions occupied in his heart that prevented him from gaining eternal life, not the mere fact that he was very wealthy.

Virtue has to be the spring of action for the hope of justice to be realized. Jesus said he came not to abolish the law, but to complete it (*Matthew 5:17*), and he did this by going beyond the letter of the law: emphasizing its spirit, placing intention above rule, substance above form. By his time the law had become complex; the six hundred and more commandments were overlaid with a myriad of rules governing even the smallest details of everyday life. It was simply impossible for ordinary people to keep all the rules, and they were looked down on by the Pharisees, the "separated brethren" who prided themselves on their own precise observance of the law. Jesus publicly criticized the Pharisees in a series of "woes".[12] The heart of his criticism was the way in which concern for the letter of the law had blinded them to the more fundamental demands for justice, that is, the demands of social solidarity that the law enshrined. So, for example, the fourth woe reads:

> "Woe to you, scribes and Pharisees, hypocrites! You pay tithes of mint and dill and cumin; but you have overlooked the weightier demands of the law—justice, mercy and good faith. It is these you should have practised, without neglecting the others. Blind guides! You strain off a midge, yet gulp down a camel!"
>
> *Matthew 23:23–4*

We really need to take this to heart. In the wake of many crises, when individual, corporate, or political behaviour has been found wanting, we hear the defence, "We have done nothing wrong!"—a mantra regularly repeated, for example, by those whose selfishness was exposed in the "Paradise Papers". Judged by the letter of the law, this protestation may be correct, but judged by the spirit of the law—the weightier demands of justice, mercy, and good faith—it most certainly is not. Laws, codes of ethics, and rules of professional practice are insufficient in themselves to prevent injustice and corruption; their purpose will only be achieved when the right spirit is brought to their implementation. (Given the scale of the problem, one could be forgiven for assuming that corporate codes of ethics are more about presenting the right image than actually governing behaviour.) Generally, we do not need to tighten up the laws; for example, the rules and the regulatory regime were both strong enough to have prevented the banking crisis. It was not so much the law that was inadequate but the people who applied it; both bankers and regulators were too much concerned with the letter of the law rather than its spirit—with maximizing profit rather than pursuing justice. Part of the problem is that corporate codes of ethics cannot reflect the *true* nature of ethics, namely a form of self-obligation by which we autonomously impose a norm on ourselves. Moreover, Christian belief connects ethics with love and grace, the source of virtue, which secular schemes cannot.[13] The Head of the House of Israel, who gave the Law on Sinai, gave a New Law for the New Covenant in which substance triumphs over form, the spirit over the letter. As John said, the spirit completes the law: "The law was given through Moses, but grace and truth came through Jesus Christ" (*John 1:17*). Law gives shape to society; the Spirit gives it life.

## The Law from Sinai

The story of Moses continues with the Exodus, the long march to freedom which I consider in the next chapter. When the Israelites gathered at Mount Sinai Moses received the Ten Commandments, the foundation of the Law of the Covenant (*Exodus 24:12*). As the journey continued, we read that the LORD summoned Moses to the Tent of Meeting and gave him further laws and commandments (*Leviticus 1:1*). The law given to Moses is an impressive code, covering all aspects of life: there are detailed rules dealing with worship and community life, land and property, trade and personal conduct—in all, well over six hundred commandments. We look to this law as the exemplar of a righteous society because, as Oliver O'Donovan says, Israel was "the theatre of the LORD's self-disclosure as the ruler of nations", and "implied in the hope of a new national life for Israel was the hope of a restored world order. The future of the one nation was a prism through which the faithful looked to see the future of all nations."[14] This is not, of course, to say that the actual conditions of life for the Israelites offer any kind of ideal or model for today; it is the hope of a just society enshrined in the law that speaks to us, a hope characterized by the concept of *shalom*.

### *Shalom*

Justice must serve *shalom*. The Hebrew word *shalom* is usually translated as "peace", but the concept is much richer than the common understanding of peace, which tends to be simply the absence of conflict. As John V. Taylor explained, *shalom* is something much broader than peace; it is "the harmony of a caring community informed at every point by its awareness of God. . . . It speaks of a wholeness that is complete because every aspect and every corner of ordinary life is included."[15] We might think of *shalom* as the love of God expressed in a communal form. Bishop Simon Phipps was once asked what love meant in business life; he replied, "Taking everybody's interests seriously." And that is what *shalom* seeks to do. Taking everybody's interests seriously means equating the interests of the rich and powerful, the movers and shakers, with the interests of the moved and the shaken: the poor, the powerless, and the dispossessed.

*Shalom* gives shape to the hope for justice, the key biblical requirement for any political order. When a new king was enthroned in Israel, the liturgy included a prayer that he would act justly:

> God, endow the king with your own justice,
> his royal person with your righteousness,
> that he may govern your people rightly
> and deal justly with your oppressed ones.
> . . . May he give judgement for the oppressed among the people
> and help for the needy;
> may he crush the oppressor.
>
> *Psalm 72:1–4*

The king must take everybody's interests seriously, coming to the aid of the poor, and overcoming those who oppress them. Justice in society requires placing the common good before individual advantage, ensuring that resources are equitably shared, and that all have a sense of participation and inclusion. Of course, these perspectives are not exclusively biblical; they are widely shared—they are precisely the issues that the survivors of the 2017 Grenfell Tower fire in London, and other members of the local community, insisted be addressed following that disaster—but they are biblical in origin, impressive features of the laws of the covenant through which the Israelites felt themselves to be part of a single living whole. The concern for those on the edge of society enjoined upon the king, which would have seemed extraordinary in other ancient cultures, was a striking feature which arose out of the awareness of the corporate solidarity basic to *shalom*. The poor, orphans, widows, and strangers were no less deserving of justice; so, for example, the law decreed:

> When you reap the harvest in your land, do not reap right up to the edges of your field, or gather the gleanings of your crop. Do not completely strip your vineyard, or pick up the fallen grapes; leave them for the poor and for the alien. I am the LORD your God.
>
> *Leviticus 19:9–10*

The same concern for the poor has characterized many Christian initiatives to secure justice, and working to transform the unjust structures of society is now generally regarded as one of the "five marks of mission".[16] The provision of education and healthcare go back many centuries; the nineteenth century saw other Christian initiatives: the campaigns to alleviate poverty, rescue women from prostitution, end the slave trade, and reform the penal system. In the mid-twentieth century, in the aftermath of the Second World War, the Beveridge Report (the impetus for which was largely Christian) identified five "Giant Evils" in society: squalor, ignorance, want, idleness, and disease; from its work flowed the institutions of the Welfare State, including the NHS. Those who have laboured to provide education and healthcare for all, to improve housing and working conditions, to bring an end to hunger and deprivation, those who have campaigned for the remission of the unpayable debts of the poorest nations, and for effective measures to combat human trafficking and climate change, these have all been working towards *shalom*, or in Archbishop Justin Welby's phrase, "enthroning Christ over Mammon", whether they knew it or not.

Alongside this practical action the Church has developed a body of social teaching, beginning in 1891 with Pope Leo XIII's encyclical letter *Rerum Novarum*,[17] which addressed the condition of the working classes following the Industrial Revolution. Over the years, other social encyclicals have developed the theme of the common good, the latest being *Laudato si'*, referred to in the previous chapter.[18] Perhaps the most fundamental issue from the perspective of justice is the Church's insistence on the universal destination of material goods, which derives from the vision in *Genesis* that God intended the earth and all it contains for the use of every human being and every people. The Christian belief is that the world is made to furnish every person with the means of livelihood and the instruments for their growth and progress; "therefore," Pope Paul VI declared, "each person has the right to find in the world what is necessary for him- or herself. . . . All other rights whatsoever, including those of property and of free commerce, are to be subordinated to this principle. They should not hinder, but on the contrary, favour its application."[19] More recently, Pope Francis, writing of God's special concern for the poor, has given a timely reminder that property has a social function, and that the private ownership of goods "is justified by the need to protect and increase them, so that they can better serve the common good".[20]

**Justice and economics**

This radical and challenging policy poses fundamental challenges to the economic assumptions which shape the contemporary world. These assumptions are so pervasive that the economist Jane Collier described contemporary culture as an economic culture:

> The language of economics is the language through which the world is understood, the language by which human and social problems are defined, and by which solutions to those problems are expressed . . . Political options translate into economic decisions; political decisions are implemented by economic institutions.[21]

We have lived so long in a world dominated by economic ideas that we have taken them on board as the warp and weft of life, just as medieval Europe accepted Christianity. Indeed, economic ideas function just like a religion, providing the basic understanding of what life is about. Because this is so basic to the hope for justice, it is important to look at these economic ideas more closely.

Collier wrote in 1992, when the change in economic policy that began in the 1970s had taken full effect. The change came about as the Keynesian[22] approach to economic management gave way to a new approach called monetarism, associated in particular with the economist Milton Friedman.[23] The two approaches rest on different analyses of the way the economy works, and also on differing political perspectives. Keynes advocated government intervention in the economy in the interests of equality; monetarists demur, maintaining that the principal duty of government is to control the money supply in the interests of stability. Monetarism provides an economic justification for those who believe in a limited state and minimal regulation of the market. "Gave way" is actually too weak a way to describe the change from the Keynesian approach; it was quite deliberate, as Margaret Thatcher made clear: "Economics are the method: the object is to change the heart and soul."[24] The effect has been to make economic considerations and market outcomes paramount in shaping both society and morality, though from the perspective of justice it ought to be the other way round. Owen Nankivell argues, in his seminal book *Economics, Society and Values*, that the drive for more and more material goods—the preoccupying concern for economic activity in Western culture—means we are putting the cart before the horse; life is more than getting and spending. He argues that society as a whole provides an overarching context in which to set economic activity. If the way the economy is managed (including both its outcomes and the particular values that shape it) conflicts with wider social aspirations, it is clear which should yield, "nevertheless, the presumption in Western market capitalism appears to be that the economic model . . . drives and dominates people's lives".[25] The drive for more and more material goods is symptomatic of a society that has lost any unifying moral vision of its aim and purpose. Equally symptomatic is the predominant use of mathematical models, measurements, and statistics in the development of public policy. Technical expertise is valued above moral vision; purely instrumental ways of thinking replace concern for values and ends, overlooking the fact that we cannot measure or model those things that make us uniquely human, as Robert F. Kennedy remarked in 1968: " . . . [T]he gross national product does not allow for the health of our children, the quality of their education, the joy of their play . . . It does not include the beauty of our poetry or the strength of our marriages . . . It measures . . . neither our wisdom nor . . . our compassion . . . It measures everything, in short, except that which makes our life worthwhile."[26]

The response to the COVID-19 pandemic has opened our eyes to the truth to which both Nankivell and Kennedy draw attention: the shocking disparity between social and economic value in today's world. It is the nurses, social care staff, cleaners, delivery drivers, and others whose economic value is low (judging by their financial rewards), upon whom we depend in the last resort, rather than the captains of industry, city traders, sports and media personalities whose economic value (judged by the same criterion) is very high. The exaltation of the economic over the social and the human can also be seen clearly in the way countless British town centres have been redeveloped, turning them into soulless places dedicated to commerce. Woking in Surrey, where the town centre consists of two large shopping malls, is one of the worst examples, utterly devoid of redeeming features. Globalization has the same effect. Capital can move more freely and rapidly than labour; capital flows cause social changes, like the loss of jobs, the effect of which endures long after capital has moved on. "Footloose financial capital" also subverts the autonomy of democratic institutions,[27] further obstructing the pursuit of justice and fuelling *ressentiment*. As in Woking, the social and the economic are uncoupled. In the Law given on Sinai the social model is fundamental, and the economic model is designed to reflect it, but monetarist theory requires society, in effect, to be re-engineered to support the market, rather than the market supporting society.

The uncoupling of the social and the economic, and the resulting disparity of value, is closely connected with another strand embedded in mainstream economic thought, namely, the conception of justice developed by the philosopher John Rawls. Rawls was one of the towering figures of moral and political philosophy of the twentieth century, and his major work, *A Theory of Justice*, heralded a new starting point in conceptions of justice.[28] His work explored the idea of justice as fairness, but oddly (one might think), this did not lead him to regard social outcomes—the actual conditions of life— as the basic criterion of whether an economic or political system is just, as it is in a society based on the principle of *shalom*. Instead, Rawls regards as fundamental the nature of the institutions of government: if the institutions are just (by which he means that they are agreed on unanimously by all through some form of social contract), then the outcomes they produce must be accepted as just. His theory has been widely criticized, notably by Amartya Sen in *The Idea of Justice*, in particular for not paying sufficient regard to outcomes.[29] As Sen says, concern about the actual conditions of life, and how they can be improved, is "a constant and inescapable part of justice". Although Rawls' theory is by no means accepted by all economists (and the fact that it is not reminds us that the economic institutions that flow from it are not "givens", but a political choice), his work is regarded as so foundational that it shapes the mainstream view that the market is a just institution, and thus its outcomes must also be accepted as just.

This goes hand in hand with the belief that economics is, in principle, independent of any particular ethical position or normative judgement. Friedman argued that economics is an "objective" science in the same way as the physical sciences, and one of the key tenets of monetarism follows logically from this belief, namely, that market forces are autonomous. If this is true then the hope for justice is no different from the hope for a fine day, subject—like the weather—to forces beyond our control. However, it is *not* true; economics cannot be equated with physical science. A major difference is the data upon which they rely. Economic data do not have the same "objective" quality as data in the physical sciences because they record human preferences, which are far from constant, and are influenced by subjective factors like fashion and the pursuit of wealth, status, and power. So upon what basis do economists like Friedman claim that their discipline is an objective science? How do they base their theories on something firmer than the shifting sands of human preference? The answer is that economists have sought to objectify their theories by basing them on a number of axioms, that is assumptions about human life considered to be self-evidently true, the most basic of which is that everyone always acts rationally in pursuit of their own self-interest. High claims have been made for axiomatic economics, including the notion that "social and economic theory is not derived from experience—it is prior to experience".[30]

This really is a piece of nonsense; the only reality that is prior to experience is God (but it does explain why economic theories are slow to adjust in the light of experience). The result of the axiomatic approach, according to Jane Collier, is that "neither the form of economic theory nor the assumptions upon which it is based accord with reality".[31]

Moreover, the quest for objectivity meant that economics moved away from classical "political economy" with its interest in the creation and distribution of wealth, to neo-classical "economic science", which defined welfare in terms of getting the most out of available resources. To quote Jane Collier again, "This was a shift with profound implications for humankind, because it committed economics to an interpretation of human benefit based on the premise that 'more is better', and to the view that human happiness or welfare is best served by the achievement of economic growth."[32] Monetarism, like all economic theories, is a creed, not a science—a creed that deprives us of one of our uniquely human qualities: the ability to step back from our situation and decide both the values that are important to us and the goals we wish to pursue. When the only objective truth is determined by the market, then all other values are no more than mere dreams and opinions. The fundamental role of the Law given on Sinai, namely shaping a just and participative society, is denied; the only choice allowed to us is the choice of what to consume.

## Containing the market

While those who hope and work for justice must take the market seriously—no better way has been found for distributing scarce resources and for lifting people out of poverty[33]—this does not mean that we have to endow its outcomes with a divine inerrancy. The market is a human institution, and like any other human institution it operates to the advantage of those best placed to operate it, namely those with economic power. It may be the best mechanism for distribution and exchange, but the market does not, of itself, have any concern for the justice of its outcomes. We see this particularly in the scandalous and ever-growing gap between rich and poor. In the UK, the richest ten per cent now earn on average almost ten times the income of the poorest ten per cent, and globally Oxfam reported in January 2016 that the richest sixty-two billionaires in the world owned as much wealth as the poorest half of the world's population, or to put it another way, one per cent of people own as much as the other 99 per cent combined.[34] We see the injustice of market outcomes in the disparity of provision in housing, education, healthcare, and employment between affluent and less well-off areas; and in the lowering of ethical and moral standards, not only in the conduct of business, but also in civil society. You cannot roll back regulation without implicitly legitimizing a more relaxed business ethic, and—because morality is all of a piece—that relaxation spills over into other aspects of personal behaviour. The Wall Street crash of 1929 prompted an outspoken denunciation from Pope Pius IX in words that ring true today. "Immense power and despotic economic domination" are concentrated in the hands of a few, "limitless free competition . . . permits the survival of those only who are the strongest, and this often means those who fight most relentlessly, . . . [and] who pay least heed to the dictates of conscience."[35] For Oliver O'Donovan the "state of pervasive moral debilitation" that characterizes Western democracies is the consequence of displacing God as the source of political authority.[36] The heart and soul have indeed changed.

However, like all human institutions, the market operates within a legal and moral framework, and therein lie grounds for hope. Adam Smith, one of the founding fathers of modern economics whose ideas are regarded with something approaching biblical authority by today's neo-classical economists, believed that the market could be justified only in terms of individual virtue, and he warned that a society governed by nothing but transactional self-interest was no society at all.[37] Free-market fundamentalists, who have given disproportional weight to Smith's words about the invisible hand,[38] need to give rather more weight to his view that markets depend for their effective operation on a string of moral virtues, not least honesty and trust, *that markets themselves cannot create or sustain*, and in some cases actually erode.[39] Divorced from virtue, the market—for all the good it produces—becomes our master, not our servant, and this underlies the widespread feelings of *ressentiment*.

Economics is best understood as a "moral science", as Keynes believed,[40] and the hope for justice needs to be focussed on reforming the legal and moral framework within which the market operates, so that the market becomes our servant and not our master, and economic power is made to serve the common good. What does this mean? At the most basic level it means acknowledging that the market is ill-suited to regulate certain areas of life, like education, healthcare, and transport, where criteria other than price are important in determining the provision of services. More widely, it means a range of things, from radical changes to the present regime of structural adjustment programmes imposed on developing countries,[41] to taking effective action on more local problems that are widely recognized. As I write, the campaign for female economic equality has stepped up several gears; recently there have been the scandals over the misuse or under-funding of pension funds of the former BHS chain and other major companies; there is now an annual denunciation of the level of executive pay and bonuses, and widespread protest at the gross disparity of executive pay compared with that of other staff. Taking effective measures to deal with these issues would be an important step along the road to taking everyone's interests seriously. Some action has been taken on equal pay, but much remains to be done, including requiring companies to act not just in the interests of their shareholders, but in the interests of all their stakeholders (employees, pensioners, customers, the local community) and of the environment; pension funds need to be ring-fenced more effectively, especially in take-over deals (as is the case in the Netherlands), and the tax system reformed so that corporations pay a fair share of tax.[42] There are hopeful signs that this message is being heard, as, for example, in the "Davos Manifesto" issued following the World Economic Forum of 2020.[43] Changes like these amount to a repurposing of the corporation, and will require a change of mindset among boards of directors who will need to see themselves as the trustees of the purpose of the company rather than as agents of the shareholders.[44] As Pope Francis has said, business is a noble vocation provided that those engaged in it see themselves as challenged by a greater meaning in life.[45] The same could be said of public and political service. It is where that challenge is absent that the seeds of injustice find fertile soil and hope is frustrated.

### Connecting economics with virtue

Governments, following the monetarist agenda and fearful of alienating powerful economic interests, have shied away from taking even modest steps towards the goal of economic justice, but in this Age of Anger, social pressure to make effective reforms is increasing. Christians ought to welcome this, as we have much to offer in reshaping the economic framework, both in terms of economic structure and the goals of human society. Structurally, the biblical vision of society challenges all economic perspectives, Keynesian no less than monetarist. Against the free-market fundamentalists Christians must assert the basic principle of the Law given on Sinai, namely shaping society so that everyone's interests are taken seriously. Socially, Christianity offers a far better goal than the economic one of increasing material prosperity, which is based on the belief that happiness comes through increasing consumption and ever-expanding choice. Here the individual is central; ethics are utilitarian, and it is assumed that human behaviour is motivated solely by the rational pursuit of self-interest—love, altruism, and charity, which have no price, have no economic value. This economic view is far removed from the Christian one which sees love, not consumption, as the primary motivation in life, placing service above self-interest, equating love of neighbour with love of self: insisting both that the common good is central, and that the condition of the poorest, rather than the general level of material prosperity, is the bottom line in determining the state of the nation. The economic model sees us as consumers, effectively defining us by our appetites and not by our hopes; it has transformed Advent from the season of hope to the main season of consumerism, a frenzy of getting and spending. Worse still is the effect on the planet of this economic stress on ever-increasing consumption: the environment is degraded, natural resources are used up faster than they can be replenished, pollution is at crisis levels, and the climate is changed. Dethroning economics from its dominating cultural position is now about survival and not just about justice. At root, the question is whether we are prepared to place faith above economics and allow it to shape our politics.

This part of the journey of hope presents a huge challenge today. In the face of economic forces we can feel hopeless, especially given the extent to which they shape our lives, but we should not underestimate the power of moral pressure. I take inspiration from those who fought to abolish the slave trade, which was justified as an economic necessity, but which in the end could not survive the moral pressure for abolition. In the same way, through moral pressure the Jubilee 2000 campaign for the remission of the unpayable debts of the world's most impoverished nations resulted in the cancellation of over $100 billion of debt owed by thirty-five of the poorest nations. The hope for justice means connecting economic theory and economic activity with virtue, morality, and the common good.[46] Two things need to be stressed: the first is that Christianity is not anti-business; its concern is that business should serve the common good. As I mentioned above, Pope Francis has described business as a "noble vocation", provided that those engaged in it see themselves challenged by a greater meaning in life; he adds that responding to this challenge "will enable them truly to serve the common good by striving to increase the goods of this world and to make them more accessible to all".[47] Secondly, this is not about pursuing a particular party political programme, but a moral requirement that any and all political programmes should seek to achieve, though clearly the more extreme political positions, both libertarian and collectivist, are ruled out. A notable pioneer of this approach was E. F. Schumacher, who tellingly subtitled his book *Small is Beautiful*, "A study of economics as if people mattered". Many economists now recognize the disjunction between economic theory and real life, prompting a vigorous debate among economists about the basis of economic theory.

At the forefront of this debate are the behavioural economists whose studies of economic activity are based on how people actually behave, rather than the axiomatic assumptions of established theories. According to Pete Lunn, these studies undermine the belief that market forces are autonomous: "Markets are not deterministic and efficient allocation machines. They behave differently according to levels of trust, common identity, the availability of information, perceptions of fair prices, and uncertainty about value and the future."[48] While this is a considerable theoretical advance, it would be sanguine to assume that the new approach will automatically result in greater justice; it might simply lead to more effective marketing—it all depends on the moral framework. If, despite the economic defeats and failures, there remain possibilities of good worth striving for, then reforming the moral and legal framework within which economic activity is conducted, to reflect both the biblical principle of *shalom* and the values of the Spirit, is foremost among them. In the Law given to Moses we are moral beings defined by our hopes, not economic beings defined by our appetites. The hope for justice in today's world is, basically, a hope for a just economic system.

## Come and ransom us

In the introduction to this chapter I said that the hope for justice will not be realized without self-giving, and the concluding petition of the antiphon helps us to explore this further. It combines two images, asking that Jesus will come with *outstretched arm* and *ransom* us. The first image, God coming to the aid of his people "with outstretched arm and mighty acts of judgement", originated in the story of the Exodus (*Exodus 6:6*), and is repeated throughout the Old Testament as a way of speaking of God's love for his people, notably in Psalm 136:

> With strong hand and outstretched arm . . .
> he divided the Red Sea in two . . .
> and made Israel pass through its midst;
> for his love endures for ever.
>
> *Psalm 136:12–14*

It summons up a dramatic picture of God, moved by righteous anger, acting powerfully against injustice and oppression. The second image, the ransom (a payment made to secure the release of a captive), is an image of atonement, which I consider more fully in chapter 7. Both are images of salvation for which we look to God, and both have spoken powerfully to people in former times, but we need to ask how they compare with God's self-revelation in Jesus. It is impossible to discern the actual events that lay behind the acts of divine power described in the Exodus story, but whatever they were they have not been repeated. God must be moved no less by righteous anger as he looks upon the injustices of today, but we hope in vain if we expect our economic system to be transformed by a dramatic act of divine intervention. God's intervention came through Jesus. At his Transfiguration the divine voice addressed the disciples with the command, "Listen to him." And it seems that God has chosen to act in the world through the minds and hearts of those who listen to his Son and nurture his Word in their hearts. There is no other way if God is to be true to the gift of freedom he has bestowed upon us; the essence of the way of Jesus is self-giving.

**The Bread of Life**

In Jesus, God replaced the image of the "strong hand and outstretched arm" with the image of the cross. It is not with one arm, but with both arms outstretched on the cross that God ransoms us in Jesus. He saves us by his own self-offering and by drawing us into the community of his disciples. John brings these themes together in the discourse about the bread of life (*John 6:22–58*). Jesus contrasted the bread that Moses gave to the Israelites in the wilderness with his gift of himself, and then added, "The bread that I shall give is my own flesh, given for the life of the world" (*John 6:51b*). Jesus is the living bread, the life-giving bread. He does not merely bestow a gift; he himself is the gift, and those who receive it will be renewed in their lives. To respond to Jesus' gift of himself, as we do in the celebration of the Eucharist, is to be drawn into the movement of his self-offering, and the more we allow him to draw us into this movement, the more the hope for justice will be fulfilled. Paying the price of sin, even if it is by the Son of God, does not eliminate sin, nor does it change the unjust structures of society; what it does is to release into our hearts the spirit of virtue. The hope for justice, for bread in this life, is here and now; it echoes the cry for bread of the Israelites in the wilderness. Law, as we have seen, has an essential part to play in changing the structures that frustrate it, but more is required: renewed hearts and a deep moral change in the nature of society. The Church, the community of Jesus' disciples, is called to be the sign to the world of this moral change, a sign of the new life made possible through being drawn into the movement of Jesus' self-offering, which becomes the pattern for our own lives and the life of the Church. This is what Paul wanted the Christians at Rome to understand:

> I implore you by God's mercy to offer your very selves to him: a living sacrifice, dedicated and fit for his acceptance, the worship offered by mind and heart. Conform no longer to the pattern of this present world, but be transformed by the renewal of your minds. Then you will be able to discern the will of God, and to know what is good, acceptable, and perfect.
>
> *Romans 12:1–2*

### A living sacrifice

Participating in the Eucharist is part of our salvation, but we do not do so in order to gain strength simply to live our present life (as many seem to think) but, as Paul says, to offer ourselves as a living sacrifice; in other words, it is so that our life becomes eucharistic: the life of Christ becomes our life; his values become our values; his Spirit moves our spirit, renewing our minds and hearts. We become what we absorb, from food and drink to ideas and values, and it is through feeding on Jesus, and taking to heart the biblical principle of *shalom*, that self-sacrifice is re-valued and the hope for justice is given life. But there is nothing automatic about this; we have to allow ourselves to be drawn into the movement of his self-offering. We may begin by moderating our demands and desires, following, perhaps, the Benedictine principles of balance, moderation, and frugality. *Enough is Enough*, the title of Bishop John V. Taylor's book, points the way. The forty years which have passed since it was published have not reduced the force of his message. Taylor is not against enjoyment and celebration; as he says, the Law given at Sinai enjoined them both, and he describes the annual celebration of God's generosity as "[a] spending-spree, whisky and all, to make our commercial Christmas look like a Lenten fast!" This "spontaneous, lavish celebration," he says, "is the absolute opposite of the greedy spirit of grasping, hoarding, exploiting and turning everything back into greater profits."[49]

For Taylor, the poison in the system is excess, which he describes as a "lust for possession and domination". Excess characterizes not only personal consumption, but also extends to corporate values like using market power to impose unfair terms of trade, and maximizing profits and shareholder value as though they are the only valid "bottom line". (As Christians and others point out, below the conventional "bottom line" there are two more "bottom lines": the people and the planet.) Turning away from these attitudes is the modern equivalent of the biblical injunction against harvesting to the edge of the field (cf. *Leviticus 23:22*). Against excess Taylor places the principle of *shalom*, which breeds the opposite of excess, "the readiness to fit one's own needs to the needs of others and to submit self-assertion to the claims of an equipoise society . . . So moderation is not . . . a yielding meekness; it means, rather, a matching, a toning in with the whole, an awareness of how one's own small piece fits into the jigsaw picture."[50]

The bread of life was broken for the many, not for the few, and moderation extends beyond personal behaviour to the way in which the economic system is operated. We hope for justice, not charity; for laws and an economic system that will reflect the values of the Law given at Sinai, and be administered with the spirit of the New Law given by Christ. Fair trade is not simply a matter of buying fairly traded products, but of creating a global trade system that takes everyone's interests seriously, as advocated (for example) by John Madeley in *Hungry for Trade*.[51] This is the outworking of the biblical principle of *shalom*; we might call it the economics of generosity.[52] The world is desperately in need of the economics of generosity, but it is only in a community that feeds on the bread of life and places an economic value on self-sacrifice that the economics of generosity can become a reality.

"I am the bread of life." The Lord who spoke the law now speaks the language of love: with arms outstretched he teaches us that it is self-giving that leads to life, fulfils the law, and undergirds justice. The Head of the House of Israel has become the Servant who gives himself for all, drawing us into communion with himself so that his values and his spirit inform our laws and shape our economics. The New Covenant is founded on love; it is love that enables us to take everyone's interests seriously, and the kingdom to come on earth as in heaven. We see in Jesus that there *is* another way and so, despite the forces ranged against it, the hope for justice is kept alive.

3

# Sign to the Nations: The Hope for Freedom

*O Scion of Jesse, standing as a sign among the nations;*
*before you kings will keep silence,*
*and peoples will summon you to their aid;*
*come and set us free and delay no more.*

*I am the offspring of David, the shoot growing from his stock.*

*I am the true vine.*

## Let my people go!

On 23 August 1989, two million people joined hands along the whole length of the Baltic Way that joins the three capital cities of Vilnius, Riga, and Tallinn. The day was the fiftieth anniversary of the signing of the Molotov-Ribbentrop Pact which divided Europe into Soviet and Nazi spheres of influence, consigning the Baltic states to a future under Russian domination. This great human chain, stretching over 370 miles, made real and visible the hope and demand for freedom. In both Riga and Tallinn the main public square is called "Freedom Square", and the freedom they celebrate is liberation, overthrowing oppression and regaining the ability to pursue their own aims and reassert their national identity—the collective equivalent of becoming your true self. The same hope motivates nations and national groups today, as they resist the way in which more powerful nations and groups endeavour to change the identity of those they dominate, importing their citizens, their language, their culture and religion, as the Russians sought to do in the Baltic and as ISIS aimed to do in Iraq. The examples could be multiplied.

It was precisely this experience of oppression that motivated the Israelites to escape from Egypt, and which led to the Exodus, the event in which Israel recognizes her beginning. "Let my people go!" Moses demanded of Pharaoh, a cry that has echoed down the centuries from the lips of every oppressed people. The long walk to freedom which followed the Exodus has become a source of inspiration and hope for other oppressed peoples, especially the American slaves, and it provided the title for Nelson Mandela's account of the struggle against apartheid in South Africa.[1]

Freedom in the Bible is first and foremost freedom from slavery. The cry of Moses has lost none of its urgency. Although the slave trade was abolished in 1807, more people are enslaved today than when it was at its height, both literally and in other forms like bonded labour, human trafficking, sexual exploitation, and conscription into labour gangs. Jean Jacques Rousseau famously observed, "Man is born free, and everywhere he is in chains."[2] He had in mind not only the oppressive use of monarchical and aristocratic power, but also the threat to freedom from the rising commercial class, a threat that has come to pass in modern life through the way the freedom of millions is constrained by the economically powerful. Many are ensnared through the practices of loan sharks, by zero-hours contracts and other oppressive conditions of employment, by the unfair terms of trade imposed on developing countries, and—much more subtly and insidiously—by the gathering of personal data by corporate giants like Facebook and Google. The professed aim of this may be to reflect better the preferences of the customer in the goods or services offered, but in practice what it amounts to is the manipulation of choice to serve the interests of the seller. Indeed, Shoshana Zuboff of the Harvard Business School, in a recent ground-breaking study of digital privacy, argues convincingly that internet surveillance is a major threat to freedom today, used not only to predict our behaviour but to influence and modify it,[3] and it is now apparent that the same techniques are used to influence the outcome of elections.[4] What these practices have in common with slavery is the denial of the full humanity, or autonomy, of the oppressed person or group. Freedom in the Bible is about restoring this fullness; it is not simply a formal freedom, like freeing a slave legally, but a substantive freedom that requires concrete and generous, even lavish, measures that will return to the slave his or her full humanity. Thus the Law of Moses went further than other codes by limiting the period of domestic slavery to six years; by extending to female slaves unconditional release in the seventh year; and by requiring former slave-owners to provide capital resources for a new start in life:

> Do not let him go empty-handed. Give to him lavishly from
> your flock, from your threshing-floor and your winepress.
> Be generous to him, as the Lord your God has blessed you.
>
> *Deuteronomy 15:14,18*

Moreover, the former owner is warned against being resentful, for the slave has been worth twice the wage of a hired man. The hope of freedom is, at root, a hope for the restoration of full humanity and autonomy for all who are oppressed.

**Scion and Sign**

After the Exodus the hope of freedom became a reality, but in the centuries that followed Israel was oppressed by her more powerful neighbours until King David ascended the throne. One of the reasons David is hailed as Israel's great king is because under him Israel enjoyed a brief period when she was the equal of her enemies (at least in the collective memory), and her hope of freedom became a reality. This new dispensation could not last—not only because of the resurgence of Israel's oppressors, but also because of corruption within the monarchy—but the hope remained. The third antiphon reflects this hope, and in doing so draws on a prophecy of Isaiah of Jerusalem. Isaiah lived some four centuries after David, at a time when Israel was constantly threatened by the Assyrian Empire; he foresaw that the hope for freedom would again be fulfilled by a new righteous ruler from the line of Jesse, the father of David:[5]

> On that day a scion from the root of Jesse
> will arise like a standard to rally the peoples;
> the nations will resort to him,
> and his abode will be glorious.
>
> *Isaiah 11:10*[6]

When quoted out of context, we miss the violent imagery behind this prophecy. In the previous chapter, Isaiah speaks of the LORD of Hosts routing the unrighteous as a mighty forest is felled with the axe (*Isaiah 10:33–4*), and just as new shoots can grow from the stumps of felled trees, so (he says) a new ruler will arise, the "Scion of Jesse", a new shoot from the root of true kingship. Christians see the prophecy fulfilled in Jesus, who "was of the house and lineage of David" (*Luke 2:4*, RSV), and the two images are brought together in one of the I AM sayings in Revelation: "I am the offspring of David, the shoot growing from his stock" (*Revelation 22:16*). As the violent image of the felling of trees suggests, Isaiah seems to have thought of the new ruler in military terms, a leader of armies like Joshua and David, but when Isaiah's prophecy was fulfilled in Jesus it was clear that the freedom that he offered was of an altogether different nature.

For Isaiah this new ruler carried the hope of true freedom. In the preceding verses of the oracle, Isaiah says that the scion from the root of Jesse will inaugurate a new era of justice and peace, when the humble will be treated with equity and the ruthless and the wicked punished; in the animal world natural enmities will be transcended, the wolf living with the lamb, and the calf feeding with the lion. In the name of the LORD he declares that on that day, "There will be neither hurt nor harm in all my holy mountain; for the land will be filled with the knowledge of the LORD as the waters cover the sea" (*Isaiah 11:9*). The hope that this prophecy expresses is for a world that is free, not only from external forces of injustice, fear, oppression, and violence, but also from those internal forces that diminish and enslave humanity. The hope is for a world in which all people and all creation can freely enjoy the peace of God. Jesus spoke to that hope when he used the image of the vine to describe the relationship between himself and his disciples: "I am the vine; you are the branches. Anyone who dwells in me, as I dwell in him, bears much fruit; apart from me you can do nothing" (*John 15:5*). Jesus, the Scion of Jesse, is the sign that points the way to freedom; he teaches us that only to the extent that we are united with him will our hopes be realized. This is particularly true of the hope for freedom, because true freedom requires us to be rooted in truth and justice, otherwise it degenerates into licence and anarchy.

## Liberation, Humanity and Wholeness

At the beginning of his ministry in the synagogue at Capernaum, Jesus said that in him the prophecy of Isaiah was fulfilled; he was the promised sign to the nations. Given the scroll of Isaiah, he chose to read this oracle:

> "The Spirit of the Lord is upon me
> because he has anointed me;
> he has sent me to announce good news to the poor,
> to proclaim release for prisoners
> and recovery of sight for the blind;
> to let the broken victims go free,
> to proclaim the year of the Lord's favour."
>
> *Luke 4:18–19 (cf. Isaiah 61:1–2)*

The prophecy that Jesus read is from Third Isaiah.[7] It comes from a period more than two centuries later than the prophecies of Isaiah of Jerusalem, and shows a different concern. While freedom in the Bible begins with freedom from slavery, it is not confined to it, and includes freedom from all forms of oppression. Third Isaiah spoke at a time when Israel had returned from captivity in Babylon; her time of political oppression was over, yet within her midst were many who were "unfree" and who yearned for liberation among their own people. His oracle gives three examples: the poor and the indebted, imprisoned by the misery of their condition (which is what "prisoners" means in this context[8]); the blind, imprisoned by their inability to find their way—the spiritually blind as well as the physically blind; and the broken victims: those imprisoned by oppression and bondage. Third Isaiah joins his voice, albeit in a different key, with the prophets who thundered against those who oppressed their fellow Israelites, referring back to Israel's experience of slavery in Egypt, from which they were delivered by the mighty acts of God. In taking these words to inaugurate his ministry, Jesus not only identifies himself as the one whom the Lord has anointed, God's sign to the nations, he also identifies himself with the substance of Isaiah's call for liberation.

Third Isaiah points to completeness about the hope for freedom uniquely expressed in the Hebrew concept of *shalom*, which underlines two important characteristics of the freedom that Jesus offers. The first is that freedom is built upon solidarity, thus guarding against the freedom of the one becoming a threat to the freedom of another. Thus Edward Schillebeeckx argues that Christian freedom "can only be liberated freedom, a freedom released from egoism and power, a freedom which rests on the acceptance of everyone by God . . . who accepts people beyond the limits of their ethical capacity and actions and regardless of the broken status of their humanity."[9]

The second is that freedom has a purposive character which takes the biblical understanding of hope for freedom beyond that of liberation. The hope of the Israelites escaping from Egypt may have been simply for freedom *from* oppression, but in the eyes of God it was also freedom *for* worship: God told Moses to go to Pharaoh and say, "These are the words of the LORD: Let my people go in order to worship me" (*Exodus 8:1*). And this is precisely the cry that Luke places on the lips of the old priest Zechariah, who praises God that he has set his people free from their enemies, *free to worship him without fear* (*Luke 1:74*). In the Bible freedom is never simply *freedom from*, that is, an escape from bondage; it always includes *freedom for*, that is, to enjoy the love of God and to contribute to *shalom*—in other words, freedom to put the right values at the heart of our life.

**Two views of freedom**

This biblical understanding has a bearing on the debate among political philosophers about the nature of freedom. On one side are those who see freedom simply as the liberty to act in accordance with our personal preferences *free from* coercion, constraint, or other disabling factors; on the other are those who see freedom as the ability to exercise certain positive rights that enable men and women both to act as they choose and to realize their own potential, setting them *free for* the life that God wills for all. Within the first view, extreme libertarians reject all constraints on personal behaviour; more moderate libertarians accept reasonable constraints, those necessary to ensure that one person's action does not unduly constrain the freedom of another. The second view of freedom, based on the concept of positive rights, generally includes freedom from poverty, starvation, treatable disease, and oppression, as well as from force and coercion. This second view of freedom requires political or communal action to ensure that an individual's positive rights are respected—a right is merely theoretical unless an individual or an institution is under a correlative duty to do whatever is required to give substance to the right. Libertarians reject this second view, certainly as far as state action is concerned, because it is incompatible with their belief in a very limited role for the state.

However, the biblical understanding of freedom is in line with this second view; it is based on the same understanding of what is required for human flourishing and rejects both the extreme and moderate libertarian positions. Its philosophy is communitarian; it is not interested in theory, but in practical action: characteristically, the Bible speaks of duties rather than rights. Thus the law does not give a slave the *right* to freedom; instead the master is placed under a *duty* to free him/her; and the concept of *shalom* places the community under a *duty* to care for its less advantaged and more vulnerable members. Placing the stress on duties rather than rights is one area where the Bible challenges both libertarians and communitarians, a challenge presented by Pope Francis in *Evangelii Gaudium*, where he argues that people being born in places with fewer resources or less development does not justify the fact that they are living with less dignity. Those more fortunate *have a responsibility* towards them, not simply of humanitarian relief, but for their "general temporal welfare and prosperity". This means, he says, education and access to healthcare, and above all, employment, "for it is through free, creative, participatory and mutually supportive labour that human beings express and enhance the dignity of their lives."[10] Pope Francis' argument is, in fact, part of the deeper challenge to contemporary ideas of freedom posed by the biblical understanding, namely that freedom has a purpose beyond individual liberty. God made us to be free in the way that he is free: freedom is the gift that enables us to love, delight in, and care for one another and for all creation.

## Seven signs

The purpose of freedom is human flourishing and wholeness, and this characterized Jesus' ministry, making real the prophecy of Third Isaiah that he read in Capernaum. We see this in his miracles, which—significantly—John calls signs. He describes seven: changing water into wine at the wedding in Cana (*2:1–11*); saving the officer's son from death (*4:46–54*); healing the paralysed man at the pool of Bethesda (*5:1–9*); feeding the multitude with a few loaves and fishes (*6:1–14*); calming the storm on the Sea of Galilee (*6:16–21*); giving sight to a man born blind (*9:1–7*); and raising Lazarus from the dead (*11:17–44*). In Jesus the hope for freedom becomes a reality, whether it is freedom from death, blindness, fear, hunger, illness, or unworthiness. The first miracle, changing water into wine, is the most fundamental of the seven signs. It points to a God whose generosity is overwhelming;[11] but more than this, it signifies a new way into his presence. The significance of the sign is that the new wine was produced by filling some of the large stone jars that were used in Jewish rites of purification; symbolically, the old rite is transcended: the water of the old covenant becomes the wine of the new covenant. The miracle prefigures the Eucharist: it is through the shed blood of Jesus that we are made clean and our sins washed away, rather than by a ritual washing with water, and we come to enjoy the freedom of the children of God. The third antiphon hails Jesus as the sign to the nations of God's way to freedom and fullness of life for all people.

## Listen to Him

At the turning point of Jesus' ministry, he was transfigured, and the divine command was heard: "Listen to him!" (*Mark 9:7*). As we have already seen, Saint Benedict urged his disciples to listen "with the ears of their heart", that is with their whole person, really taking to heart what is heard.[12] The antiphon echoes this when it says that kings will keep silence before God's sign to the nations. The image comes from Isaiah of Babylon. In the last "Servant Song" he describes the transformation in the way that the servant of the Lord will be regarded:

> Look, my servant will prosper,
> will grow great, will rise to great heights.
> As many people were aghast at him—
> he was so inhumanly disfigured

> that he no longer looked like a man—
> so many nations will be astonished
> and kings will stay tight-lipped before him,
> seeing what had never been told them,
> learning what they had not heard before.
>
> *Isaiah 52:13–15 (New Jerusalem Bible)*[13]

The prophet compares the revulsion of the people at the sight of the grossly disfigured servant with their astonishment at the divine favour now heaped upon him, so much so that kings will be reduced to silence, overwhelmed at the revelation before them. The prophet foretells the effect of God's self-revelation in Christ: nothing less than a revolution in the understanding of God and in what he requires of kings and their peoples. Can we hope that kings and rulers today will, in the same way, acknowledge the authority of Christ and the truth of God? It is a hope that flies in the face of experience; today it is the economic gurus before whom kings and rulers keep silence, not Jesus: they are the bearers of light, the heralds of a new dawn, while the Christian witness is largely ignored. Although those who seek political power generally do so to make life better and the people more free, there are powerful forces that combine to prevent these ambitions from being realized. What *Word* would today's kings and rulers hear from the Lord if they did indeed fall silent before him? I believe that there are four *Words* in particular that they need to hear if the hope of freedom is to be realized.

**Economics is not the whole story**

The first *Word* concerns the place of economic ideas and models in modern life considered in the previous chapter. I return to this issue because of the fundamental place that economic ideas occupy in today's world; not only are they a source of injustice, as we have seen, but they also lead to an attenuated concept of freedom. In 1971, Pope Paul VI asked rhetorically if there was not "a radical limitation to economics", which rendered it inappropriate to determine social structures.[14] It is clear today that Pope Paul was right; economics is not the whole story, because its conception of the nature and destiny of human life is flawed, and because in the developed world bigger no longer means better.

Taking the second point first, paradoxically, economic ideas have come to hold an unrivalled sway precisely at the time when, in the developed world, further economic growth has ceased to contribute in any meaningful way to increased happiness and wellbeing, as Richard Wilkinson and Kate Pickett point out in *The Spirit Level*:

> [F]or the vast majority of people in affluent countries the difficulties of life are no longer about filling our stomachs, having clean water and keeping warm . . . Economic growth, for so long the great engine of progress, has, in the rich countries, largely finished its work. Not only have measures of wellbeing and happiness ceased to rise with economic growth but, as affluent societies have grown richer, there have been long-term rises in rates of anxiety, depression and numerous other social problems. The populations of rich countries have got to the end of a long historical journey.[15]

I think most of us in the rich countries feel the truth of this, but we have become so accustomed—"programmed" might be a better word—to life being about getting and spending, getting more and bigger, that we fail to make the connection between our feelings of dissatisfaction and the economic imperatives that drive everyday life. The evidence presented by Wilkinson and Pickett in their ground-breaking study is compelling, and it adds powerfully to the argument that accepted economic ideas and institutions no longer serve us well.

This is clearly illustrated by the inadequacy of the most basic economic axiom, namely that humans act rationally in order to maximize their utility. Rational behaviour is defined exclusively in terms of pursuing one's self-interest; other motivations are regarded as non-rational. This axiom rests on the assumption that we are possessed of all the relevant information we need to decide what we want, and how to achieve it, from all the possibilities before us. No more than a moment's reflection is required to realize that the real world is not like that. Rarely, if ever, do we have full information, and we all know the effect of fashion, advertising, and peer pressure on the choices we make, as well as the altruistic motives of love and charity, and the needs of family and friends. As David Marquand has said, "In real life, atomistic individuals, solitary captains of their own souls . . . are so rare that we have a special label for them: 'autistic.' The vast majority of us are linked to others by ties of kinship, education, ethnicity, religion, locality, and occupation . . . "[16] Although there are leading economists who dissent from the established view—notably Amartya Sen, who has described it as "an exceedingly narrow approach"—it remains the mainstream view. (Sen also notes that many leading economists, who in their writing accept the assumption of the completely egoistic human being, have, in other contexts, also "expressed their serious doubts" about its veracity.)[17] Economists may argue that we act out of love, friendship, or charity because to do so has utility for us, but that is to fit the facts to the theory. As the economist Joan Robinson remarked, the concept of utility is endowed with an "impregnable circularity": "utility is the quality in commodities that makes individuals want to buy them, and the fact that individuals want to buy them shows they have utility".[18] Better to abandon the economic understanding of rationality as the sole source of human motivation, and to learn from modern research on the brain which confirms the "non-rational" way in which all humans actually behave.

In truth, we need to re-define what we mean by rational. Behavioural economists (the emerging school of economic thought mentioned in the last chapter) argue that our basic economic instincts are not simply self-serving: rather they are for fair shares, co-operation, and group identity. It *is* rational to work towards these goals. Nor do people work simply for money, or see work as a "disutility", as some economists assume; having good and meaningful work is basic to our sense of self-worth and fulfilment. Nor is work to be equated solely with paid employment; we work whenever we occupy our skills, talents, and time in the service of others and of the world. We might say that we work whenever we "add value", so long as we do not confine this to monetary value. Kahlil Gibran offered a beautiful description of work as something undertaken to keep us in rhythm with the soul of the earth: work is "love made visible".[19] What is self-evident is that many people are prepared to forego monetary rewards for the intrinsic satisfaction that their work provides. As Pete

Lunn says, "We are routinely selfless and our economy would not work as well as it does if we were not."[20]

It is also evident that the theory justifying minimal regulation of the economy, particularly financial services, was hopelessly flawed.[21] To quote David Marquand again: "The rational economic actor that economists put at the center of their conceptual universe had turned out to be a chimera. The financial services sector had been driven by the wild stampedes of what George Soros . . . called 'the electronic herd.' J. M. Keynes's mordant warning against allowing capital investment to become the 'by-product of a casino' had turned out to be as pertinent in the 2000s as it was in the 1930s."[22] Although the theoretical basis of neo-liberal economics is widely believed to be inadequate, it is difficult to avoid the conclusion that it is so deeply embedded in the way the modern world works that it simply cannot be disavowed. It is notable that in spite of the near collapse of the financial sector in 2008, nothing of substance has changed, either in the way it is operated or is regulated. In marked contrast to the new economic thinking that followed the crash in the 1930s, the response today has been—perversely—to reaffirm the validity of the very system that led to it! However, it takes time for the heavy structures of society, like the economic system, to change. It is like turning around a super-tanker rather than a racing yacht. If the behavioural economists are right, as they must be, then there are real grounds for the hope of fundamental change, though it will be hard fought, and will take time.

**Freedom is founded on equality**

The second *Word* concerns the link between freedom and equality. The disjunction between economic theory and social reality is one of the main causes of *ressentiment*, the sense of alienation and apathy, and of being trapped, that many feel—what Rousseau described as our "chains". Alienation is now much deeper than the alienation of the worker from both the product of his/her labour and its value described by Karl Marx. Today the "haves" as well as the "have-nots" feel left out of account, and that there is a basic unfairness and inequality at the heart of life. As I mentioned in the Prologue, it is impossible to understand the support for Brexit, or the rise of Donald Trump, or the election of right-wing regimes in Hungary, Turkey, India, and Brazil, or the way middle classes in many developed countries reject the regimes from which they have benefited materially, if this sense of alienation and inequality is ignored. David Harvey suggests that what people yearn for is dignity, and not being bought off with material goods, which he describes as the compensatory materialism that "limits and imprisons rather than liberates the horizons of personal fulfilment".[23]

While the Bible does not have a doctrine of equality in the modern sense of the term, it does have a doctrine of solidarity that placed upon the rich a duty of economic generosity towards the poor, an example of which I mention above in relation to the release of slaves. Modern ideas of equality are a development of the biblical concept: an example, I would argue, of the Holy Spirit leading us into the truth as Jesus promised. Equality is basic to our health and wellbeing. The evidence presented in *The Spirit Level* shows convincingly that in the developed nations inequality (as measured by income) is *the one factor* underlying poor levels of trust, health, and education, and high levels of obesity, violence, crime, teenage births, and infant mortality. The most unequal societies, like the UK and the USA, have the highest levels of health and social problems; in the more equal societies of Japan and Scandinavia these are uniformly low. It was shocking to read that in the USA, the richest country in the world, with the most sophisticated medical services, the rate of infant mortality is the highest in the developed world! Contrary to popular ideas, Wilkinson and Pickett show beyond doubt that greater equality does not just benefit the poor, but everyone—everyone's freedom is diminished by inequality, rich and poor alike. If the Christian concept of freedom, as I argue above, includes not only freedom from force and coercion, but also freedom from poverty, starvation, treatable disease, and oppression—the very things that inequality increases—then the hope for freedom requires that we strive to create a more equal society.[24]

If this is the case for those in the developed world, it is massively more so for those living in the rest of the world, for whom inequality and exclusion are ineradicable effects of the global economic system. For most people in the world there is nothing liberating about modern economic liberalism; from their perspective it must seem like "a bourgeois ideology" which refuses to respond to the problems of mass-pauperization[25]. Globally, the terms of trade are stacked in favour of the rich countries.[26] Structural adjustment programmes based on neo-liberal theories advocated by the IMF and World Bank have generally had a negative effect on the economies of the poorer nations, and result—through the mechanism of debt repayment—in a net transfer of resources from the poor to the rich. The belief that wealth would "trickle down" from the movers and the shakers to the moved and the shaken has proved completely mistaken; similarly, the claim that a rising tide lifts all boats has not been substantiated. The economic tide does not work like the ocean; economically, the bigger the boat the higher it rises. The use of theories to sustain a lifestyle that excludes others and perpetuates inequality is only possible because a "globalization of indifference" has developed.[27] It blinds us to reality. Economic liberalism is not the way to true freedom because its understanding of the human person and of human motivations is flawed, as I argued in the previous chapter; it works against community and equality. In other words, it is not rooted in truth. By contrast, to be rooted in Christ is to discover a much truer understanding of humanity with its recognition of kinship and community, finitude and sin, faith and hope.

**Community comes first**

The third *Word* concerns the nature of human society. Understanding the biblical conception of society requires a close reading of the laws set out in the first five books of the Bible, particularly the so-called Holiness Code in *Leviticus*.[28] We often skip over these books with their detailed laws and rules, but study of them is repaid if done with the aim of discovering the values implicit in the laws. Socially, the basic unit is "the-person-in-community"; the communal and individual interests are held in a creative balance, acknowledging both our interdependence and our individual worth. Social justice is the basis of the wellbeing of the community, and it is seen typically in a solidarity between the classes, with the duty of generosity towards the poor being accepted by the rich. We live in an age in which this divine concern for social solidarity is all but drowned out by a consumerist and highly individualistic culture. This culture has little sympathy for the idea that enabling the kingdom to come "on earth as in heaven" requires, as Schillebeeckx argues, "a partisan choice for the poor and oppressed, against the oppression of powerful people and structures which grind down men and women".[29] (The poor and oppressed in this context are not simply the desperately poor, but also those described by Theresa May in 2016 as "just about managing".) Typically, in today's managerial state the poor are spoken *about*, and spoken *for*, but not spoken *with* and really listened to. This denial of effective participation in society lies at the heart of the deeply felt anger over the fire at Grenfell Tower.[30] God's sign to the nations is simply not seen, and his word is not heard. And if it is seen or heard, it is acknowledged formally rather than substantively in changed lives and in an economic policy which aims to reduce inequality.

There is a wealth of evidence not only that the unequal distribution of resources underlies many social problems, but also that when things go wrong the cost is borne mostly by the poor. This, alas, is nothing new. Almost two and a half millennia ago, the Greek historian Thucydides, in his *History of the Peloponnesian War* (431–404 BC), described the unjust terms of peace imposed by the economically powerful Athenians upon the poorer Melians; when the Melians appealed to divine justice, the Athenians replied, "The strong do what they have the power to do and the weak accept what they have to accept." It is precisely this arrogant, oppressive, and self-serving use of power that the principle of *shalom* overcomes. Looking at the world from a European perspective, it is easy to miss the scale of the problem of inequality, as the liberation theologian Jon Sobrino pointed out:

> The world is not just a planet with typical European problems like secularization and agnosticism. It is a planet of poverty where the main issue for human beings is to live and survive . . . [T]he problem in the world is not, as they say in Europe or the United States, that there are pockets of poverty: in the world there are pockets of abundance, and the rest is poverty.[31]

The hope for freedom calls us to align policy with faith, really heeding God's sign to the nations. Third Isaiah thundered against the oppression perpetrated by those who outwardly conformed to the faith, but inwardly remained unchanged. He condemned those who kept the customary fasts, but served their own interests on the fast-day by keeping all their servants hard at work. "On such a day the fast you are keeping is not one that will carry your voice to heaven," he warned (*Isaiah 58:4b*). Personal mortification without works of mercy was not a fast acceptable to the LORD; the fast that the LORD required was:

> . . . to loose the fetters of injustice,
> to untie the knots of the yoke,
> and set free those who are oppressed
> . . . sharing your food with the hungry,
> taking the homeless poor into your house,
> clothing the naked when you meet them,
> and never evading a duty to your kinsfolk.
>
> *Isaiah 58:6–7*

If Jesus is a sign to the nations, then his way is deeply challenging to modern Western life and to our understanding of community. The divine concern for the liberation of the poor echoes throughout the Old Testament, for example in the prayer of Hannah:

> "He raises the poor from the dust,
> he lifts the needy from the dunghill
> to give them a place with princes,
> to assign them a seat of honour . . . "
>
> *1 Samuel 2:8 (New Jerusalem Bible)*

A reversal of fortune that Luke placed on the lips of the Virgin Mary in dramatic terms:

> "He has shown strength with his arm
> and has scattered the proud in their conceit,
> casting down the mighty from their thrones
> and lifting up the lowly.
> He has filled the hungry with good things

and sent the rich away empty."

*Luke 1:51–3 (Common Worship version of the Magnificat)*

As Donal Dorr comments trenchantly, Mary's song "makes no concession at all to those who would like to imagine that the oppressed can be set free without disturbing those who hold power and without dismantling the structures of oppression".[32] How often do we repeat Mary's words and the meaning passes us by?

**We are all in it together**

The fourth *Word* concerns the mutuality of freedom. In the biblical understanding, freedom is not something that we achieve one by one, individual by individual; it is something that we achieve together, and this requires a heartfelt recognition that we are all in it together—a truth that the COVID-19 pandemic has made inescapably clear. The biblical principle of solidarity arises out of this conviction. The duty of generosity that the rich accept towards the poor is not done out of charity, but because they accept that their good fortune is given to them by God to share, so that all can enjoy his good things. The desire to hang on to what we have is natural, part of the instinct for self-preservation, but in a consumer culture where worth is measured by wealth and possessions, it goes *well beyond* self-preservation. Rich and poor alike need to learn that it is not through selfishness that we grow, but through generosity and self-giving. Rowan Williams asks why we should be concerned about this, and his response is worth quoting in full.

> The answer is seen in what is happening in urban America, as in many Third World cities: heavily protected areas of extreme wealth growing up in the middle of what's seen as a threatening underclass. Individual countries are made insecure by this kind of juxtaposition; what if the whole world were an inflated version of such a picture? For the dispossessed and hopeless don't disappear conveniently; they have to eat. At whose expense? If not at the expense of our voluntary help, then at the expense of our security. If at

> the expense of our security, then, ultimately at the expense of our prosperity, as we have to devote higher budgets to small and large-scale defence. If at the expense of our prosperity, then at the expense of a shrinking market.[33]

He spoke in 2001; since then, the insecurity that globalization exports to many weaker countries, and then visits on the rich, has come home to roost. An economy which privileges one section of society or part of the world above the rest cannot be regarded as good in Christian terms, and a global economic ethic that sets light to the indefinitely continuing poverty or disadvantage of some has to be decisively rejected. Returning to this issue nine years later, Williams emphasized the need for those who *have* to recognize their "own need and dependence even on those who appear to have nothing to give. To separate our destiny from that of the poor of the world . . . is to compromise that destiny and to invite a life that is less than whole for ourselves."[34]

The example of the self-giving of Jesus to the point of self-sacrifice should lead us to see the spiritual value of economic generosity; the evidence presented by Wilkinson and Pickett in *The Spirit Level* shows us its practical importance—indeed, as the title of their study indicates, spirituality and practicality are linked. Until we create a more equal society the kingdom will not come "on earth as it is in heaven", and all are diminished: the poor by their lack of resources, the rich by their meanness of spirit. As Julius Nyerere, the former president of Tanzania, said, if the kingdom (heaven on earth) does not come for all, it does not come for any. We cannot believe as Christians that God does special deals.[35] *Shalom* is communal, not individual, and the kingly rule of God is seen in a life dedicated to justice and equality. Paul put it well: "[T]he kingdom of God is not eating and drinking, but justice, peace, and joy, inspired by the Holy Spirit" (*Romans 14:17*). The hope for freedom yearns for the time when the kingly rule of God shall come on earth as it is in heaven, and kings shall recognize Jesus as God's sign to the nations and keep silence before him.

## The Vine and the Branches

Implicit in the hope for freedom is the hope for a new order in human society built upon social justice, equality, community, and mutuality. It has been suggested that primitive societies were based on these virtues,[36] but they have been eclipsed over the centuries by other motivations, and to many this hope will seem no more than a dream. But the hope will not go away, and it remains a powerful motivating force for those who work for justice and freedom. The third antiphon pictures the peoples summoning Jesus to their aid. His response is to remind us that we cannot achieve our hopes in our own strength; it is only to the extent that we are united with him that our hopes will be realized.

> "I am the true vine . . . dwell in me, as I in you. I am the vine; you are the branches. Anyone who dwells in me, as I dwell in him, bears much fruit; apart from me you can do nothing. No branch can bear fruit by itself, but only if it remains united with the vine; no more can you bear fruit, unless you remain united with me."
>
> *John 15:1,4a,5,4b*

The vine and the vineyard are biblical images for Israel, but Israel, for all God's tending, had not been the vine that he intended it to be. Israel had, in Isaiah's words, brought forth "wild grapes". Isaiah's Song of the Vineyard (*Isaiah 5:1–7*) begins as though it were a love song, as might have been sung at a wedding, but ends on a note of judgement. In response to his love God expected faithfulness and righteousness, but instead his laws have been ignored and "the piercing cry of the oppressor and the oppressed rings in his ears".[37] Isaiah asks: What more could God have done for his vineyard? The question is rhetorical; the prophet declares that God is about to abandon it, and let it go to waste. But this was not God's final word: Jesus proclaimed that in himself the purpose entrusted to Israel by God was being fulfilled. When he spoke of himself as the True Vine it was with deep prophetic meaning: he applied to himself a social image which had hitherto been used only of the community; he is not just the vine-stock, but the whole vine. Just as in the Ancient Near East, a king was thought of as embodying the nation, so Jesus presents himself as embodying the true Israel, the new and true people of God. He says to his disciples, "You are a people in me." Daniel Stevick points out that the striking thing about the way Jesus uses the image of the vine is that "*all is now*". He does not tell a story, as Isaiah did; there is no development, no reckoning. "Even though something may happen to individual branches, nothing happens to the vine." There is no planting, no maturation, no destructive enemies, no blighting of the crop, no harvest.[38] The emphasis is entirely on the connectedness, the unity of the vine. And it is only by remaining within that connectedness that the true fruit which God's vineyard was created to produce will be brought forth. Those who hope in him must be joined to him, as the branches are joined to the vine, if their hopes are to be realized. He is the source from which all our hopes receive their life. As the branches of the vine are fed by the root and the stock, so the aid Jesus offers to those who call upon him is his own spirit. To be free, he says, you have to be grafted into what is real, rooted in the source of true life.

**Rootlessness**

Some years ago I caught part of a radio broadcast in which the speaker said that the problem with our present age was not meaninglessness, but rootlessness. I have no idea who he was, but his words have remained with me. Meaning, strength, and values come from our roots. As Jesus said, we shall achieve nothing if we are not rooted in him, nor shall we be truly free. Apart from him we will be like a withered branch that is gathered up, thrown on the fire, and burnt (*John 15:6*). To be free we must be rooted; the importance of roots cannot be over-stressed. Roots anchor us: they give us our identity, and our place in society and in history. Roots sustain us: through them flows the source of life; through our roots we are fed and formed; without roots we cannot grow—cut off from them we wither and die. Roots keep us earthed: they keep us in touch with what is real; roots are the source of meaning. Saint Benedict understood the spiritual importance of roots, and the first of the vows he required his monks to make was a vow of stability, a promise of commitment to a community, where (as we say) we put down our roots, and let its life, its identity, and its values form the person that we shall become. Benedict contrasted the rooted monk with those whose way of life allowed them simply to please themselves and wander rootless from place to place, those whom he called "sarabaites" and "gyrovagues", those who had the appearance of freedom, but not its substance. Rachel Srubas, reflecting on this, wrote:

> Gathering God,
> you fashioned me
> not for isolation, but community . . .
> let me experience as true
> what, deep down, I always knew:
> to surrender independence
> is freedom. To serve other people
> is to be made whole in you.[39]

**Restraint and commitment**

"*Come to our aid!*" To all who are truly united with him, Jesus promises his spirit, his strength, and his values. Jesus' call to be rooted in him challenges modern ideas of freedom as the condition of being unattached and uncommitted. Our individualistic culture and utilitarian morality encourage us to believe that we are our centre of concern, our own source of moral authority. This is better described as licence or anarchy rather than freedom—in truth it is a condition more of slavery than freedom, in which people are impoverished materially, morally, and spiritually. The truly free are those who have room to grow, who enjoy personal and moral security; and this freedom, paradoxical as it may seem, requires restraint. Jordan Peterson, author of *12 Rules for Life*, is convinced that "we have got to a point in our culture . . . where all the talk of infinite rights and continual freedom has just left a huge gap on the other side of the equation, which is order and discipline and responsibility . . . " He believes that "a glib, juvenile search for happiness . . . has bewitched modern culture".[40] Without discipline there is no freedom. This is, or ought to be, a matter of common experience. Those who have acquired an artistic or technical skill, or have acquired a professional expertise, have only done so because they have given themselves to their calling or profession, to the exclusion of other possibilities, and spent long hours in disciplined training. They will know the truth of Jesus' words about the work of the gardener: "Any branch of mine that is barren he cuts away; and any fruiting branch he prunes clean, to make it more fruitful still" (*John 15:2*). The decision to become a violinist, for example, excludes other possibilities, but once trained and accomplished, the player acquires a freedom that she lacked before. She is rooted, and she is free.

Attaining true freedom also requires commitment, both to each other and to a source of authority that is beyond ourselves. The bishops of the Church of England put it well in their statement on marriage: "There is a great deal in our culture which discourages us from making binding and public promises . . . But the promises are liberating. Through them we focus our intentions, and offer one another a shared future in a way that we could hardly dare to do otherwise."[41] Commitment is the virtue that enables us to be rooted, and being rooted actually expands our lives, opening up new dimensions that we would otherwise be denied; non-attachment is a rootless, dysfunctional understanding of freedom.

## Set us free!

"*Let my people go!*" The story of the liberation of the Israelites from slavery has been the inspiration of all oppressed peoples, not least the American slaves. Their lack of freedom was clear for all to see, and was cruelly enforced, but those who enslaved them were no more free, although their liberty was not constrained. Unjust and repressive ideas corrupt and enslave the spirit; they also create no-go areas for the oppressors, thus limiting their physical freedom. I remember my visit to South Africa before the end of apartheid. The blacks suffered cruel restrictions on their freedom and were housed in shocking conditions; the whites and coloureds who oppressed them sheltered at night behind high walls and security alarms. The system of strict racial segregation that they enforced imprisoned them also: to some extent physically, but more importantly, morally and spiritually. Economic and political inequality imprisons everyone, rich and poor alike, though the privileged life of the oppressors blinds them to the reality of their situation. Try pointing this out, and you are met with a wall of incomprehension and the assertion of rights and worthiness. This was the experience of Jesus in an encounter with some Jewish converts, recorded by John. Jesus said to them, "If you stand by my teaching, you are truly my disciples, you will know the truth, and the truth will set you free." The Jews responded indignantly, "We are Abraham's descendants; we have never been in slavery to anyone. What do you mean by saying, 'You will become free?'" (*John 8:31–3*). Jesus replied by saying it is sin that enslaves; it is their wrong devices and desires that imprison them. This truth needs to be heard by both oppressed and oppressor alike. It is just as easy for the oppressed, as well as the oppressors, to have the wrong ideas about freedom, as the immediate aftermath of the French Revolution (and, indeed, of most other revolutions) showed appallingly clearly, with the newly liberated installing their own oppressive regime of terror. As the Jews who argued with Jesus discovered, the truth that will set us free faces us in a person, not in a creed or ideology, nor in a political, economic, or social system. The truth that liberates is personal not propositional; it is rooted, not free-standing, communal, not individual.

Liberation comes through a personal relationship with Jesus, and it demands a generosity of spirit that takes everyone's interests seriously; but before it can liberate us we have to overcome the insidious way in which we become acclimatized to injustice, so that while we might recognize it in the abstract we no longer see it under our nose. This is well illustrated by Sue Monk Kidd in her novel *The Invention of Wings*, based on the life of Sarah Grimké, one of the pioneer campaigners against slavery in the USA in the mid-nineteenth century. Sarah's awakening is described through an episode when her female slave Hetty takes a bath in Sarah's bedroom while she is away. When Sarah returns earlier than expected and discovers Hetty in her bath, her first reaction is anger that Hetty has assumed a forbidden privilege. But then Sarah sees what she had not seen before, that she was "very good at despising slavery in the abstract, in the removed and anonymous masses, but in the concrete, intimate flesh of the girl beside me, I'd lost the ability to be repulsed by it. I'd grown comfortable with the particulars of evil. There's a frightful muteness that dwells at the centre of all unspeakable things, and I had found my way into it."[42] It is the same with the way in which neo-liberal economics has become the new religion. Most of us have grown comfortable with the particulars of the new economic dispensation; perhaps we are aware that the heart and the soul have changed, but like Sarah we feel this in the abstract, and not personally. We have lost the ability to be repulsed by it, mute in the face of the new religion to which we have been converted.

Lying behind Sarah's failure to let the truth really touch her was the personal and social cost that acknowledging it would entail. We learn later in the story that her father, a judge in South Carolina, believed slavery to be evil, but was unable to acknowledge this, because in doing so he would forfeit his judicial position, his social standing, and his friends. The truth that faces us in Jesus is, more often than not, rejected or glossed over because it is politically or socially inconvenient. It is easy to put aside concerns about the poor as "left-wing", conveniently overlooking the fact that this concern was biblical long before there was any left or right wing. Concern for the poor reflects God's priorities, and part of our worship is to bring our priorities into line with his. It is also easy to overlook the fact that both Left and Right equally exclude the spiritual dimension of life from their conception of the nature and ends of human life, an inconvenient truth to which Pope St John Paul II drew attention in 1991:

> [When] the affluent society or the consumer society seeks to defeat Marxism on the level of pure materialism by showing how a free-market society can achieve a greater satisfaction of material needs than Communism, while equally excluding spiritual values . . . it agrees with Marxism, in the sense that it totally reduces [humans] to the sphere of economics and the satisfaction of material needs.[43]

The Bible has no conception of religion and politics occupying separate spheres, and one of the malign effects of secularism has been to persuade us that this is so, effectively confining religion to private life. Archbishop Desmond Tutu said that when he heard people say that the two should be kept apart, he asked what Bible they were reading. If the truth is to set us free, then it has to be brought out of the holy place, into the marketplace. Despite failure, the hope for freedom persists. While we do have to accept a great deal of unfairness in life, it remains an affront to our being. In the end, we cannot settle for a morally neutral life, nor for a morally inadequate politics. It is in Christ alone that we shall find the truth that sets us free.

# 4

# Open Door: The Hope for a New Beginning

*O Key of David and Sceptre of the House of Israel;*
*you open and none can shut,*
*you shut and none can open;*
*come, and free the captive from prison.*

*I am the door of the sheepfold.*

## The Open Door

"I have set before you an open door which no one can shut" (*Revelation 3:8*). The idea of an open door leading to a new beginning and a new life speaks to all our hopes—not simply because we yearn for something better, but also because the fulfilment of hope involves personal renewal. For some, a new beginning will mean an escape from the past, perhaps in a dramatic way like taking on a new identity, cutting all links with their former life. The Christian idea is rather different. It *is* about being freed from past failures and receiving new strength for the future, but not in any escapist way in which the past is denied and obliterated from memory. In the new beginning that Jesus offers us we take our past with us, not obliterated but healed. We need to own the past if we are to learn from it and avoid simply repeating it, but in Christ's new day we are no longer determined by it, nor weighed down by it; we are made new. Someone I was speaking to recently put it beautifully when he said of his decision to follow Jesus, "I became a new version of me."

Jesus is both the key to this new life and its guardian. He is the key because he makes it possible through his divine gifts of forgiveness and of the Holy Spirit; he is the guardian because he himself is the door, the entrance to the place where newness of life can be found. Using the image of the sheepfold to describe that place, he said:

> "I am the door; anyone who comes into the fold through me will be safe. He will go in and out and find pasture."
>
> *John 10:9*

Jesus is not just the key, but the door itself. In his day the shepherd used to sleep across the entrance to the fold; his body kept the sheep safe, and entry to the sheepfold was—quite literally—"through" him. In Orthodox Christianity, this image is transposed to the church building: an icon of the head and shoulders of Christ is often placed above the entrance; if the whole figure were represented the doorway would be his body so that, in effect, the faithful enter through him. The two images of the key and the door belong together, and they are brought together in the Revelation to John:

> These are the words of the Holy One, the True One, who has David's Key, so that when he opens the door, no one can shut it, and when he shuts it, no one can open it: I know what you are doing. I have set before you an open door which no one can shut.
>
> *Revelation 3:7b–8a*

The claim to have the "power of the keys" is a claim of authority. Jesus can offer the gifts of forgiveness and the Holy Spirit because of the authority committed to him—an authority symbolized throughout the New Testament by the image of Jesus being seated at God's right hand (e.g. *Ephesians 1:20*). The Key of David is one of two symbols used by the fourth antiphon to speak of Jesus' authority; the other is the Sceptre of the House of Israel, and it is helpful to consider them both before looking further at the gifts that he offers.

**Key of David**

The first symbol comes from an incident in the story of the kings of Judah. Isaiah of Jerusalem relates that Eliakim was appointed comptroller of the royal household in place of Shebna, who had abused his position, seeking advantage for himself by building a prestigious tomb. The prophet spoke the word of the LORD to the disgraced steward:

> The LORD will shake you out, shake you as a garment is shaken out to rid it of lice . . . On that day I shall send for my servant Eliakim son of Hilkiah; I shall invest him with your robe, equip him with your sash of office, and invest him with your authority; he will be father to the inhabitants of Jerusalem and to the people of Judah. I shall place the key of David's palace on his shoulder; what he opens none will shut, and what he shuts none will open . . . I will fasten him firmly in place like a peg. On him will hang the whole glory of the family.
>
> *Isaiah 22:17,20–24a*

The story works on two levels, the historic and the prophetic. On one level, it is history: Eliakim did replace Shebna; he represented a new beginning for the royal household, and on him hung the whole glory of the king's family. But on another level, it is also prophecy: as God has set a new ruler over the king's house, so he will set a new ruler over his people, through whom they will have a new beginning, and the glory of Israel will hang upon him. The fourth antiphon hails Jesus as the fulfilment of this prophecy; he is the Key of David who will unlock a new beginning for the House of Israel, seen particularly in his authority to forgive sins. However, this new beginning was not only for Israel but for all peoples, as Simeon prophesied: "He will be a light to lighten the Gentiles and the glory of his people, Israel" (*Luke 2:32*).

**Sceptre of Israel**

The second image—of the sceptre, a sign of royal authority borne by kings and by their high officials—reflects the same messianic theme. This image reaches back to the patriarch Jacob, who at the end of his life appointed his third son Judah to be his heir, investing him with the Sceptre of Israel:

> The sceptre shall not pass from Judah,
> nor the staff from between his feet,
> until the day when he comes
> who is to be sent to us,
> he, the hope of the nations.
>
> *Genesis 49:10 (free translation)*[1]

Jacob decrees that Judah and his descendants will hold the sceptre of Israel, but only until the coming of the One to whom it is destined to belong. The expectation of the One to come is a consistent theme of the prophets, perhaps most eloquently Daniel, who in a vision saw:

> one like a human being coming with the clouds of heaven; he approached the Ancient in Years and was presented to him. Sovereignty and glory and kingly power were given to him, so that all peoples and nations of every language should serve him; his sovereignty was to be an everlasting sovereignty which was not to pass away, and his kingly power was never to be destroyed.
>
> *Daniel 7:13–14*

This image appears also in *Revelation*. John of Patmos, in a vision, sees God holding a scroll in his right hand sealed with seven seals (*Revelation 5:1*). An angel asks, "Who is worthy to break the seals and open the scroll?" The only One who is worthy is "the Lion from the tribe of Judah, the shoot growing from David's stock". This One appears before the heavenly court as a Lamb bearing "the marks of sacrifice"—a clear reference to Jesus, the Lamb of God—who alone has the divine right to break the seals and to open the scroll; and as this divine authority is conferred on him, the host of heaven sings a great song of praise:

> "Worthy is the Lamb who was slain, to receive power and wealth, wisdom and might, honour, glory and praise!"
>
> *Revelation 5:12*

Just as the full authority of the king passed from Shebna to Eliakim, so the fourth antiphon praises Jesus as the One who possesses the full authority of God. He now bears the sceptre of Israel and is endowed with the same plenitude of power as the royal steward; it is to him that full authority in heaven and on earth has been committed (*Matthew 28:18*). Just as he was the sign of God's new beginning for Israel, so he is the sign of God's new beginning for all people.

**Full authority**

Right from the beginning of his ministry it was his authority that marked Jesus out. It is almost the first thing that Mark tells us about him. At Capernaum, he says, Jesus "went to the synagogue and began to teach. The people were amazed at his teaching, for, unlike the scribes, he taught with a note of authority" (*Mark 1:21–2*). Not long before, Simon and Andrew, James and John had responded to that authority by obeying Jesus' call to follow him, and later on in the synagogue, Mark records the universal sense of awe after Jesus had healed a man with an unclean spirit: "They were all amazed and began to ask one another, 'What is this? A new kind of teaching! He speaks with authority. When he gives orders, even the unclean spirits obey'" (*Mark 1:27*). As the Gospel unfolds, it becomes clear that Jesus' authority extends not only over demons, disease, and death, but also, and most controversially, it extends to the forgiveness of sins, a power that belongs to God alone. Jesus is the One whose authority is truly divine, seen not only in his power over all that is opposed to God, but also in the divine gift of forgiveness, and on another occasion in Capernaum this was dramatically and pointedly made plain (*Mark 2: 1–12*). A paralysed man was brought to him for healing; Jesus said to him, "My son, your sins are forgiven." These words aroused the wrath of the scribes who were present. To them this claim was blasphemy; God alone had the authority to forgive sins. Jesus, knowing what was in their hearts, said to them, "Is it easier to say to this paralysed man, 'Your sins are forgiven,' or to say, 'Stand up, take your bed, and walk'? But to convince you that the Son of Man has authority on earth to forgive sins"—he turned to the paralysed man—"I say to you, stand up, take your bed, and go home." And he did!

## What he opens none will shut

The plenitude of royal authority conferred on Eliakim empowered him to control access to the royal presence, with power to admit or exclude those who sought admittance to the palace. The same power is part of the full authority bestowed on Jesus: "No one comes to the Father except by me" (*John 14:6*). He has the power of the keys, but this power is given to him to bring people to God, to open the door in welcome, not to shut the door in condemnation and exclusion: "I have come," he said, "that you may have life, and may have it in all its fullness" (*John 10:10*). Adapting what Isaiah said about Eliakim, we may say about Jesus that on him hangs the glory of God's family, that is, men and women fully alive. The second-century theologian Irenaeus of Lyons put it memorably: "The glory of God is the living man; and the life of man is the vision of God."[2] The door which Jesus opens is the gateway to that glory and to that vision, and it is made real sacramentally in the rite of baptism. Baptism is, above all, the sign of God's new beginning, when the new Christian symbolically dies and rises with Christ. Alas, the attenuated form in which it is generally administered today robs baptism of its symbolism; it was otherwise in the Early Church.

The ceremony was held just before dawn on Easter Day. The candidates would face west, the direction where the sun had set, and pushing out their hands towards the darkened sky and turning their heads away in a gesture of rejection, they repudiated the darkness and all it stood for. They were divested of their clothes, symbolically putting off the old nature, and then turning around and facing east towards the light of dawn—the new light of Christ in which they would live—they stepped down quite naked into the water. As they stood, water was poured over them three times, initially for the Lord's three days in the tomb, and later also for their trinitarian faith. They came up out of the water and, as was usual after a bath, were rubbed with oil (this later became an anointing, or christening: a "making bright" with Christ). They were clothed in new clothes, symbolically putting on the new nature, and brought before the assembled church where the bishop received them by laying hands on their heads, with prayer that the Holy Spirit would, by his gifts, confirm the candidates in their new faith.

The reality of a new beginning was palpable. The question, "Do you turn to Christ?" was answered in body as well as in mind: with the words "I turn to Christ" the candidates literally turned around, showing outwardly in their bodies the inward desire to re-orient their lives away from self-concern and towards God. The symbolism of dying and rising with Christ was experienced bodily as water was poured over them, reflecting the ancient belief that those who had drowned did not come up for the third time. In baptism the new Christian receives the gift of the Holy Spirit; it is a new birth in the Spirit, a new birth from above, and like natural birth cannot be repeated—the new Christian has passed through the door that Christ holds open, and there is no going back. There is nothing magical about the gift of the Spirit; like any gift we can put it in the cupboard and forget about it, or we can treasure it and enjoy it, and this means nurturing the gift and learning to live by it, rather than by the devices and desires of our own hearts. The re-orientation that baptism requires is not achieved in a moment, but in a lifetime's endeavour; yet such moments are the way we grasp our hopes: they are pursued rather than possessed.

## An integrated life

God's new beginning is nothing less than life in all its fullness. Rowan Williams has described it as an integrated life, "living in a way that expresses with complete integrity who and what we really are. Living in a way that weaves together knowing and loving and judging and forgiving in one act of self-sharing that is somehow beyond the fragmented and reactive ways we so often live."[3] This is a richer and deeper understanding than the conventional claim to be living life to the full, with its associations of a wealth of experiences and adventurous activity. Life in all its fullness may well include these things but essentially, in the Christian understanding, it is a foretaste of life in communion with God, eternal life, the life of heaven. "Eternal life" does not refer simply to life after death; it is more a quality of life, a mode of being, that can be experienced here and now within the fellowship into which the Christian is initiated in baptism, and in which we are sustained by our communion with Christ—the bread and the wine are given with the prayer that the divine gift will *keep us* in eternal life. It is the fullness of human life offered by God. "It is to be able to receive from God the richness of intimacy, liberty and love we were made for, and to be free to give this love back to God and outwards to others."[4] In spiritual terms a full life is a connected life, in which our beliefs, feelings, values, intuitions, and actions form a unity. E. M. Forster, in his novel *Howards End*, speaks of connecting the prose and the passion; without that connection, he says, "we are meaningless fragments, . . . unconnected arches that have never joined into a man." I am inclined to think that the problems of modern life—the sense of dislocation, lack of meaning, high levels of stress, fractured relationships—derive from the lack of connection in our lives; our lives are unfulfilled because they are disconnected and unbalanced, part of the rootlessness described in the last chapter. We know that life should be different, and we hope for something better. This hope is made real in Christ whose life was completely integrated, the truly human life. E. M. Forster's heroine, Margaret, felt that it was hard-going in the roads of her husband's soul; she longed for him to build "the rainbow bridge that should connect the prose in us with the passion", a gift that she believed was latent in his own soul, but which he had so far not been able to discover. "Only connect! That was the whole of her sermon. Only connect the prose and the passion, and both will be exalted, and human love will be seen at its height. Live in fragments no longer."[5]

*"I have set before you an open door which no one can shut"* (*Revelation 3:8*). Jesus fulfils our hope for an integrated life by setting before us a door that is permanently open; anyone may pass through it, no one is excluded. Faith in him gives us the power to gather the fragments of life into a connected whole, but something is required of us if we wish to do so, because integration is not something that happens automatically; we have to want it. To borrow E. M. Forster's phrase, we have to play our part in building the rainbow bridge that connects the prose and the passion of our lives. God comes to our aid, but we have to seize our hope and work towards its realization. Opening ourselves to receive forgiveness is

where we start. It is freely given, but for it to be received we have to offer in return both reciprocity and repentance. And if the new beginning that we seek seems to elude us, it may be because we have not taken these two things to heart.

**Reciprocity**

Reciprocity means that those who seek forgiveness must also have a forgiving heart. We are reminded of this each time we say the Lord's Prayer: "Forgive us our sins *as we forgive those who sin against us*." As we pray these words we remind ourselves of our own need to forgive, a point that Jesus explained time and again; for example, "When you stand praying, if you have a grievance against anyone, forgive him, so that your Father in heaven may forgive you the wrongs you have done" (*Mark 11:25*). In the Sermon on the Mount, Jesus drove the point home, adding, "For if you forgive others the wrongs they have done, your heavenly Father will also forgive you; but if you do not forgive others, then your Father will not forgive the wrongs that you have done" (*Matthew 6:14–15*). The measure of forgiveness expected of us is just the same as the measure we hope for from God. When Peter asked Jesus if he should forgive those who kept on wronging him "as many as seven times", Jesus replied, "I do not say seven times, but seventy times seven" (*Matthew 18:22*—a point graphically driven home in the parable of the Unmerciful Servant which follows: *Matthew 18:23–35*).

The full meaning of Jesus' response is seen in the way he countermands the cultural norm which lay behind Peter's question. For the Hebrews, and some other ancient cultures, the number seven signified completion or perfection, as with the seven-day creation. Thus forgiving someone seven times was, for Peter, as much as could be expected, the complete fulfilment of moral duty. Jesus firmly rejects the idea that forgiveness is conditioned by cultural norms: just as there is no limit to the number of times that God will forgive, so also there can be none for us. For Jesus, reconciliation with those we have wronged was so important that it took priority even over worship: anyone who is presenting a gift at the altar, and remembers that someone has a grievance against them, must leave their gift, make peace with their brother or sister, and then return to offer their gift (*Matthew 5:23–4*). As Joachim Jeremias said, "God can forgive only if we are ready to forgive. . . . [Our] willingness to forgive is, so to speak, the hand which [we] reach out toward God's forgiveness."[6] God is a loving Father who longs to forgive, but he is not an indulgent parent. Our turning to him must be from the heart, and among other things this means that we must find in our hearts the love to forgive those who have wronged us. Just as Eliakim will not admit all comers to the king's presence, so those who seek forgiveness must humble themselves, not in self-abasement as an earthly ruler might require, but because humility—aligning our attitudes and values with God's attitudes and values—is an essential part of faith. In the parable of the Lost Son (*Luke 15:11–32*), the elder brother stands for those who cannot do this. In his own way he is turned in upon himself just as much as his younger brother was, in his self-centred, prodigal life.

**Repentance**

The second thing we must find in our hearts is repentance. Repentance is a strong word. The Greek *metanoia* means, literally, "mind change", which we speak of as "a change of heart". Repentance is a deliberate, willed action, a determination to do and to think differently; it is not about simply feeling sorry for, or feeling bad about, what we have done wrong; that is contrition. Repentance goes beyond contrition; it implies a will to change direction, a decision to face another way, to embrace different goals, to seek a different path. It is repentance, not contrition, that is required for forgiveness to take root and change our lives. Repentance is the path that leads to the open door, the way we enter the sheepfold, and as we have seen, early rites of baptism symbolized this dramatically as the candidate turned bodily from darkness to light. It is easy to say, "I repent of my sins," but no one pretends that it is equally easy to make these words real; any kind of re-orientation is personally demanding, as are all liminal experiences, of which baptism is one.

Anthropologists use the concept of liminality (from the Latin *limen*: "threshold") to describe the quality of ambiguity or disorientation that occurs in the middle stage of an initiation ritual, when the participant no longer holds her pre-ritual status but has not entered upon the new status which the ritual is designed to bring about. During the ritual's liminal stage, she stands at the threshold between the old and the new, like a candidate for baptism who has made her commitment but awaits her immersion in the renewing waters through which she will become one with Christ. “Liminal” has come to be used as a spiritual term describing the situation in life where we find ourselves in a state of waiting, when one reality has ended and the next has yet to begin. The liminal space is where we prepare for a new beginning and, as the Franciscan Richard Rohr says, to live in the liminal space we need to allow ourselves to trust.[7] If we can trust as we move through the door that Jesus holds permanently open, then the transition becomes a time of grace, and our hope for a new beginning becomes a reality. This is the kind of spiritual journey that repentance makes possible, and through which we know that we are forgiven. The open door is a powerful symbol of hope, and the promise that it is permanently open means that our hopes are assured.[8]

## What he shuts none will open

Forgiveness shuts the door on our sin. In the parable of the Lost Son Jesus gave a dramatic picture of forgiveness (*Luke 15:11–32*). The younger son asks his father for his share of the property which he then squanders in loose and extravagant living; his care is only for himself and his pleasure. When he has spent all his inheritance and is reduced to destitution, the only occupation he can find is to look after pigs, the most despised of tasks. In his misery he comes to his senses, deciding to turn his life around and return to his father. He will confess his wrongdoing, well knowing that he has forfeited any claim on his father, and expecting only to be treated as a servant, no longer as a son—in a word, he repents. But his father sees things differently: he has never ceased to love his son, nor has he ceased to desire his safe return, and when he sees him afar off, he hastens to meet him and to welcome him home. The son asks his father to take him back as a “hired servant”, but his father will have none of it; he restores him to the family, clothes him in a fine robe, and throws a great party to celebrate. This, said Jesus, is how the angels of God rejoice over the sinner who repents. Divine forgiveness is not grudging, but generous and overflowing; the sin is shut away, not to be reopened. Forgiveness restores the sinner’s lost status in the love of God, as the father restored the status of his lost son; but forgiveness does not excuse the sin, nor remit the penalty due for wrongdoing. There will always be a penance to make, an act of restoration or amends: in the case of criminal sin, for example, it will include surrendering to the police and accepting the punishment due.

**Sin and sins**

When we talk about sin, it is generally in terms of wrong actions and desires, like the fornication, drunkenness, and debauchery that characterized the younger son's life; and because most of us live good and moral lives, our sense of sin tends to remain on the surface. Jesus invites us to go deeper. When the son came to his senses, he realized that he had forfeited all claim to be part of his father's family, and this is what he confessed: "I am no longer fit to be called your son; treat me as one of your hired servants." His repentance expresses not just what he has done wrong, but that his whole life had become disordered; he had put himself at the centre of his own concerns, consumed solely with his wants and his pleasures, and heedless of his family and social obligations. Jesus is not so much concerned with *sins*, as with *Sin*, the state of being in which our lives are off target, like an arrow that misses the mark. This state of sin is not simply an individual thing, but a reality that pervades the structures of society: the term "structural sin" has been coined to describe it, from institutional racism in public life to the reckless pursuit of financial gain in the banks. So much of our common life is off-target and, like Sarah Grimké and slavery, because we have grown up with it we take this disorder as normal, seeing only the symptoms and not the cause; we focus on what we have done or failed to do, rather than on whatever it is that causes our life to be off-target, whether that be selfishness, immaturity, pressure to conform, fashion, or wrong devices and desires. True repentance means changing our focus away from the symptoms towards the cause. This is made all the harder today by the way that the sense of sin has largely atrophied. We believe we are our own moral authority and we don't want to be told what to do. While we denounce serious sin (as seen, for example, in the outrage at child abuse and financial greed), generally we accept the lax standards in most aspects of life—public, corporate, and private—dismissing shameful words as "locker room talk". As one of the characters in Anita Brookner's novel *Hotel du Lac* says, "People feel at home with low moral standards."[9] This is true; our lives have become disordered, missing the mark. It is this state that needs to be acknowledged and confessed, not simply a list of transgressions—whether minor or more serious—if our repentance is to be real, and if God is to be able truly to shut the door on our sins.

**Renouncing evil**

"I turn to Christ" and "I repent of my sins" are the first two baptismal promises. The third takes the matter deeper: "I renounce evil."[10] In the Lord's Prayer Jesus taught us to pray to be saved from evil. He closes the door not just on sin, but also on evil, the source of sin. It was customary in his time to personify evil; for example, Jesus warned us to fear *him* who can kill the soul (*Matthew 10:28*). This personal image speaks powerfully to us, but we must not allow it to blind us to the fact that the source of evil is not some external force or devil, but is within us. As Jesus said, the things that defile us come from within: "It is from the human heart that come evil thoughts, acts of murder, adultery, greed, fraud, malice, envy, slander . . . " (*Mark 7:21–3*). Walter Wink puts it well: "When we fail to bring a committed ego to the struggles for choice, and yield ourselves to compulsive gambling, or to overeating or drinking, or to sexual promiscuity, or to compliance with corporate directives we know are unethical—then to a degree we place ourselves in the power of [evil]."[11]

The common idea of the devil, or Satan, as the source of evil is a corruption of the original conception of Satan as the Accuser, the servant of God who brought sinners before God for judgement.[12] This earlier understanding has been lost sight of, although it runs through the New Testament alongside the idea of Satan as the Evil One. We see it, for example, in Jesus' warning to Peter: "Simon, Simon, take heed: Satan has been given leave to sift all of you like wheat . . . " (*Luke 22:31*). It is, I think, impossible to reconcile belief in the existence of Satan as an independent source of evil with belief in an omnipotent God. If Satan exists as an independent source of evil, who created him? It cannot have been God; in which case we are driven to the conclusion that either God is not the only creator, or he is not almighty, or both. Walter Wink rightly says that Satan is best understood as an archetype, the real inner spirit of a person or society idolatrously pursuing their/its own enhancement as the highest good: "'Satan' is the actual power that congeals around collective idolatry, injustice, or inhumanity, a power that increases or decreases according to the degree of collective refusal to choose higher values."[13] It is appropriate to speak of this power in personal terms, as Jesus did, because that is what it feels like.

W. H. Vanstone explained the existence of evil as the expression or consequence of the precariousness of the divine creativity. "Evil," he said, "is the moment of control jeopardized and lost; and the redemption of evil is inseparable from the process of creation."[14] God's desire to create free, creative, and responsible beings necessarily admits the possibility of that freedom being abused—that is, it admits the possibility of evil. The Letter of James accepts that "envious longings" are part of being human, but adds that "the grace God gives is stronger" (*James 4:6*). In other words, we have within ourselves both the source of evil and the means to overcome it.

However we explain its source, the reality of evil is beyond doubt—my most chilling encounter was when I visited the Nazi concentration camps at Auschwitz and Birkenau—and if we seek God's new beginning, it is a force we have to renounce. The reality of evil lies behind the feeling that dark, capricious powers are at work in the world. In earlier times, disease and disaster, war and pestilence, flood and famine were ascribed to the work of demons. Today we may know more about the causes of these things, but there is still a sense that dark forces have the world in their thrall, especially in the political and corporate worlds. We still have our demons; we see them in "that real but invisible spirit of destructiveness and fragmentation that rends persons, communities, and nations".[15] We have seen this evil spirit in the Nazi rallies at Nuremberg, in the desire for ethnic cleansing and revenge in Rwanda, Bosnia, and Myanmar, in the abuse of prisoners at Abu Ghraib, in the Tottenham riots of 2011 and the looting and destruction which followed, in the terrorist atrocities of Paris, London, Barcelona, and elsewhere; and as I write, we see it in the callous indifference of the warring parties in Syria and Yemen to the suffering and starvation of their innocent victims. But we see an evil spirit too, though it is not always named, in the sharp and corrupt practices of business and politics—in the modern world, the forces of evil seem particularly to incarnate themselves in institutional structures. Again, Walter Wink puts it well:

> The demonic in our time has a peculiar proclivity for institutional structures. It is as if the demons of the Bible grew up along with us and, while leaving some of their smaller cousins to continue harassing individuals, swelled to the gigantic proportions of our transnational corporations, military establishments, university systems, and governmental bureaucracies.[16]

Institutions have replaced individuals as the locus of power; it is through political, corporate, and social institutions that personal power is exercised today, and not through individual claims of divine right, aristocratic inheritance, or social status. Political, corporate, and social structures develop ways of doing things, collective attitudes and values, that shape those who work for them. These attitudes and values survive changes in management or personnel, manifesting a virtually independent existence. We see these institutional "demons" at work as they seek to enhance the power of the institution rather than to pursue justice and the common good. The fulfilment of financial targets becomes more important than meeting need; senior executives are grossly overpaid compared with their employees; men and women are unequally rewarded for doing the same job; and pension funds are wantonly depleted. The connection between these injustices and evil is simply not seen; institutions fail to connect. But this evil has to be renounced if God's new beginning, enshrined in the hopes for truth, justice, and freedom, is to be realized.

**Shutting the door**

As with Shebna, it seems that much of modern life is like a garment infested with lice. It needs to be shaken out! We still need deliverance from the demons, even if today they go by different names. The ancient language of evil spirits does not seem inappropriate to describe the wrong devices and desires that possessed those making the myriad fateful decisions which led to the banking crisis, and the many corporate scandals like the collapse of Enron; nor does it seem an inappropriate way to describe the corrupt behaviour that characterizes so many political elites, and poisons political debate even in so-called mature democracies, or the wickedness that drives people to abuse women and children, employers to exploit their employees, traffickers to take advantage of refugees, and spectators to hurl racial abuse at black soccer players. I am not suggesting that evil spirits have any kind of independent existence in some kind of parallel spirit world. The language of evil spirits is symbolic, but the evil it symbolizes is very real. Evil originates in the wrong devices and desires of the human heart, as Jesus said; everyone has a shadow side, and evil is the result of allowing it to rule one's life. This, of course, is usually an unconscious process, but the outpouring of evil can be so strong and palpable, especially in group situations, that it can seem to have an independent existence.

Today we might think of an evil spirit as something within us that subverts our nature: something that mars the image of God in us, and leads us down the wrong path, just as Shebna's greed led him to abuse his office. We all know what this feels like, though it may not always be greed that leads us astray. The image of God in us is subverted in many ways, from evil acts and deliberate wrongdoing to the way we let ourselves down by saying and doing the wrong thing, or just going along with the crowd. The Gospels show Jesus to be in a constant battle against the forces of darkness, and he has authority over them: he brings order to those whose lives are disordered; he rebukes the wrong use of power, and he confounds false teaching. When the man in the synagogue with an unclean spirit was healed, it was by the *command* of Jesus (*Mark 1:27*; cf. *Luke 4:33–6*). It is the word of God that restores order and gives new life. That word is authoritative, and I think we may say that in the end, evil is about authority: who rules our lives? Jesus has the authority and the power to shut the door on the powers of darkness, as we see in the many signs that he performed. He holds the key of David; he is the sceptre of the House of Israel, and we reach out to him in hope as the One whose authority is divine, as we pray that he will lead us in a personal journey from darkness to light and dethrone the dark powers which disorder our lives.

## Free the captive from prison

The cry for freedom echoes throughout the antiphons because it is basic to our hope and to God's purpose for his creation. Freedom is what new beginnings are all about. In the fourth antiphon, the cry for freedom is based on an oracle of Isaiah of Babylon:

> "I the LORD have called you with righteous purpose . . . to open eyes that are blind, to bring captives out of prison, out of the dungeon where they lie in darkness."
>
> *Isaiah 42:6–7*

It is impossible to know how "bringing the captives out of prison" was understood by the author of the antiphons—most likely in the spiritual sense of being set free from sin and evil, which fits with the antiphon's earlier petitions. While that is a perfectly understandable reading—linked as it is with opening eyes that are blind—this was not Isaiah's meaning. The reference to freeing captives reaches back to the Exodus, to the experience of Israel as slaves in Egypt: an experience which shapes the whole understanding of God in the Scriptures. The captives of whom he speaks are all who are oppressed and in bondage through the actions of others, in particular those bound by the bonds of debt,[17] a bondage that has much in common with slavery. In this final petition of the antiphon, hope faces in a new direction as it picks up the hope of a new beginning that comes with the *release from debt*. To those in the bondage of debt, as to all the enslaved, the image of the open door speaks powerfully, and it was *their* hope, in particular, that Jesus said was fulfilled in his own person, in words (as we have seen) that clearly link poverty with imprisonment: "[The LORD] has sent me to announce good news to the poor, to proclaim release for prisoners . . . " (*Luke 4:18*).[18]

In ancient Israel, as today and throughout history, debt is chiefly a problem of poverty, especially among those looking after families on low incomes and in insecure housing.[19] Debt creates a bond akin to slavery: "The rich lord it over the poor; the borrower becomes the lender's slave" (*Proverbs 22:7*). Debt becomes a prison and, like all imprisonment, it is dehumanizing. The Law of Moses recognized the imprisoning effect of debt, and made provision for the release from debt, a very practical example of God's new beginning and of his special concern for the poor. Charging interest on loans was prohibited,[20] as was the complete harvesting of a field or vineyard, so that something was left for the poor to glean (*Leviticus 19:9–10*). Every seven years debts had to be remitted and slaves released, and this was not to be done grudgingly (*Deuteronomy 15:1–3, 9–10*). These laws were crowned by the Jubilee that was to be proclaimed every fiftieth year when, in addition to the release of slaves and the remission of debts, land that had been sold was to be returned to its ancestral owners (*Leviticus 25:10*). The effect of the Jubilee was to re-set the economy every fifty years; this was the LORD's new beginning, and on an epic scale! The whole thrust of these provisions was to avoid ingrained poverty and the social problems that come in its wake: "There will never be any poor among you if only you obey the LORD your God . . . " (*Deuteronomy 15:4–5*). This is an astonishing example of how Israel was socially far in advance of other nations, showing "an independence of thought, which is not content to surrender economic development to the section of the nation with capital resources for its own private profit".[21] *Free the captive from prison!* This is indeed a hope rooted in the actual conditions of life, and which takes seriously the biblical view that it is the condition of the poor, not the general level of prosperity, that determines the justice of an economic system.

The extent to which these laws were enforced is uncertain—it is clear from the protest of Jeremiah and other prophets that there were those who ignored their obligations (e.g. *Jeremiah 34:14*). But whether or not the laws were properly enforced is not really the point from the perspective of hope; the point is that they show God's intention for the way we should live together, and a society that does not provide equal justice for the poor misses the mark. From a biblical perspective such a society is disordered, a society in which structural sin is enthroned—though this glaring example of structural sin is not generally perceived. This is a hard truth for the modern world, built as it is upon a culture of debt, albeit attractively packaged, from the slogan used for the old Access credit card—"Take the waiting out of wanting"—to invitations to run up debts described in banker new-speak as "extending your credit". Compared with the biblical perspective, this is nothing less than a cultural earthquake. Debt has become not merely acceptable, but essential to the working of the modern economy, and the way in which the imprisoning effect of this economic imperative is ignored is nothing less than wicked. The level of personal indebtedness has now reached unsustainable levels, as we saw only too clearly in the sub-prime mortgage scandal. From a Christian perspective, it is outrageous that today the rich, far from accepting a duty of generosity *towards* the poor, benefit from a net transfer of resources *from* the poor in the form of interest payments—the precise opposite of the biblical principle. The extent to which we are off-target is shown in the proliferation of schemes to ensure not only the preservation, but the enhancement of the fortunes of the ultra-rich, as the leaked financial documents known as the "Paradise Papers" disclosed in 2017. There is even a so-called "professional" body, the Society of Trust and Estate Practitioners, to certify the credentials of those who create and manage such schemes. As Brooke Harrington makes clear, these practitioners largely operate in an "ethical grey area", helping their clients to evade the rule of law, "a realm of activity that is formally legal but socially illegitimate".[22] Their role, she says, is to secure the freedom, mobility, and privacy that the ultra-wealthy crave—in other words, a life without obligation, the wilful and deliberate negation of the biblical principle.

The door that Jesus holds open leads in a different direction, and to a pasture in which personal salvation is linked to the salvation of our neighbour. To return to *Howards End*: Margaret, the main character, comes from a rich and privileged family; however, she is aware that the rich stand on "islands of money", lifting them above the common condition, and that they forget that they do so. As she gets to know her husband Henry, she notices in him "the inner darkness in high places that comes with a commercial age. . . . He had refused to connect . . . ". And, as Forster himself observes, "It is those who cannot connect who hasten to cast the first stone."[23]

While the Jubilee principle of re-setting the economy every fifty years just would not work today (if it ever did), some kind of basic readjustment is needed. If Jesus is the key to the cry and hope for freedom becoming a reality, then in this Age of Anger we have to learn to connect and take steps to realize in modern society the sense of corporate solidarity that the Bible sets before us, and which is re-emerging in response to the COVID-19 pandemic. Hope will be fulfilled, and *ressentiment* lessened, when we recognize the true extent of structural sin as much as personal sin; that rights of personhood are more important than rights of property;[24] and that giving people life, freedom, and security is a greater priority than preserving private wealth and privilege. In a phrase, we need to learn the truth that we are all in it together. No one has expressed this truth better than John Donne in his poem "No man is an island":

> No man is an island,
> Entire of itself,
> Every man is a piece of the continent,
> A part of the main.
> . . . Any man's death diminishes me,
> Because I am involved in mankind,
> And therefore never send to know for whom the bell tolls;
> It tolls for thee.

This, perhaps, is the realization that dawned on Zacchaeus, the tax collector, who had climbed a tree to see Jesus pass by. Zacchaeus had not been altogether honest in his dealings, but the call of Christ changed him: there and then he said, "Here and now, sir, I give half my possessions to charity; and if I have defrauded anyone, I will repay him four times over" (*Luke 19:1–10*). For Zacchaeus, his encounter with Jesus was a new beginning. If he was true to his promise (as we must assume), he entered a new world where things would be valued very differently from his old way of life. This transition would have been disorientating, but in Christ he had a new identity and a new security, with a new authority governing his life; he became a new version of himself. Accepting that authority and growing into that new identity and new security will not have been an instant process, but a time of transition, a time of living in liminal space where new beginnings occur. In the liminal space we know that new life is ahead of us, but that it will take time to feel at home. Ways of life, habits, attitudes, and values can easily become ingrained, and if left unexamined, they become a prison as we grow older. Growing into new truths takes time, as Zacchaeus doubtless discovered. If we want our own new beginning, we have to make the same journey through the door that Jesus holds open.

5

# New Dawn: The Hope for Light

*O Morning Star,*
*Splendour of the Light eternal and Bright Sun of Justice;*
*come and enlighten all who dwell in darkness*
*and in the shadow of death.*

*I am the bright star of dawn.*
*I am the light of the world.*

## Light of the World

Light is essential for life and growth. Without light, the natural world withers and dies; it is the same for us: without light we wither away. We need light to guide us, to know where we are, and to make judgements, and this is as true of our inner lives as it is of our physical lives. Without inner light or insight, we are diminished as people; and it is the hope for inner light, or enlightenment, that the fifth antiphon reflects. I imagine it is no accident that it is set to be sung on 21 December, the shortest day, the longest night. This is the turning point when the days begin to lengthen and we start the journey from the darkness of winter to the light of spring; similarly, gaining inner light is an important turning point in our spiritual lives.

Light is one of the universal symbols used to speak of divinity, and there are many examples in the Bible, not least in the Psalms:

> O Lord my God, you are very great,
> clothed in majesty and splendour,
> and enfolded in a robe of light.

*Psalm 104:1–2*

The Bible describes the creation of light as the first act of God in bringing order to the world, and Third Isaiah foresaw that this divine light would shine forth in all its splendour as the last things were fulfilled:

> The sun will no longer be your light by day,
> nor the moon shine on you by night;
> the LORD will be your everlasting light,
> your God will be your splendour.
>
> *Isaiah 60:19*

At the end of the Bible, John of Patmos beholds the fulfilment of this prophecy in his final vision. As he looks upon the new Jerusalem coming down out of heaven, the city of peace that God has created, he says, "The city did not need the sun or the moon to shine on it, for the glory of God gave it light, and its lamp was the Lamb" (*Revelation 21:23*). Similarly, the Letter to the Hebrews speaks of Jesus as "the radiance of God's glory" (*Hebrews 1:3*), and at the Transfiguration, the disciples closest to Jesus—Peter, James, and John—saw for themselves the radiance of God's glory shining forth from their Master, a divine sign of who he really was; and from the splendour of the light they heard the divine voice declare: "This is my beloved Son; listen to him" (*Mark 9:7*). So the fifth antiphon praises Jesus as "the splendour of light eternal"; he is the One in whom our hope for inner light will be fulfilled, and it was this gift that Jesus promised to all who put their faith in him:

> "I am the light of the world. No follower of mine shall walk in darkness; he shall have the light of life."
>
> *John 8:12*

**True enlightenment**

For a Christian, living by the light of Christ is true enlightenment, and this is rather different from the secular understanding of the word. The Enlightenment of the eighteenth century put its faith in reason as the source of knowledge and morality, searching for the universal laws of a "pure" human nature, a kind of "universal self". Initially, the movement was not hostile to religious faith, but sought to re-interpret it in the light of reason, moving away from the idea of revelation as a source of understanding. It brought many benefits, not least the scientific method of discovering new knowledge, but it does not always live up to the high claims made for it, failing to acknowledge that its roots are often deeply Christian. A good example is the concept of human rights, which, although *developed* by Enlightenment thinkers, actually *originated* with the canon lawyers of the Middle Ages, as Tom Holland has shown.[1] In time, "enlightenment" came to imply the rejection of religion, and today to be "enlightened" is to profess the so-called progressive, liberal, secular values of an educated elite, and to reject any claim of religion to be a purveyor of truth. The Enlightenment was also marked by an elitist spirit (particularly in the thought of Voltaire, 1694–1778), which modern secular liberals tend not to acknowledge. Serving the interests of the mercantile class, it paved the way for modern economic theories, which, as we have seen, work against the fulfilment of hope. The Enlightenment was not at all about taking everybody's interests seriously, and something of that persists today in the "*de haut en bas*" attitudes often found among intellectuals. Although materially our lives have been transformed, spiritually we have hardly moved on from the eighteenth century, with its rational, utilitarian values that made humankind the measure of all things. In truth, the modern liberal society is just as controlling as the religion it rejects, with its own constraints on what is acceptable, evident, for example, in the notion of political correctness.

Although hailed by many as a new dawn, the Enlightenment has many of the characteristics of a false dawn: it is simply not possible to talk adequately about the nature and destiny of human society while ignoring the spiritual dimension of humanity. In the aftermath of the fall of the Berlin Wall, Salman Rushdie put it eloquently:

> As we witness the death of communism in central Europe, we cannot fail to observe the deep religious spirit with which so many of the makers of these revolutions are imbued, and we must concede that it is not only a particular political ideology that has failed, but the idea that men and women could ever define themselves in terms that exclude their spiritual needs.[2]

**Bright star of dawn**

False dawns are nothing new. Centuries before Jesus, one of the kings of Babylon described himself (anticipating Enlightenment thought) as the morning star, the brightest in the sky, the most glorious of men, even one of the gods, saying to himself, "I shall ascend beyond the towering clouds and make myself like the Most High!" He was, of course, no such thing, and in anticipation of his downfall, Isaiah taunted him: "Bright morning star, how you have fallen from heaven!" Like all who exalt themselves, Isaiah said, he will be "brought down to Sheol, into the depths of the abyss" (*Isaiah 14:1–15*). In contrast to such self-exaltation, the Book of Revelation uses the same image of the morning star and applies it to Jesus, whose life was one of self-offering. After his visions have ended, John of Patmos hears the voice of the Lord proclaiming, "I am the offspring of David, the shoot growing from his stock, the bright star of dawn" (*Revelation 22:16*). It is Jesus, not an earthly monarch, who is the true morning star, whose dwelling is in heaven, whose appearance is like the Most High, and who heralds the new dawn. And it is his teaching, not a secular creed, that is the true source of light.

Dawn is a time of hope and awakening; the shadows of the night are dispersed, the deeds of darkness are banished, and the soft light of dawn suffuses our lives. One dawn I will not forget was on the summit of Mount Sinai, as part of a pilgrimage following the route of the Exodus. We had reached the Sinai desert where the Israelites had assembled as they fled from the wrath of Pharaoh, and in the early hours, under the stars, we ascended the holy mountain on camels. It was a timeless experience. On the mountain-top it seemed as though I was on the roof of the world. The dawn light had a special quality, illuminating the mountains in a way that the harsh light of day cannot. The light of dawn is soft, more varied and subtle, less blinding. At the dawn you see differently, and in the same way the light of Christ enables us to see differently, offering a new view of God and a new view of ourselves: a vision of hope. For Christians, Jesus is the bright star of the morning who heralds God's new day, "the true light", as Saint John says, "which gives light to everyone" (*John 1:9*).

What star are we following? If we hope for light, then we need to be clear upon whom our hope is placed, or—to put it another way—we need to be clear about whom we worship. Today, as in Jesus' day, people are captive to false ideas about God, and the false hopes that these engender. As I have said, the twentieth century was marked by false hopes on a grand scale: fascism, communism, liberalism, science, the free market, all have been hailed as the harbingers of the new age—and they have all been found wanting because, like the King of Babylon, they have tried to do without God. The same is true of the many sects and false prophets promoting wrong and distorted beliefs. Compared with faith in Christ they have very little of substance to offer, and the result has been darkness, not light; a death of the spirit, an inner decay. And if we ask why Jesus is the key to the proper understanding of God and the way we should live together, the answer is to be found in the resurrection, an event unique within history, which gives to Jesus' ministry and teaching an unsurpassable authority. Richard Harries put it well:

> The resurrection is God's unqualified seal of approval on all that Jesus was and stood for. The authority with which he taught, his claim to forgive sins, his special care for the lost and outcast, his relationship of a son to the Father—all this is revealed to be grounded in God himself. The resurrection does not make these things true: they were always true. The resurrection is the clearest demonstration of their truth. The resurrection is the most profound statement of what God is like.[3]

The resurrection was, for the first witnesses, an experience of light (*Matthew 28:3*; *Luke 24:4*). If we hope for a God who is merciful and just, who moves towards us in love and compassion, whose gift is inner light, then that hope is fulfilled in Jesus. In him we catch a glimpse of the splendour of the light eternal, and what that light illuminates is not just new knowledge about God, but a new relationship with God, a relationship that is personal and gracious. Jesus made this plain in the way he taught us to address God as *Abba*, "Father". Through Jesus we see God as a loving father whose loving-kindness shines upon us, bringing new hope like the dawn.

**Bright sun of justice**

In enabling us to see more clearly, light is also the instrument of judgement. The antiphon speaks of this through an image from the prophet Malachi, who was active in the years immediately after the return from the Exile in Babylon, somewhere between 500–450 BC. These were restless years, when serving the LORD seemed futile and going along with the ways of the world seemed the better course—a common response throughout history to the hard and difficult challenges which, after liberation, have to be surmounted if a new life is to be built. Malachi warned against such attitudes, reminding the people of the need to honour the LORD properly and not to follow leaders who turned away from the path of righteousness, tolerating evil-doers. The LORD warned them that he was about to send his messenger to clear a path before him, and that he would suddenly come to his Temple. "Who can endure the day of his coming?" Malachi demanded. "Who can stand firm when he appears? He is like a refiner's fire, like a fuller's soap; he will take his seat, testing and purifying . . . " (*Malachi 3:1–3*). Malachi warned that the arrogant and the evil-doers would be destroyed, but that over the righteous the LORD would shine like the sun:

> The Day is coming, burning like a furnace; all the arrogant and the evil-doers will be stubble, and that Day, when it comes, will set them ablaze, leaving them neither root nor branch, says the LORD of Hosts. But for you who fear my name, the Sun of justice will rise with healing in his wings . . .
>
> *Malachi 4:1–2*[4]

The judgement of which Malachi speaks is not just for the wicked; those who place their hope in God must also reckon with his judgement—you cannot have the one without the other. A traditional theme for Advent sermons is the Four Last Things (death, judgement, hell, and heaven), combining preparation for the coming of the Saviour with preparation for our own coming before God. We lose this connection at our peril, because the coming of Jesus cannot be other than a time of judgement: just as light cannot but illuminate the darkness, so the coming of the Light of the World cannot but show up the dark places of our hearts.

Knowing these dark places, and acknowledging them, is part of our own journey from darkness to light, through which our hope for inner light is fulfilled. Judgement is an inescapable part of this journey: "Nothing in creation can hide from him; everything lies bare and exposed to the eyes of him to whom we must render account" (*Hebrews 4:12–13*). And although the image of God sitting in judgement in the heavenly court is much used in the Bible—as in the Letter to Hebrews which describes the word of God as alive and active, keenly dividing soul and spirit, and disclosing the purposes of the heart (*Hebrews 4:12*)—the truth is that we judge ourselves according to our acceptance or rejection of the gospel:

> "This is the judgement: the light has come into the world, but people preferred darkness to light because their deeds were evil. Wrongdoers hate the light and avoid it, for fear their misdeeds should be exposed. Those who live by the light come to the light so that it may be clearly seen that God is in all they do."
>
> *John 3:19–21*

Judgement is basic to Jesus' message; he warned continually about the importance, the inevitability, and the consequences of judgement in a series of parables, but he struck a different note to the condemnatory understanding of Malachi.[5] God has no desire to see his creation perish; he judges so that we might see ourselves clearly, repent and turn to him, and receive his gift of life. In the light of Christ we see that God is love, not wrath; that all are equal in his sight, and that his gifts are for all. This view challenges popular ideas of a wrathful God who is demanding and angry, and who needs to be propitiated; the fact that Jesus felt the need to stress the *love* of God suggests that such a view was widespread in his day too.[6] While there is much in the Old Testament that can be read as supporting the popular view, the wrath of God should be understood as speaking not so much of God's anger with sinners, as of his utter opposition to sin, selfishness, social injustice, and the ruthless exploitation of his creation. To describe God as wrathful is to speak of the seriousness with which he regards human sin and all that prevents us from living in communion with him. Understood in this way, God's wrath is an aspect of his love. In the light of Christ we see that God goes in search of those who are lost and brings them home, placing mercy above judgement, bearing the burden of our sin, so that nothing in creation shall be lost. This is a profoundly hopeful picture of God.

For Jesus, judgement is about salvation, not condemnation; he is risen with healing in his wings, and the believer has nothing to fear from judgement, as John affirmed: "No one who puts his faith in him comes under judgement" (*John 3:18*). And in words often overlooked, Jesus himself extended the non-judgemental approach even to those who reject him: "I have come into the world as light, so that no one who has faith in me should remain in darkness. But if anyone hears my words and disregards them, I am not his judge; I have not come to judge the world but to save the world." However, he continues, "There is a judge for everyone who rejects me and does not accept my words; the word I have spoken will be his judge on the last day" (*John 12:46–8*). Again, Jesus reminds us both of the inevitability of judgement, and also of its salvific purpose. The two-fold nature of the Christian understanding of judgement is often forgotten, but its non-condemnatory character does not mean that the believer can behave as she or he chooses. Although through baptism the believer has symbolically undergone judgement, baptism does not confer an automatic salvation that cannot be forfeited. It is described by Peter as a pledge made to God from a good conscience (*1 Peter 3:21*); as such, baptism emphasizes the seriousness of the moral and spiritual endeavour in the Christian life: those who have received God's grace must work out their own salvation in fear and trembling (*Philippians 2:12*). In seeking enlightenment, the believer cannot escape the eternal conflict between light and darkness, one of the principal themes of the fourth Gospel, used by John to present the radical choice Jesus sets before the world and before each individual person. Judgement focusses that choice, reminding us that our hope is in him. Without judgement there is no true enlightenment.

True enlightenment is to see from within: to be stripped of illusion, to perceive things as they truly are, in other words, to see as God sees. This is to have the light of life. In his letter to the Romans, Paul urged them to cast off the works of darkness and to put on the armour of light (*Romans 13:12*); his advice holds good for us today. On the Damascus road, Paul literally "saw the light", and it changed him, turning him round to face in a new direction, leading him in a way he had not known before (*Acts 9:1–22*). For over two thousand years we have been living in the true Age of Enlightenment, and the same promise is held out to all who hope in Christ. He is the light of life, the source of true enlightenment, uniting both our spiritual and our material needs, and enabling us to see them anew. In his light we are able to recognize the gods of the age for the deceits that they are.

## Enlighten all who dwell in darkness

One of those gods is the cult of the individual, to which the Enlightenment gave birth when it made humankind the measure of all things. The self has replaced God and the community as the focus of moral concern, a "bounded masterful self", to use the psychoanalytic description.[7] A widespread modern ideal is the self-sufficient, self-made person, recognizing no obligations to others for whom he/she is, nor for what he/she has achieved or become, and characterized by "a wish to manipulate the external world for one's own personal ends"—a clear parallel with "economic man". Such a self is deeply averse to judgement and, as Philip Cushman argues, "experiences a significant absence of community, tradition and shared meaning" (which all communities of faith take as their bedrock), creating an inner emptiness that manifests itself through a sense of a lack of personal conviction and worth, which in turn is embodied as "a chronic, undifferentiated emotional hunger".[8] This is the darkness in which many people dwell in this Age of Anger. Much modern literature and drama, with its focus on fractured serial relationships, stifled ambition, and unfulfilled lives, brings the reality home.

Modern psychology has enabled us to understand that the self is a social construct; we are "completed" by our culture which explains and interprets the world, defines our sense of obligation, and shapes the choices we make. We become a person through our relationships with others: "Each of us has a presence or a meaning in someone else's existence."[9] It follows that there is no universal self, contrary to the ideas of the Enlightenment thinkers who divorced the understanding of the human person from its social context. Among other things, this has brought about the deep fracture in modern Western societies between public values and private virtues. The public realm has become objective and technocratic, devoid of feeling and depth, where people and the environment are manipulated in the name of utility, and we become pawns in someone else's game: people are no more than instruments, relationships are commodified, and the commercial contract is the template for every relational encounter. At the same time, the spiritual, moral, and artistic values that humanize us and create depth, both in society and in personal relationships, are regarded as purely subjective and are relegated to the private realm—a position termed "emotivism": values are matters of personal feeling or taste, no more than the lifestyle choices of individuals. In personal morality there has been a marked move from the given to the chosen.[10] The feelings of emptiness resulting from this fracture are fed by consumption: on the one hand by an ever-increasing supply of consumer goods—the consumer-based economy is inconceivable without the empty self—and on the other hand by the prescriptions of an army of therapists, personal trainers, and lifestyle gurus—the priests of the modern age. Our preoccupation with image and lifestyle is a sign of an inner emptiness that makes us vulnerable both to religious cults and spiritual charlatans, and also to highly authoritarian and controlling romantic partners and political leaders. Economically we may, in Harold Macmillan's famous slogan, have never had it so good, but spiritually we have never had it so empty. True enlightenment goes hand in hand with spiritual growth, not economic growth. Writing to the Ephesians, Paul describes the goal of the spiritual life as attaining a maturity measured by nothing less than the full stature of Christ (*Ephesians 4:13*). This personal journey to maturity is made possible through the enlightenment of love rather than the enlightenment of reason: in the light of Christ we discover a God-centred understanding of self-fulfilment, depth of character, and growth in virtue.

**Self-fulfilment**

Jesus said that he had come not to do his own will, but the will of him who sent him (*John 6:38*), so we believe that seeking the will of God and following where it leads is the path to true self-fulfilment. Seeking this path is bound up with the question of personal identity: "Who am I?" Jürgen Moltmann points to the different ways in which this question is answered in anthropology and in the Bible.[11] Anthropologists approach the question by comparing humanity with other forms of sentient life. In the Bible the answer arises through the divine mission—that is, from the call of God: we know who we are through what God calls us to be. To hear God's call is humbling, not self-exalting. Thus Moses exclaims, in the face of his call to lead the Exodus, "Who am I that I should go to Pharaoh and bring the children of Israel out of Egypt?" (*Exodus 3:11*). In the same way, when Isaiah received his call, he responded, "Woe is me! For I am undone; I am a man of unclean lips, and I dwell among a people of unclean lips" (*Isaiah 6:5*). When Peter, at Jesus' prompting, made a huge catch of fish, he fell before Jesus and in amazement exclaimed, "Go, Lord, leave me, sinner that I am!" (*Luke 5:8*). From the biblical perspective, self-knowledge comes about in response to the call of God; we discover who we are through comparing ourselves, not with other creatures, but with what God calls us to become. What we are, and what we can become, we learn in hopeful trust in the One who said, "I am with you always" (*Matthew 28:20*; cf. *Isaiah 41:10*). The call of God does not simply reveal us to ourselves but opens up new possibilities, with the result that we can become what we are not yet, often symbolized by the giving of a new name: Jacob becomes Israel; Simon becomes Peter; Saul becomes Paul. When we know what God calls us to become, we can set out on the path to true self-fulfilment.

Some people believe that God calls us to become something we are not, to some kind of denial of who we are. This is a mistaken belief. It was not the experience of Moses, Isaiah, Peter, and Paul, who found in their calling who they really were and the gifts that they really possessed. God desires that the gifts and abilities he has given us are used to the full; God calls us along the grain of our being, not across it; he calls us to fulfil who we are, not to deny it. Seeking the will of God is not to discover some purpose that goes against the way we are made, but to release in us our God-given talents and energies. This may bring the surprise of a talent that had remained hidden to us, or a way to use our talents that had not occurred to us or which we had rejected. The sense of becoming "a new version of me" describes it exactly. What God has given is to be used in the service of others; this does not rule out personal profit, but I think it does rule out seeking wealth simply for its own sake, and also work that is entirely self-centred or immoral, or which does not, in some way, serve the common good. Seeking the will of God requires the spiritual virtue of obedience, through which we acknowledge that it is God, not the self, who is the source of value. This is profoundly counter-cultural in today's world, where doing your own thing, adopting a chosen lifestyle, and measuring personal worth by material criteria are widely accepted norms. There is also the sense that "I have no need to change. I am as I am. These are the impulses and desires that I have, and therefore they must be fulfilled." This crude claim of a right to an unexamined, instinctual life, in which we are spared the burden of choice, is widespread.[12] Frank Sinatra's song "My Way" is the anthem of the generation who seek to live by their own lights and not by the Light of the World.

Contrary to the way of the bounded masterful self, Jesus teaches that the way to happiness and fulfilment is to accept a source of authority *outside* the self. The path of obedience means learning to grow in humility and learning to heed voices other than our own. In 1995, the Doctrine Commission of the Church of England warned that "the secular quest for self-fulfilment can today so easily become self-seeking individualism, and a claimed duty to be oneself and to fulfil oneself can be used to justify disregarding one's responsibilities for others." More disturbingly, they added: "Freedom—in the sense of the absolute autonomy of the individual—has become the single, overarching ideal to which all other goals are subordinated." It is not simply that there *are* no normative goals, "but that there *must* be none, if I am to be truly free to be myself—to be the self I choose to make myself."[13]

In a characteristic paradox, Jesus challenged such views:

> "Whoever wants to save his life will lose it, but whoever loses his life for my sake and the gospel's will save it. What does anyone gain by winning the whole world at the cost of his life? What can he give to buy his life back?"
>
> *Mark 8:35–7*

This saying exists in all four Gospels, thus underlining its importance for all who place their hope in Jesus, and it offers a markedly different goal to the modern idea of self-fulfilment, as is evident in Jesus' reference to the futility of winning the whole world. He speaks of an eternal goal; and the truly enlightened are those who see that losing oneself and fulfilling oneself are divinely linked. Perhaps the best analogy is love. Those who truly love another put their beloved before self, they lose their life for the sake of the other, but at the same time they find their completion in the one they love: self-loss leads to self-gain. In any deep experience of love, we discover that losing oneself and fulfilling oneself go hand in hand. There are many everyday examples of the selfless service that we render one another, from parents caring for disabled children to organizations like Médecins Sans Frontières working on the front line in the world's most desperate situations. This is the work of love, and hope calls us to follow, moving away from self-seeking to true self-fulfilment.

**Character and personality**

Living in the light of Christ is to invite him to shape our character, a word that comes from the Greek *kharasso*, which means to engrave. Our character is the sum of the enduring or engraved marks of our being which define us and motivate our behaviour. One of the effects of today's economic culture has been that the formation of *character*, essentially a religious and moral process, has been displaced by the quest for *personality*, a more superficial, secular attribute—the word derives from the Latin *persona*, meaning an adopted role, like that of an actor in a play. In *The Corrosion of Character*, Richard Sennett provides an excellent description of the personal consequences of work in the modern economy, where character is corroded in the same way that acid corrodes metal, eating it away.[14] Sennett tells the story of Rico, a second-generation Italian American. By any standards Rico was well off: upwardly mobile, well housed, and able to afford the best education for his children. But to achieve this, Rico had moved house four times in fourteen years, each time having to start his life over again. After being downsized he set up in business on his own, but the demands of his work meant that he was at his clients' beck and call with no time for his family; he said, "It's like I don't know who my kids are." His fear was that they would become "mall rats", hanging about aimlessly in shopping centres. Rico felt he belonged nowhere and could not offer the substance of his life as an example to his children of how they should conduct themselves ethically. Rico's life had been shaped by the values of the modern economy, and they had corroded his character. He no longer felt able to sustain social relations or to offer durable guidance to his children. The world in which he had to behave flexibly in order to survive had taken its toll; his character had become flexible, and he was no longer sure what he stood for.[15]

In adapting himself to the needs of his clients, it seems that Rico had adopted a *persona*, a role that had corroded his character. Creating the right personality is said to be an important part of personal advancement, and thus "impressing others and gaining their approval [has become] an important aim in life, far outstripping the value of doing the morally correct act . . . dictated by one's character."[16] Changing the emphasis from personality to character is to become "inner-directed": that is, to be guided in thought and action by one's own conscience and values rather than by external pressure to conform. Conscience, however, needs to be properly formed. Christopher Jamison has described conscience as "the inner process that enables you to listen to voices beyond your own feelings and desires".[17] There are many people who signally fail to do this, like those who have no conscientious objection to perpetrating appalling acts of terrorism, or to abusing children, or who avoid paying their fair share of tax. In the Christian tradition the formation of conscience, becoming inner-directed, is essentially about growing in virtue.

**Growth in virtue**

The hope for light and for growth in virtue go together:

> Gods and frail mortals seek refuge in the shadow of your wings.
> They are filled with the rich plenty of your house,
> and you give them to drink from the stream of your delights;
> for with you is the fountain of life,
> and by your light we are enlightened.
>
> *Psalm 36:7b–9*

The psalmist describes virtue in some beautiful images: *the rich plenty of God's house, drinking from the stream of God's delights, the fountain of life.* An image that I find helpful when thinking about virtue is the fountain or well that stands in the centre of the cloister of a monastery. The cloister is an enclosed space at the heart of the monastery around which the life of the monastic community revolves; the cloister connects the various parts of the monastery: church, refectory, dormitory, meeting room, and places of work. Our inner life is our enclosed space around which the rest of our life revolves, the part of us that connects, brings together, and integrates the various aspects of our being, and virtue is like the fountain in the midst of the cloister, a fountain of life welling up inside us and nourishing our life. Virtue is the source of inner light and life, "the recognition of the sacred in daily life".[18] Virtue must present something of a puzzle to enlightened liberals who view morality as a set of universal rational principles, rather than habitual, embedded ways of life and practice. If, as has been argued, Enlightenment thinkers likened humans to machines, this opened the way for managers, technocrats, and social engineers to manage those lacking their expertise for the good of society and for their own good. "Virtue was thus no longer embodied in noble character; it was the practice of actions useful to the greatest number. Happiness was no longer a state of blessedness; it was reducible to pleasure, where all values became mere matters of taste."[19] Unsurprisingly, we do not hear much about virtue today; we hear more about values, but virtue is prior to values: it is an inner quality, a fountain of grace, enabling us to live a life that is morally good. Virtue is the light of Christ within, the agent of inner change and growth; the pursuit of virtue gives us the inner strength to live by higher values, qualities, and standards (particularly those that are altruistic) than the values which simply serve our self-interest. We think of values today as personally chosen, as part of our lifestyle. Virtue, by contrast, is something given, and it is not concerned so much with lifestyle as with life-giving style.

In classical philosophy there are four cardinal virtues: prudence, justice, temperance, and fortitude. "Cardinal" comes from the Latin *cardo* meaning hinge or centre point, and these are the central virtues on which the others hinge. In a public discussion with the psychoanalyst Susie Orbach and the sociologist Richard Sennett, Rowan Williams summarized them neatly: prudence is "good judgement", temperance is "emotional intelligence . . . understanding our desires and bringing them into self-critical awareness", fortitude is "courage . . . without being deflected by circumstance", and justice is "doing what is due to the individual, society and environment".[20]

To these the monastic tradition has added a fifth: the virtue of humility, to which I referred in chapter 1. Humility is the doorway to our true self. It is an inner strength that comes from a true appreciation of our place before God and within the community; a strength that means you do not have to have your own way all the time. Humility is what Paul had in mind when he warned the Romans not to think too highly of themselves, nor to be conformed to the pattern of the world, but to be transformed by the renewal of their minds (*Romans 12:2–3*). As Christopher Jamison said, "Humility helps us to achieve an inner freedom that frees us from selfish impulses and allows us to be shaped by other people's lives."[21] Humility is an essential foundation for the cardinal virtues. It is like a narrow door that you have to go through in order to find the treasure within—in other words, your true self. Humility opens the door to true enlightenment, allowing the light of Christ to illuminate our darkness. Humility enables us to be grasped by our hopes.

## The shadow of death

The light of Christ also shapes our hopes at the end of life. The shadow of death lies over the whole of life, even if awareness of it is greater in our later years. Spiritually, death is a necessary horizon, a limiting point without which life would be deprived of vitality and meaning. If all could be achieved in an infinity of time, we would be drained of motivation and moral purpose. The fact that we shall die concentrates the mind, and highlights the ultimate questions we all face: What is my purpose in life? Where am I going? Who shall I become? Death poses an agenda for living:

> The important thing is this:
> to be able
> at any moment
> to sacrifice what we are
> for what we could become.[22]

The Christian vision of our becoming is a growth in Christ-likeness, "until we all attain to the unity inherent in our faith and in our knowledge of the Son of God—to mature manhood, measured by nothing less than the full stature of Christ" (*Ephesians 4:13*). This inner growth is an experience of enlightenment. Through the Resurrection we see what we shall become, and we are assured that our hope is not in vain. As John Macquarrie said:

> Death has not quenched hope. Unclear though the hope may be, there has always been a hope that has stood out against death. Life has seemed stronger than death, and in the face of the total threat of death there has arisen the total hope that even death can be transformed and made to contribute to life.[23]

The Christian hope is that nothing, not even death, can separate us from the love of God in Christ Jesus (*Romans 8:38–9*).

In biblical terms, this hope came late in the day. The Old Testament, for the most part, reflects the belief that after death people went to *Sheol*, the place of shadows, the underworld, and there they languished. *Sheol* did not connote the extinction of life, but rather a descent into a shadowy existence separated from God—seen, for example, in the story of the Witch of Endor who summoned up the shade of Samuel at the request of King Saul (*1 Samuel 28*). Death was not the gateway to new life, but the end of meaningful existence, a belief expressed poignantly in a poem by King Hezekiah of Judah:

> Sheol cannot confess you,
> Death cannot praise you;
> nor can those who go down to the pit
> hope for your faithfulness.
>
> *Isaiah 38:18*

By Jesus' time this view had begun to change—as is apparent from the question about resurrection put to him by the Sadducees (*Mark 12:18*)—and the Resurrection changed it utterly.[24] The Resurrection is described as an experience of light. Those who went to the tomb saw angels in dazzling garments, with faces that shone like lightning. John speaks not of Jesus' death, but of *his dying*; not as something that was done to him, but as something that he did:

> "I lay down my life to receive it back again. No one takes it away from me; I am laying it down of my own free will. I have the right to lay it down, and I have the right to take it back again; this charge I have received from my father."
>
> *John 10:17–18*

Jesus is the subject, not the object; John affirms that he is the one who has authority over life and death. His resurrection is the sign that this affirmation is true. As Bishop Simon Phipps once said to me, "In the resurrection, God says, 'You can trust me with your life.'" What is true for Jesus allows us to hope that it will be true for us, and that this hope will not be disappointed.

Today many, including some Christians, believe that there is nothing beyond death; it is the ultimate darkness, extinguishing all existence. Against this, Tom Baker argued persuasively that the belief in the life to come flows inevitably from the nature of God.[25] If God is love, then God cannot have created life in all its wonder and diversity and richness simply to see it perish. When God is conceived in personal terms as all-loving and all-good, as Jesus taught, it becomes difficult to make religious sense of life if everything is bounded by the grave, Baker argued. "If God is to carry out his allegedly loving purposes for all mankind, then, to put it crudely, he needs more elbow room than this life alone can offer.

If an afterlife is declared out of bounds, it is extremely difficult to go on believing in a loving God, in a world where the vast majority of people end their lives with their potential of spiritual growth largely unrealized, where many die prematurely and in conditions of tragedy and suffering, and many others meet their death having known nothing but grinding poverty, cruel maltreatment, relentless pain, or bitter disappointment."[26]

Baker wrote in response to Don Cupitt, a fellow priest, who believed that it was spiritually important *not* to believe in the life to come. Cupitt taught that our need was for a spirituality to direct our freedom and make it fruitful, "so that human lives can gain something of the never wasted integrity and completeness of a work of art. When lives are rounded off in that way, death loses its sting." As Baker says, it sounds marvellous, and there is truth in what Cupitt says, but even so, just how many people have any real chance of a life "rounded off" this side of death? As Baker says, "Some, no doubt; favoured by birth, circumstances, upbringing or temperament. But what about the others? . . . [What] about the majority of the human race? In what sense can it be said that their lives can be 'rounded off' like a completed work of art, thus making any kind of future hope unnecessary?"[27] If God is the God of whom Jesus is the human face, then of necessity there must be a life to come, and death becomes the gateway to a new life, and continuing enlightenment. Confident in this belief, Paul could rejoice: "Death where is thy sting, grave thy victory?" (*1 Corinthians 15:55*). In Jesus the power of death was broken and life and immortality were brought to light (cf. *2 Timothy 1:10b*).

Dispersing the shadow of death, the resurrection of Jesus points to a continuity between earthly life and the life to come, which distinguishes resurrection from other conceptions such as the immortality of the soul and reincarnation.[28] Paul poses the question of how the dead are raised: "In what kind of body?" he asks, and although he describes such questions as "senseless", nevertheless he proceeds to offer an answer by drawing an analogy with the transformation of a seed into a plant (*1 Corinthians 15:35ff.*). While it is only an analogy, and Paul misunderstands the biology,[29] it is still helpful. The image is profoundly hopeful: all the potential in the seed comes into full flower in the plant; nothing is lost, all is gain; and there is a continuity between the two, even though the physical nature is completely transformed. Thus Paul speaks of our own resurrection as our transformation from a physical body to a spiritual body where all our potential is realized. Many have offered their own speculations on the nature of the life to come,[30] but in the end I think we have to be content to accept it as a mystery—in the sense, as I have said before, of something that can be experienced but not explained. This was the experience that changed the disciples, transforming their fear into boldness. They knew that the person who had appeared to them was one with the person they knew as Jesus of Nazareth. While his resurrected body was not physically constrained in the way that our earthly bodies are, he was not a ghost; he ate with them, and was demonstrably the same person that his disciples had known, and they found in him a continuing source of grace and hope. This continuity is explored by T. S. Eliot in his poem "East Coker". He observes that home is where we start from, but as we grow older the world becomes stranger and life's pattern more complicated, the intense moments of experience of our younger days giving way to the sense of "a lifetime burning in every moment". The poem concludes with these lines:

> Old men ought to be explorers
> Here or there does not matter
> We must be still and still moving
> Into another intensity
> For a further union, a deeper communion
> Through the dark cold and the empty desolation,
> The wave cry, the wind cry, the vast waters
> Of the petrel and the porpoise. In my end is my beginning.[31]

The final words—"In my end is my beginning"—are the mirror image of the opening words of the poem—"In my beginning is my end." These two statements are complementary rather than contradictory; our beginning and our end are part of a continuum, the one inseparably involved in the other. The One from whom we came, who gave us life, is the One to whom we shall return, and from whom we shall receive new life. This continuity characterizes the gift that Jesus offers those who put their faith in him, the gift of eternal life. When he was asked how eternal life was to be gained, he told his questioners that the quest began in this life. In response to a lawyer, Jesus told the parable of the Good Samaritan: those who wish to inherit eternal life must show kindness to all and to any in need, regardless of race, religion, and status. Speaking to one of the rulers, Jesus said that if he wanted to inherit eternal life, he should sell all that he had and give to the poor (*Luke 10:25–37*; *18:18–23*). Eternal life is the life lived in communion with God; it is shaped by the teachings and values of Jesus; we can experience it in this life, and we shall experience it in its fullness in the life to come. This was so real for Paul that he said that his mortal life was the faith that he had in the Son of God (*Galatians 2:20*).

I think the sense of this continuity is widespread. As Eliot says, advancing years bring glimpses of it as the pattern of life becomes more complex, and perhaps, like him, we have the sense of a lifetime's experience "burning in every moment". We can leave it at that, or we can take a further step towards turning our hope into a reality. While eternal life is a gift freely given, it is also a gift that requires of us the will and the effort to possess it. Eliot describes laying hold of this hope as a never-ending exploration. "Home is where one starts from," but it is not where we remain. "Old men ought to be explorers," and in "Little Gidding", the final poem of the *Four Quartets*, he speaks of the culmination of the spiritual journey:

> We shall not cease from exploration
> And the end of all our exploring
> Will be to arrive where we started
> And know the place for the first time.[32]

The path of exploration that leads to eternal life is one where we need to be both "still and still moving", that combination of prayer and action we see in Jesus himself. The quest for depth in faith—"a further union, a deeper communion"—is never going to be easy. Eliot likens it to being tossed on "the dark cold and the empty desolation" of the ocean, where other creatures—the petrel and the porpoise—are at home. Nothing worthwhile is achieved without effort, and the goal of this journey is that true enlightenment which I have explored in this chapter.

Unlike the dawn on Mount Sinai, the new dawn in Christ will not happen again; it does not need to, for Jesus promised that no one who followed him would wander in the dark, but would have the light of life. The hope for light finds its fulfilment in him. In good times and in bad, in joy and in sorrow, we carry his light with us; in the darkness of pain and suffering, conflict and war, and in the shadow of death his light shines, "and the darkness shall never overcome it" (*John 1:5*). Christ is the new light of dawn by which we see anew and glimpse the continuity between this life and the life to come. St John of the Cross said that God has "no more faith to reveal nor anything more to say, for in his Son all has been accomplished for us, all has been given to us, and more besides".[33] The tender compassion of our God has broken upon us like the dawn from on high, shining on those who dwell in darkness and the shadow of death and guiding our feet into the way of peace.

# 6

# Cornerstone: The Hope for Peace

*O King of the Nations;*
*you alone can fulfil their desires;*
*Cornerstone, you make opposing nations one;*
*come and save us, whom you formed from clay.*

*I am the good shepherd.*

## King and Peacemaker

The sixth antiphon praises Jesus as the One who alone can fulfil the desires of the nations. The most basic of those desires is to live in peace, both at home and in the world, and to ensure the wellbeing of their peoples. The prophets taught that fulfilling this desire was one of the duties placed on the king, part of the covenant between king and people. The king embodied the nation—or perhaps we should say he embodied his people, for the idea of nationhood came late on the scene. It is said that King Louis XIV of France proclaimed, "*L'état, c'est moi*"—"The state, it is me"—which expresses the idea exactly. King and people were bound in a personal relationship: in a real sense the people owed their lives to the king, and they looked to him for security and protection, and to fulfil their hopes and desires. The antiphon praises Jesus in precisely this way. The final petition, reaching back to the story of the creation of Adam from the dust of the earth, recognizes Jesus as the one through whom we were created, the one in whom "we live and move and have our being", as Paul put it, quoting the Greek poet Aratus (*Acts 17:28*). Jesus embodies all of humanity; and so he is praised not simply as the king of a nation, but of all the nations.

As we have seen, the biblical and Christian understanding of peace and wellbeing is rooted in the concept of *shalom*, the pursuit of which, the prophets believed, would characterize the rule of the righteous ruler. He would be the shepherd of his people:

> He shall appear and be their shepherd
> in the strength of the LORD,
> in the majesty of the name of the LORD his God . . .
> and he shall be a man of peace.
>
> *Micah 5:4–5a*

"Shepherd" was frequently used in Israel to mean "ruler",[1] as in this prophecy, and one of the signs of the peace that the righteous ruler would bring was reconciliation, both within the community and with God. Jesus described himself as the Good Shepherd, the one who knows his sheep and is prepared to lay down his life for them (*John 10:14–15*). Shepherd and sheep are bound in a personal relationship, akin to that between king and people, which derives from the relationship between Jesus and the Father, based on love, not on institutional authority, status, or power. The good king binds the people into one, and the shepherd binds the flock into one, as a cornerstone binds two walls together. The antiphon builds on the image of the good king as a reconciling presence. The "man of peace" knows his people as persons, not simply as the instruments of his purposes, and seeks to reconcile them to one another, and with the other nations.

The binding together that a cornerstone achieves is basic to the Christian hope for peace, which is not fulfilled simply by the absence of war. As we see in Northern Ireland, wherever there has been conflict and war, the hard and exhausting work of building peace follows the cessation of fighting—and it will be all the harder and more exhausting in places like Syria and Yemen. Those who have been divided need to be reconciled, bound together, if justice, wellbeing, and support for the common good are to be established. This is what a "man of peace" seeks to achieve, and the hope for peace rests on the conviction that Jesus, in his own person, is the source of reconciliation, the cornerstone who makes opposing nations one.

Isaiah of Babylon saw peace as a gift of God, a gift only God can bestow:

> From every corner of the earth turn to me and be saved;
> for I am God, there is none other.
>
> *Isaiah 45:22*

And Paul saw that divine gift as the great work of God achieved by the sacrificial death of Jesus. Writing to the Gentiles, from whom the Jews were separated, he said:

> Once you were far off, but now in union with Christ Jesus you have been brought near through the shedding of Christ's blood. For he is himself our peace. Gentiles and Jews, he has made the two one, and in his own body of flesh and blood has broken down the barrier of enmity which separated them . . .
>
> *Ephesians 2:13–14*

The sixth antiphon praises Jesus as the source of unity and reconciliation without which the hope for peace and wellbeing will not be fulfilled. However, before considering the Christian understanding of reconciliation, and how it is achieved in Christ, it is helpful to look at what Jesus had in mind when he described himself as the Good Shepherd, and also to give some shape to the desire of the nations for peace.

## The Good Shepherd

Kings came late on the scene in Israel. When political necessity required the appointment of a king, a vital factor in the acceptability of the first king, Saul, was his charisma, the outward sign that he was inwardly possessed by the Spirit of God.[2] The kingship in Israel was always predominantly a religious institution, "far more profoundly involved with the nation's innermost experience than any element of political life could ever be".[3] After a promising start, Saul turned out to be a disappointment;

and thereafter, apart from his immediate successor David (and one or two others), the kingship—in religious terms—was on a continual downward path. The prophets, particularly Hosea, were outspoken in their criticism of the kings and the extent to which they forsook the ways of the LORD, and as we have seen, the conviction began to grow that God would himself appoint a righteous ruler. Ezekiel notably uses the image of the shepherd to describe this ruler, whom he identifies as God himself: "I myself shall tend my flock, and find them a place to rest, says the Lord GOD" (*Ezekiel 34:15*). This prophetic presentiment was fulfilled in Jesus, who showed forth in his own person both the charismatic endowment of the Spirit and a profound involvement in the innermost life of Israel, but in the purposes of God his authority extended beyond Israel to all the nations, as Isaiah of Babylon had prophesied:

> "It is too slight a task for you, as my servant,
> to restore the tribes of Jacob,
> to bring back the survivors of Israel:
> I shall appoint you a light to the nations
> so that my salvation may reach earth's farthest bounds."
>
> *Isaiah 49:6*

When Jesus used the image of the shepherd to describe his ministry, he gave it a particular emphasis: the king of the nations is to be understood as the *good* shepherd, an image that Jesus merges with the image of the door of the sheepfold. In the discourse on the Good Shepherd (*John 10:1–21*), Jesus spoke about the nature of his authority and the way in which it is exercised. The discourse follows the account of Jesus' healing of the man born blind and his subsequent exclusion from the synagogue by the Jewish authorities (*John 9*). John Marsh suggests that the discourse is designed to answer the question, "Who is the true leader and ruler of the true people of God? Who has the proper authority to include or exclude a man from the society of God's chosen people?"[4] Jesus' criticism of the rulers of Israel as *false* shepherds—"thieves and robbers" were his words—should have been familiar to his hearers from the prophecy of Ezekiel, who had condemned the rulers for abandoning the flock committed to their charge and caring only for themselves.[5] Jesus likens them to thieves who climb into the sheepfold not through the door but by some illegitimate way; by contrast, the shepherd who has charge of the sheep enters legitimately by the door, and the sheep follow him because they know his voice. John says that the people did not understand this parable (despite the familiar imagery), so Jesus spoke again:

> "In very truth I tell you, I am the door of the sheepfold. The sheep paid no heed to any who came before me, for they were all thieves and robbers. I am the door; anyone who comes into the fold through me will be safe. He will go in and out and find pasture."[6]
>
> *John 10:7–9*

As John Marsh explains, the good shepherd "exists, and exercises his authority, solely for the good of the sheep, while the thieves and robbers think of the sheep only in terms of what profit they can make for themselves, or how they can best secure their own safety".[7] Later in his Gospel John describes how Jesus washed the feet of his disciples at the last supper (*John 13:1ff.*). The washing of the feet—usually performed by a servant for the guests as they arrived, the same kind of menial task that a good shepherd is prepared to do for his sheep—is a lesson in servant leadership. Jesus wants to show what true kingship is like—indeed, more than this, he shows what true divinity is like. How does he do this? asks William Temple. "Does he order a throne to be placed that he may receive the homage of his subjects?" No, he rises from table, lays aside his garments, takes a towel, ties it round him, pours water into a basin, and begins to wash his disciples' feet, and to dry them with the towel.[8] This is God the servant of whom Isaiah spoke. This is the King of the Nations showing the full extent of his love, and it is upon this love, that does not disdain the most menial task, that the hope for peace is founded.

## The Desires of the Nations

The prophet Haggai spoke of the desire of the nations when he urged those who had returned from exile in Babylon to show as much concern for restoring the Temple in Jerusalem as they did for rebuilding their own homes. He encouraged the people and their leaders to take heart, for the LORD was with them despite their neglect; his spirit remained among them, and the new Temple would be filled with splendour:

> I will shake all nations, and the desire of all nations shall come: and I will fill this house with glory, saith the LORD of Hosts.
>
> *Haggai 2:7 (King James Version)*[9]

While both this prophecy and the antiphon are messianic in intent, they strike subtly different notes. The prophecy clearly looks forward to the coming of the "*desire* of all nations", namely the Messiah;[10] the antiphon takes this expectation a stage further: speaking of the "*desires* of the nations", namely their hopes for peace and wellbeing, it affirms that only in Christ can they be fulfilled. The nature of desire has an important bearing on the hope for peace.

### Desire and restraint

Desire is one of the basic human motivations, and the disciplining of desire is one of the main themes of most spiritual traditions. Desire and its perils are the theme of the opening story of the Bible. Adam and Eve were placed by God in a garden in which there were many trees pleasing to the eye and good for food, and in the midst of them God set the tree of life and the tree of the knowledge of good and evil. Eve saw that the fruit of the tree of knowledge (nowhere is it described as an apple) was good to eat and pleasing to the eye, and "to be desired to make one wise" (*Genesis 3:6*). Although God had expressly forbidden her and Adam to eat of the fruit, Eve, led on by the serpent, ignores the divine command, takes the fruit, and eats it; she gives some to Adam, and he also eats it. The result is that they are driven out of the garden, expelled from paradise. The clear message is that desire has to be constrained by moral norms, and if it is not it will lead us astray. Desire tends not to be viewed in this way in the world. The manipulation and manufacture of desire is one of the driving forces of our consumer society, creating its own powerful hopes and firmly resistant to any idea of restraint or discipline. The consumer society has taken to heart the view of the philosopher Thomas Hobbes (1588–1679), that the desire for pleasure is the fundamental motivation of all human action, ignoring the wisdom of the ages which says that unbridled desire is the path to hell. Wellbeing demands the restraint of desire; the destructive effects of unrestrained desire are all too evident in the over-consumption of alcohol, for example, or in the exercise of overweening political power.

Perhaps the best statement of the desires of the nations is the Preamble to the Charter of the United Nations (1945), which sets out the purposes for which the United Nations was founded:

- to save succeeding generations from the scourge of war, which twice in our lifetime has brought untold sorrow to mankind, and
- to reaffirm faith in fundamental human rights, in the dignity and worth of the human person, in the equal rights of men and women and of nations large and small, and
- to establish conditions under which justice and respect for the obligations arising from treaties and other sources of international law can be maintained, and
- to promote social progress and better standards of life in larger freedom.[11]

The UN Charter, and other international obligations like the Paris Treaty on Climate Change (2016), put some flesh on the bare bones of the desire for peace and wellbeing. The pursuit of these desires, like the pursuit of personal desires, requires restraint. Moving away from war, affirming the rights of others, respecting international obligations, and promoting social progress all impose restraints on giving unbridled scope to national interests narrowly conceived, which, alas, increasingly characterizes politics today. What the Charter's aims actually require is that national interests be defined to include promoting the common good. (The decision of President Trump in 2017 to remove the USA from the obligations of the Paris Agreement, and more recently to impose punitive tariffs on certain imports, are particularly egregious examples of the rejection of restraint in pursuit of national interests, narrowly conceived.) Just as Adam and Eve had to learn that their desire for paradise would only be fulfilled if their bodily desires were disciplined by moral restraints, so likewise it is true that the desires of nations for peace and wellbeing will only be fulfilled if their behaviour is also disciplined by moral restraints. In both cases, personal and national, the challenge is spiritual (as we saw with the hope for justice), but in the hope that Jesus sets before us we can rise to it.

There are, I believe, three reasons underlying this belief. Firstly, there is the Christian understanding that peace is not just the absence of conflict but the presence of justice and the pursuit of the common good. The priority of justice goes back a long way; in the words of the psalmist, "Justice shall march before [the Lord] and peace shall follow his steps" (*Psalm 85:13*). The pursuit of justice is basic to any realistic hope of peace. Secondly, the pursuit of peace and wellbeing requires the servant leadership that we see in Jesus. It is only through those whose aim is to serve, and to place the good of others above self or party, that we have any chance of establishing a lasting peace. Thirdly, pursuing peace requires spiritual resources strong enough to discipline desire (including political ambitions) and to equate the interests of others with our own. The Christian experience is that these resources come only as a gift when—with the aid of the Holy Spirit—we seek to align ourselves with the will of God. "The harvest of the Spirit," said Paul, "is love, joy, peace, patience, kindness, goodness, fidelity, gentleness, and self-control." And he added, "We must not be conceited, inciting one another to rivalry, jealous of one another" (*Galatians 5:22–6*). These virtues are prior to desire and shape it; they cannot be prescribed by law, nor can they be acquired by an act of will alone; they are a divine gift—in a word, they are charismatic. Haggai's insight remains true: the hope and desire for peace and wellbeing will only be fulfilled if faith is first enthroned.

**Desire and fulfilment**

Desiring rightly is the key to the fulfilment of desires, a truth that Thomas Traherne (the seventeenth-century poet and spiritual writer) helps us to understand. He talks of want, which—he says—is in God himself:

> [T]he Lord God of Israel the Living and True God, was from all Eternity, and from all Eternity Wanted like a God. He Wanted the Communication of His Divine Essence, and Persons to Enjoy it. He Wanted Worlds, He wanted Spectators, He wanted Joys, He wanted Treasures. He wanted, yet he wanted not, for he had them.[12]

Want, says Traherne, is the "very ground and cause" of the infinite treasure that God longs to share with his human creation, and if we wish to possess that treasure then we must want like he wants, a truth which Traherne expresses in an arresting phrase: "You must Want like a God, that you may be Satisfied like God."[13] As Traherne says, want in God is of an altogether different order from our basic human wants—for warmth, food, and shelter, for example; want in God, he says, "is the very Ground and Source of infinit Treasure . . . Want is the Fountain of all His Fulness. Want in God is a Treasure to us."

Denise Inge explains that when Traherne was writing, "to want" meant "to lack" as much as it meant "to desire", and this adds a depth of meaning that is not so apparent to us today.[14] Want in God speaks to me of the divine desire for completeness—that the whole of creation should be reconciled to God; this suggests that for us, his creatures, desiring rightly comes from an acknowledgement of our incompleteness, an acknowledgement of what we lack in the moral rather than the material sense. Want is not just about fulfilling our desires, but about desiring rightly so that our desires can fulfil us. I understand want in God to be about bringing to fullness what God has started; God yearns for his creation to achieve the fullness in Christ that is our destiny, and I think it is in these terms that the antiphon speaks when it praises Jesus as the one who alone can fulfil the desires of the nations: those desires are their deepest wants, the things that—like a cornerstone—will bind them together, fulfilling their God-given destiny of peace and wellbeing, and for these to be fulfilled we must want like God.

**Desire and peace**

The hope for peace requires a genuine desire for peace, a desire that is often missing in those who lead us, displaced by other desires—for empire, a greater presence on the world stage, for personal authority and prestige—or by feelings of racial superiority, or national interests narrowly conceived. The absence of a genuine desire for peace is seen in the readiness—even today—to resort to war in the pursuit of national or sectional interests. Walter Wink has described this readiness as "a form of religious piety" based on the "myth of redemptive violence" (the belief that the threat of violence alone is able to deter aggressors), which he traces back to ancient Babylonian religion.[15] The extent to which this attitude is endemic in the world is seen clearly in the way even religious leaders are prepared to resort to violent means in pursuit of their aims.[16] This was very much the way of the world in Jesus' day, and he spoke of this at the beginning of his Passion. When Jesus came within sight of Jerusalem, he wept over it because it did not know the way that leads to peace. "But no," he said, "it is hidden from your sight" (*Luke 19:41–2*). Peace had been sacrificed on the altar of racial and religious exclusiveness; the divine vocation of Israel to be a light to the nations had been ignored by a self-serving and inadequate leadership. In the same way, peace eludes us because the way that leads to peace is hidden from us by our wrong desires, and we Christians have to acknowledge that we have too often taken the path of racial and religious intolerance and oppression. As I said in the Prologue, the world has for some years been coming to terms with the advent of ISIS, and more recently with Brexit and Trump and the rise of populist movements in Europe, Turkey, India, and Brazil. While the factors that have led to them are many and diverse, one common factor is *ressentiment*, the angry demand for justice from those who feel left out or oppressed by the world of power that does not know the way that leads to peace. The response in each case has been one of division and separation, of emphasizing difference and demonizing opponents. This may lead to some kind of short-term gain, but it will not lead to peace. Justice, as we have seen, is the pre-condition for peace; injustice leads to conflict. Our hope for peace will only be fulfilled when we take to heart the divine desire for justice:

> I will hear what the Lord God has to say,
> a voice that speaks of peace,
> peace for his people and his friends,
> and those who turn to him in their hearts.
> His help is near for those who fear him
> and his glory will dwell in our land.
> Mercy and faithfulness have met;
> justice and peace have embraced.
> Faithfulness shall spring from the earth
> and justice look down from heaven.
>
> *Psalm 85:8–11 (The Grail version)*

As Jesus parted from his disciples, he gave them his peace: "Peace is my parting gift to you, my own peace, such as the world cannot give" (*John 14:27*). The way of Christ is not the way of separation: emphasizing difference, rejecting the stranger, and building walls to keep out those who are different. The way of Christ is to bind people together, overcoming difference and reaching out to those who are estranged: in a word, completeness. The world cannot give this gift because it is only in the love of God that mercy and faithfulness meet, and justice and truth embrace. If we want his glory to dwell in our land, then we need to seek his help. "Be Sensible of your Wants," advised Thomas Traherne (i.e. be fully aware of them), "that you may be sensible of your Treasures." Reconciliation and peace are no less than the Want for completeness that is in God, and it is a Treasure for the nations.

## Christ the Cornerstone

There is no true peace without reconciliation. The Korean War ended in 1953, but almost seventy years later there is no peace between North and South, just a dangerous and unstable stand-off—although there are faint signs that this may change. It is the same with India and Pakistan over the status of Kashmir. As I have already noted, reconciliation moves beyond the cessation of conflict and brings about a unity, in the same way that a cornerstone joins two walls together, effectively making them one. The sixth antiphon uses this concrete symbol to speak of the work of Christ: he is the cornerstone that makes opposing nations one and gives substance to the hope for peace.

The image of the cornerstone reaches back to the prophecy of Isaiah of Jerusalem. More often than not in the history of Israel (as with most of the world), the absence of a good and just ruler—a good shepherd—was keenly felt, and Isaiah prophesied at such a time. He warned King Hezekiah against the policy he was pursuing in the face of the threat from Assyria, namely to form alliances with other nations rather than to trust in the LORD[17] Caustically, he asks if Israel thinks she has made a pact with death that will spare her from the might of Assyria. No, he responds, she has made lies her refuge and in falsehood she has taken shelter. This false security, he says, will be swept away, just as hail beats down the fields. A later hand inserted the cornerstone prophecy into Isaiah's oracle to reinforce his message:

> I am laying a stone in Zion, a block of granite,
> a precious cornerstone well founded;
> he who has faith will not waver.
> I shall use justice as a plumb-line
> and righteousness as a plummet . . .
>
> *Isaiah 28:16–17a*

Quite what the image of the cornerstone represented originally is unclear; many suggestions have been made, among them that it symbolized the Messiah,[18] and this is the sense in which it was understood by Jesus and the first Christians. Just as a cornerstone binds two walls together, so the Messiah would bind his people together on the foundation of justice and righteousness—the very foundation on which Isaiah urged Hezekiah to build. One of the first truths that the apostles proclaimed was that in Jesus the cornerstone prophecy was fulfilled—as, for example, in the words of Peter defending himself before the Sanhedrin: "This Jesus is the stone rejected by you, the builders, which has become the cornerstone"

(*Acts 4:11*). This bold statement recalled Jesus' pointed accusation at the end of the parable of the Tenants and the Vineyard, when he applied the image to himself (*Mark 12:10–11*). He referred to Psalm 118, where the psalmist rejoices that the one rejected, persecuted, and despised by mortals has been saved and honoured by God, and has become his chosen instrument:

> The stone which the builders rejected
> has become the main corner-stone.
> This is the LORD's doing;
> it is wonderful in our eyes.
>
> *Psalm 118:22–3*

**Reconciliation**

The Parable of the Tenants is one of judgement, designed—as always by Jesus—to bring his hearers to a new view about themselves. Coming to a new view, seeing ourselves and other people in a new light, is basic to allowing ourselves to be bound together, to be reconciled; without it there is little hope of a lasting peace, whether in Korea or Kashmir, or in any other place of conflict (nor of healing the deep polarizations—the culture wars—that now characterize the democratic West). Paul saw reconciliation as *the* work of God in Christ, and also as *the* basic task of the Church:

> All this has been the work of God. He has reconciled us to himself through Christ, and has enlisted us in this ministry of reconciliation: God was in Christ reconciling the world to himself, no longer holding people's misdeeds against them, and has entrusted us with the message of reconciliation.
>
> *2 Corinthians 5:18–19*

Christians see the creation of a new reality as the goal of reconciliation, a characteristically deeper understanding than that which generally obtains. Paul was writing to a church that had experienced sharp differences among its members which they had not been able to overcome. His great insight is that reconciliation is a divine gift, not a human achievement. It is by opening themselves to receive this gift that the Corinthian Christians will be reconciled. Reconciliation tends to be equated with conciliation, a process of conflict mediation whose goal is to lessen conflict, to broker a compromise, which will enable those at odds to find a way forward and live with their differences. Reconciliation has a more fundamental character: conciliation tends to find a way around differences, but reconciliation looks at conflict and its causes head on, seeking a different outcome—it strives, not to enable the parties to *live* with their differences, but rather to *transcend* them. Like Christian hope, Christian reconciliation is rooted in the future, not the past, as Robert Schreiter explains: "[It] never takes us back to where we were before. It is more than the removal of suffering for the victim and conversion for the oppressor. Reconciliation takes us to a new place."[19] As Paul said, when we are united in Christ "there is a new creation; the old order has gone; a new order has already begun" (*2 Corinthians 5:17*). Reconciliation is more received than achieved. Schreiter puts it well: "reconciliation is not a skill to be mastered, but rather, something discovered—the power of God's grace welling up in one's life. . . . Reconciliation becomes more of an attitude than an acquired skill; it becomes a stance assumed before a broken world, rather than a tool to repair that world . . . reconciliation is more spirituality than strategy."[20] He likens the process of reconciliation to entering a *mysterion*, a pathway in which God leads us out of suffering and alienation into the grace of his new reality. This grace is transforming, and creates the conditions not only for forgiveness, but also for those estranged to rediscover their humanity.[21] A good example is the Peace and Reconciliation Commission in South Africa through which the victims of apartheid not only affirmed their own humanity, but did so in a way that affirmed the humanity of their oppressors.[22]

### Uniting the personal and the political

Reconciliation unites the personal and the political. The desire to be reconciled comes more from our spirit and emotions than from our intellect. It requires a spiritual depth and integrity of character, a willingness to walk in another's shoes, raising the individual above institutional and tribal perceptions and ideology. Donald Nicholl, reflecting on the mutual hostility between Arab and Jew in Israel (mirrored in many other national divisions, e.g. black and white, Sunni and Shia, Muslim and Christian, Hutu and Tutsi, Rohinga and Burman), recounts a story told by Karl Stern in his autobiography *Pillar of Fire*. Arriving in Bavaria as Nazism was beginning to take hold in the minds of Germans, the young Stern noted as he walked home from the station, where his father had met him, that some of those of their acquaintance refused to greet them, being Jews, as they passed by. Nicholl comments:

> It is precisely with such little acts of cowardice and hostility that all the terrible events of our terrible world begin—the lying, the tortures and the killings. Likewise the work of reconciliation begins with an act of greeting. Simply to greet another person, to recognize that person, is to participate in the sacrament of peace.[23]

Bringing the personal and the political together is basic to the hope for peace. It enables us to recognize another as a child of God like ourselves; seeing the world through their eyes is to acknowledge their humanity, and to put it on a par with our own. In the Parable of Dives and Lazarus Jesus issues a clear warning of the consequences of failing to do this (*Luke 16:19–31*). Dives, the rich man, perhaps a Sadducee—one of the establishment—who used to dress in purple and the finest linen, and who feasted sumptuously every day, had no concern for the poor man Lazarus, covered in sores, hungry and in rags, who lay at his gate. Although Dives knew Lazarus by name, he cannot have regarded him as a human being like himself; his utter lack of charity, in the sense of genuine concern for other people, meant that he failed to see life from Lazarus' position. Nor had his faith shaped his life. He was a glaring example of those who ignored the duty, placed on the rich by the Law of Moses, to aid the poor. It would have cost Dives little in economic terms to save Lazarus from his life of wretchedness, but spiritually the cost was too great. He could not acknowledge that Lazarus was a human being equal to himself—even in hell he treats Lazarus as a lackey, asking Abraham to send him as a messenger to his family. Jesus talks of a "great gulf" that separates Dives from those who see the truth and act upon it—those who take to heart the Law and the prophets. Peace and reconciliation require a change of outlook; the contrast between the outlook of Dives and of Jesus is telling: Jesus denied no one's humanity, praying—as he died—for those who killed him. Jesus shows us the way of peace; do we, like Dives, find it too costly?

It seems that generally we do. It is easier to keep the personal and political apart. Rowan Williams points to what is lacking in most peacemaking today, resulting in what he calls a "false peace": namely that reconciliation is a drawn-out process which takes time and requires a lasting commitment (as in personal friendship), elements that are cast aside by the urgent modern desire for "closure". The premature declaration of victory when fighting ceased in the second Iraq War is a good example. As the continuing conflict so tragically shows, it is not until we can see that the broken relationships have been properly mended that we can talk of victory, nor indeed of endings. Mending the wounds of war and arriving at a new place takes time and commitment from both sides. The hope for peace poses some hard questions for victors and vanquished alike, but most challengingly for the victors, as Williams points out:

> Are we capable, as Western societies, of a peace that is not "false" . . . ? That is, are we sufficiently alert to the agenda we are bringing to international conflict—resentments, the sense of half-buried impotence that sits alongside the urge to demonstrate the power we do have, the desire to put off examining the unfinished business in our own societies? And, for that matter, there is the falsity that can also afflict would-be peacemakers, who are more concerned with condemning what's wrong than with planning for what might change things, and who derive some comfort from knowing where evil lies (i.e. in someone else, some warmongering monster).[24]

### Reconciliation and judgement

That reconciliation involves judgement is implicit in Isaiah's prophecy: there is no true reconciliation if justice and righteousness are not present. Indeed, I think that the biblical view is that God becomes judge at every crisis in history, and his judgement is to hold before us the vision of a better way, in a word, of *shalom*. If I and my neighbour are at odds with one another, any attempt to resolve our conflict will not really succeed until we both feel that we have been fairly treated, and that our concerns have been heard. Only then can we move forward into the divine gift of a new reality. Unreconciled differences are often to do with identity, and identity is bound up with the story that we tell of ourselves. For example, when nations are divided, as with Iraq, or split over major issues, as with the debate about Brexit in the UK, the different sides are telling different stories about the nation, its history, identity, and destiny. Usually both stories are true, but only partially, their advocates generally being selective about those things upon which their version is based. The conflict is about whose story is to prevail, whose story will become the only story. No peace is built that way, as we have seen (for example) in Northern Ireland, or in Iraq where the West attempted to impose a new story with no Iraqi roots. The failure of many peace plans teaches us that reconciliation cannot be imposed; it is not sufficient that the concerns of the powerful have been heard and addressed; everyone's interests need to be taken seriously. The obstacles to peace in the former *status quo* have to be removed, and this is part of the judgement that reconciliation involves: old divisions and attitudes of superiority have to be overcome; a new bond has to be established between those estranged, in the same way that a new cornerstone is inserted into a collapsing wall. From the Christian perspective, true reconciliation provides a new vision in which the former reality is transcended and raised to a new level.[25] For this to happen, the old stories that justify the conflict have to give way to a new, more complete story in which both parties can locate their own narrative.

## One in Christ

The Christian gospel is such a story. In it we find the cornerstone on which justice and righteousness are founded, the Great Story in which our own story finds its place. The most dramatic example of this in the Early Church was the decision to admit Gentiles to its fellowship. God made clear to Peter, in the vision he had in Joppa of the sailcloth let down from heaven, that this was his will, and it was confirmed by Peter's subsequent visit to the house of the Roman centurion Cornelius when the Holy Spirit fell on all who were assembled (*Acts 10*). For Jews brought up with the belief in their racial and religious exclusiveness, enforced by Ezra after the return from the Babylonian Exile,[26] this must have seemed an unbelievable possibility; indeed, when Peter returned to Jerusalem, some believers of Jewish birth took issue with him, accusing him of "visiting men who are uncircumcised, and sitting at table with them". He had to give a full explanation before they would accept it (*Acts 11:1–18*). The Book of Acts records the decision of the nascent Church to admit Gentiles to its fellowship, and says no more about this momentous new departure apart from recording the way the faith spread among the Gentile communities. It fell to Paul to explain what God had done in Christ, and to reflect deeply on its meaning.

In his Letter to the Ephesians,[27] Paul describes the effect of Jesus' self-offering as nothing less than the creation of a new humanity built "on the foundation of the apostles and prophets, with Jesus Christ himself as the cornerstone. In him the whole building is bonded together and grows into a holy temple in the Lord" (*Ephesians 2:20–1*). Through Jesus' sacrificial death the barrier between peoples formerly estranged has been overcome: "For he is himself our peace. Gentiles and Jews, he has made the two one, and in his own body of flesh and blood has broken down the barrier of enmity which separated them" (*Ephesians 2:14*). In particular, he abolished the one thing that marked out the Jews as a separate people, namely the Law, with its commandments and ordinances which provided the path to holiness. Not only was keeping the law an impossibility for the Gentiles, it could not be kept by the majority of the Jews. The way to holiness henceforth was to be through obedience to Christ, and by becoming a member of his community. Jesus, says Paul, has created out of the two "a single new humanity in himself, thereby making peace. This was his purpose, to reconcile the two in a single body to God through the cross, by which he killed the enmity . . . through him we both alike have access to the Father in the one Spirit." (*Ephesians 2:15–16, 18*)[28] This is the outworking of Jesus' words over the cup at the Last Supper: "This is my blood of the new covenant, shed *for you and for many* for the forgiveness of sins."

Jesus had foreshadowed these words, and indeed the whole of his Passion, in his discourse on the Good Shepherd. "The good shepherd," he said, "lays down his life for his sheep" (*John 10:11*). But he went further. The concern of the Good Shepherd is not just for his own flock, but also for those who are outside it: they too must be brought into the fold so that there shall be one flock, one shepherd (*John 10:14–16*). And this, Jesus tells us, is also God's concern, for the shepherd's knowledge of his flock, and their acknowledgement of the shepherd, is based on his relationship of mutual love and care with the Father. The Church has found in this divine concern for inclusion a powerful incentive to pursue the path of unity between the different Christian denominations, but when Jesus spoke there was no Church and the concern for Christian unity lay far in the future. The concern of the King of the Nations, of the Good Shepherd, is with the unity of humankind. Through him a new humanity was brought into being. Paul spells it out in his letter to the Galatians where he says that for those who have been baptized into Christ, "there is no such thing as Jew and Greek, slave and freeman, male and female; for you are all one person in Christ Jesus" (*Galatians 3:28*). In Christ the three basic social barriers of race, class, and gender are transcended. John Macquarrie says that this was no pious hope, but a concrete reality: "From the beginning, [the Church] was a people embracing 'Jew and Greek and barbarian', and it was precisely this transracial and transnational character of the people that was so deeply impressive in the early centuries that it seemed like the advent of a new humanity."[29] Alas, the Church has in subsequent centuries fallen far short of this, mirroring rather the old humanity but with religious labels. But human failure is not the end of the story; the hope persists, and in Jesus we find the cornerstone that makes opposing nations one, giving substance to our hope for peace.

## Come and save us

The high view that Jesus took of reconciliation is evident from the Sermon on the Mount where, as we have seen, he makes it plain that reconciliation takes priority over our other concerns and duties, including worship: "[I]f you are presenting your gift at the altar and suddenly remember that your brother has a grievance against you, leave your gift where it is before the altar. First go and make peace with your brother; then come back and offer your gift" (*Matthew 5:23–4*). Anyone who has made peace in this way knows that it is costly. There is no reconciliation, no peace, without cost. Pride and self-assertion have to be surrendered, and it may be that we also have to accept some difficult home truths—and, perhaps hardest of all, come to see things through the eyes of our former adversary as well as our own. Any true peace process involves this element. We may know from our own experience how challenging this is, and we see the same in the peace process in Northern Ireland and in the Truth and Reconciliation Commission in South Africa.

The last of the titles that Isaiah of Jerusalem ascribed to the Saviour was "Prince of Peace" (*Isaiah 9:6*). That title rightly belongs to Jesus because he was prepared to bear the cost of making peace, even to the point of laying down his life. This was not, I imagine, the way in which Isaiah expected his prophecy to be fulfilled, nor indeed Jeremiah, who had later prophesied that God would raise up a new king like David (*Jeremiah 23:5–6*). Jesus was not a king like David, a secular ruler, able to command obedience, to make laws, and defend his people by force of arms. When the disciples were arguing among themselves about who was the greatest, he rebuked them, saying, "If anyone wants to be first, he must make himself last of all and servant of all" (*Mark 9:35*). And on another occasion he said:

> You know that among the Gentiles the recognized rulers lord it over their subjects, and the great make their authority felt. It shall not be so among you; among you, whoever wants to be great must be your servant, and whoever wants to be first must be the slave of all. For the Son of Man did not come to be served but to serve, and to give his life as a ransom for many.
>
> *Mark 10:42–5*

The greatest rulers are those who serve those whom they rule, and the advent of the servant king was the only way in which Jeremiah's prophecy could be fulfilled if reconciliation and peace among the nations was to be achieved. Only love can reconcile; only love can break down barriers; only love can make one those who are separated; only love can make peace and create a new humanity—because it is only love that can bear the hurt and the pain of those estranged. This is the leadership of a servant, and suffering is inevitable.

Jesus was the suffering servant who built the bridge of reconciliation between God and his people that no one else could build. He was the man for others, as is often said, and when the multitudes sought out Jesus, this—I imagine—is what they sensed deep in their hearts, even if the need that drew them to him was more immediate. He was the good shepherd who laid down his life for the sheep. This is the way Jesus saves those whom he formed from clay. This is atonement, the source of our peace and reconciliation with God. Atonement through self-sacrifice is part of human experience, and it is a mystery: that is, a reality that can be experienced but not explained. The Atonement is the deepest mystery of all. The knowledge that Jesus' death was reconciling is not intellectual, but felt or intuited; it is the knowledge of the heart. We can affirm with Paul that "God was in Christ, reconciling the world to himself" (*2 Corinthians 5:19*), but beyond that affirmation the analytical mind cannot go; the best we can offer is a metaphor. A modern metaphor is that of the peacemaker. Making peace through self-giving is part of the ordinary experience of most people. When we are divided against one another, whether individuals, groups, or nations, reconciliation requires a peacemaker. We appoint people to do this work (for example, counsellors, industrial and international mediators, and diplomats), and it is costly work, because the peacemaker will have to give something of him- or herself in building the bridge of reconciliation. The hurt, anger, and lack of trust is projected on to them, and they have to bear it—and in doing so they gradually take the sting out of the conflict. If this is true of the sons of men, how much more is it true of the Son of Man who, bearing the sins of the world, built the bridge of reconciliation between God and his creation. It might not be a ransom in the strict sense of the word, but in his or her self-giving the peacemaker pays the price of peace. In Christ we see that the hope for peace, like the hope for justice, is inseparable from self-giving.

7

# Emmanuel: The Hope for Love

*O Emmanuel,*
*Hope of the nations and their Saviour;*
*come and save us, Lord our God.*

*I am the resurrection and the life.*

## Emmanuel

Of all the words used to describe our hopes, love is perhaps the most misunderstood. When we speak of "love", our meaning will vary from the erotic and the romantic to nurture and care, support and self-giving. We may hope for love in all these senses at some time in our lives, and all are basic to being human, but the hope for love that I consider in this chapter is a little different, namely the understanding of love conveyed by the name "Emmanuel", *God-with-us*. It is the most familiar of the names used in the antiphons to refer to Jesus, bringing together the other names, and expressing clearly the essence of his ministry. At one level, Jesus fulfils the hope that God will be "with us" through his physical presence. He is the living sign that God is with his people, both in salvation and in judgement; but Jesus also fulfils the hope at a deeper level: he was the sign, in time, that God is eternally with us in the moral sense of taking our part, bearing our burdens, supporting and caring for us, and also rebuking us and calling us back when we go astray. Being *with* someone in this sense is to love them; we all need this depth of love if we are to grow and flourish in our humanity, and it is in this sense that I explore the hope for love. Caring and compassionate love is the most basic of our needs. We can face pain, suffering, hardship, persecution even, if we do not have to do it alone. The love of the God who is *with us* is beautifully expressed in this prayer by Richard Harries:

> O God, Father,
> moment by moment you hold me in being,
> on you I depend.
> O God, Eternal Son,
> friend and brother beside me,
> in you I trust.
> O God, Holy Spirit,
> life and love within me,
> from you I live.

The Christian hope for love is rooted in the belief that God *is* love, and that Jesus is indeed the "friend and brother beside us", the one who stands with us, come what may. The ground of our hope is that in him God's very being is revealed. When Jesus said, "I am the resurrection and the life," he summed up the being of God: God is Life, the ground of our being, our creator, and the source of our life and our flourishing; God is Resurrection, the source of new life, hope, justice, and reconciliation. The sign of this is the resurrection of Jesus himself. His resurrection did not annul his passion; rather God absorbed it into himself, showing that his own life of love is stronger than the sins of human beings, opening a new way forward.[1]

Life and resurrection are the gifts of love; they cannot exist without love—they proceed from love and they enfold us in love. Together they assure us of our eternal destiny in communion with God, his ultimate desire and purpose for all humankind. As the Father sustained Jesus and brought him to new life, so he will sustain us. God is love and cannot be other than on our side, and—as Paul said—"If God is on our side, who is against us? He did not spare his own Son but gave him up for us all; how can he fail to lavish every other gift upon us?" (*Romans 8:31–2)*. And so Paul can affirm in ringing terms his conviction "that there is nothing in death or life, in the realm of spirits or superhuman powers, in the world as it is or the world as it shall be, in the forces of the universe, in heights and depths—nothing in all creation that can separate us from the love of God in Christ Jesus our Lord" (*Romans 8:38–9*). The hope expressed in the final antiphon encompasses all our other hopes; to hope for love is to hope for God.

**The young woman and her child**

Given the very appropriateness of the name Emmanuel, *God-with-us*, to describe Jesus, it is ironic that when first used by Isaiah of Jerusalem it had no messianic connotation at all! Isaiah used the name in a confrontation with King Ahaz of Judah over the defence policy that the king was pursuing, namely an alliance with Assyria. Isaiah believed this policy was contrary to God's will, and that it would lead to disaster. He told Ahaz to change course and invited him to ask God for a sign to confirm the truth of his words. Ahaz refused, feigning piety; in response, Isaiah said God would give him a sign anyway: a child would shortly be born to a young woman who would call him Emmanuel, and by the time that the child had grown to maturity (i.e. about twenty years hence) the lands of Ahaz's enemies would be left desolate. But this was not all: because Ahaz had not believed, disaster would also come upon Judah. Although not messianic, the symbolic nature of the child about to be born could hardly be clearer: he was to be a living sign from God that God was with his people—both in salvation and in judgement.

Matthew, whose account of the birth of Jesus is presented throughout in terms of the fulfilment of prophecy,[2] alighted upon Isaiah's words as a prediction of the virgin birth:

> All this happened in order to fulfil what the Lord declared through the prophet: "A virgin will conceive and bear a son, and he shall be called Emmanuel," a name which means "God is with us".
>
> *Matthew 1:22–3*

However, not only did Matthew misunderstand the original meaning of the prophecy, taking it out of context, he also made two crucial changes: he wrongly translated the term "young woman" as "virgin", and he said that she was about to conceive when Isaiah had said she was already "with child".[3] It is impossible to know how these changes came about—simple human error? Corrupt sources? Too zealous a desire for proof?—but what is clear is that by the time of Jesus, any interpretation of Isaiah's words in their original military terms had become impossible to maintain, given the varying fortunes of Israel and Judah, even though the idea of God as the vanquisher of Israel's enemies persisted, even among the disciples (*Luke 24:21*). Notably, Jesus did not present himself as the fulfilment of that image, and after the resurrection it was the prophecy of Isaiah of Babylon, not Isaiah of Jerusalem, that provided the picture of the God who is with us, namely the Suffering Servant, who took upon himself the sins of his people. This is how God is with us, and this is how God loves us, and it is this prophecy that Matthew actually shows to have been fulfilled as his Gospel develops. As the Suffering Servant, Jesus was—and is—Emmanuel, God-with-us—both in salvation and in judgement.

## God with us

Like other basic aspects of the faith, the understanding of the love of God developed over time, and it was not until after the resurrection that the full truth dawned that God *is* love. John the Elder expressed the belief succinctly: "God is love; he who dwells in love is dwelling in God, and God in him" (*1 John 4:16b*). Karl Barth put it this way: "God is love before he loves us and without his loving us. He is Love as he is everything that he is, as the triune God in himself. Even without us and the world and its reconciliation he would suffer in himself no lack of love."[4] The prophets came close to this belief, but Israel never quite understood God as love. That God loved Israel was never in doubt. After the Exodus Moses had declared, "It was because the Lord loved you that he brought you out with a mighty hand, and redeemed you from the place of slavery" (*Deuteronomy 7:8*). And Jeremiah believed that God loved Israel as a child in whom he delighted, for whom his heart yearned and was filled with tenderness (*Jeremiah 31:20*). God's love came from his innermost being, part of the mystery of his divinity; it was seen in the way he chose and called his people, unlike the pagan gods whose relationship with their people arose out of an earthly attachment to both land and race. The God of Israel was not an ethnic God but an ethical God,[5] and—again in sharp contrast to paganism—the prophets saw clearly that God's love is not given because of any worth or attractiveness in its object, but comes spontaneously from him and creates worth in its object. God's love has no cause prior to itself. Isaiah of Babylon came closest to taking the further step of seeing love as the essence of God's being when he said that God was the One who bore the sins of his people (*Isaiah 53*), and this, of course, is the most profound insight into the way God is with us.

**Wrath and compassion**

Although it was believed that God loved Israel, and that his love came spontaneously from the personal being of God himself, there was a tension in the relationship: despite the prophetic insistence that God would not abandon his people, the continuance of God's love was felt to be conditional upon Israel's behaviour. It is easy to see how this tension arose. God's love cannot be separated from his righteousness; he seeks moral fellowship with his people and demands an undivided allegiance; his love is given in deadly earnest and can be severe. Such love can feel like a conditional love, but it is not; it is a love given despite wrongdoing in order to save the beloved from themselves. God was involved in a struggle for the soul of Israel and was willing to hurt in order to save. While love offers unconditional acceptance, this is not to be equated with unconditional approval. This resonates with our own experience: being *with* someone does not mean unconditional approval for all that they do, but it does mean unconditional commitment to their welfare, whatever they do. It is because God is like that, that we, his creatures, are also called to be like that. God is with us both in care and in judgement, in compassion and in wrath, and both are expressions of love.

Among the prophets it was Hosea who felt and expressed the two-fold nature of God's love most keenly. Most of his prophecies denounce Israel for her sins, and he took two unchaste women as his wives as a symbol of Israel's faithlessness. His first wife, Gomer, bore him children whom he named "Not-loved" and "Not-my-people" to show God's rejection of his people, even to the point of renouncing the covenant (*Hosea 1:9*). Unsparingly, Hosea pronounces God's condemnation of Israel as a harlot and threatens to expose her nakedness and her shame, but then, his anger spent, he sees that God cannot reject his people, and his tone changes from anger to tenderness:

> But now I shall woo her,
> lead her into the wilderness,
> and speak tenderly to her.
> . . . I shall show love to Not-loved,
> and say to Not-my-people,
> "You are my people,"
> and he will say, "You are my God."
>
> *Hosea 2:14,23*

God cannot abandon Israel. He will be true to the covenant. He cannot be other than *with* his people.

Hosea offers a tender, moving picture of the God who is with us. If he were not with us, then he would not be so angry at our waywardness; the denunciation of Israel's sins that Hosea speaks in God's name is part and parcel of God's love. But because God is with us, he cannot suffer the separation of his people from himself; he works tirelessly at their reconciliation, and it is on this note of healing that the prophecy of Hosea concludes:

> I shall heal my people's apostasy;
> I shall love them freely,
> for my anger is turned away from them.
> I shall be as dew to Israel
> that they may flower like the lily,
> strike root like the poplar,
> and put out fresh shoots,
> that they may be as fair as the olive
> and fragrant as Lebanon.
>
> *Hosea 14:4–6*

**The human face of love**

Despite Hosea's conviction that God took Israel's sin so seriously precisely because of his love for her, and that God's severity was never separated from his tenderness,[6] this was not how it felt. The severity was felt more deeply than the tenderness, and the true character of God was not fully apprehended. Eight centuries later the true character of the God who is with us was disclosed in Jesus of Nazareth; as we sing each Christmas, he is our Emmanuel.[7] He made plain the truth that Hosea and the prophets had glimpsed, that God *is* Love, the One who is *with* us, and who never ceases to desire and work for our reconciliation. As we have seen throughout this exploration of hope, "God's nature is liberating love in Jesus Christ. God, the creator, the one who can be trusted, is love that liberates humanity, in a way that fulfils and transcends all human, personal, social, and political expectations."[8]

Jesus spoke of God as a loving Father whose love was so great that he had counted even the number of hairs on our heads (*Matthew 10:29–30*). All that we know about Jesus—what he said and taught, the way he treated others, his death and resurrection—is shot through with the love of God, manifesting the same two-fold nature that we see in Hosea. On the one hand, Jesus speaks of God's compassion: in his miracles and acts of mercy and forgiveness he shows God's love in action, and at the same time he extends the moral demands of God's love: for example, in the requirement that we are to love not just our neighbours but also our enemies and to pray for our persecutors. On the other hand, Jesus speaks of God's wrath: in his parables of judgement and in his condemnation of hypocrisy he is unsparing in his warnings to those who turn away from God and his laws. In Jesus we see a love that is both demanding and tender, offered with the same purpose of salvation as Hosea understood. As Jesus himself said, he came not to judge the world, but to save it (*John 12:47*), a truth which he demonstrated in his forgiveness of the woman taken in adultery (*John 8:10–11*), and which John expressed memorably:

> God so loved the world that he gave his only Son, that everyone who has faith in him may not perish but have eternal life. It was not to judge the world that God sent his Son into the world, but that through him the world might be saved.
>
> *John 3:16–17*

### *Agape*

The love that God shows towards the world, Paul believed, was the greatest of the three things which last for ever. We may say, quite simply, that God's love is the foundation of hope; Saint Paul described it beautifully in his "Hymn to Love":

> Love is patient and kind. Love envies no one, is never boastful, never conceited, never rude; love is never selfish, never quick to take offence. Love keeps no score of wrongs, takes no pleasure in the sins of others, but delights in the truth. There is nothing love cannot face; there is no limit to its faith, its hope, its endurance.
>
> *1 Corinthians 13:4–7*

Writing in Greek, Paul had to choose one of seven words for love, ranging from *eros* to affection and friendship.[9] He chose *agape*, the least used of the seven, a word not found in the Bible until Paul adopted it to describe the love that we experience in Christ. *Agape* describes an unconditional love, selfless to the point of self-sacrifice, refusing to count the cost. *Agape* expresses the love of God for his creation simply for its own sake, not for any need or desire that he may have, but because it is good. Men and women are loved not only for what they are, but also because of the potential that God has placed within them. Humans too are capable of this love, and Edward Schillebeeckx sees in this a sign of the reality of God. If we look for God in this scientific, technological world, he says, we might see him in the capacity of humans to love without having any reason to: "In such a context God would then be experienced by believers as pure gift, even pure freedom. . . . God is not there as an 'explanation' but as a gift."[10]

*Agape* is a selfless love that is passionately committed to the wellbeing of others; it is truly "with them", a love that is self-sacrificial and which expects nothing in return. *Agape* creates the conditions in which *ressentiment* dies. There is a great strength to such a love, and in speaking of *agape* Paul helps us to appreciate that love is not just an emotion, but an act of the will, an orientation of the whole person, as we see in Jesus. Selfless love frees us from those things that separate us *from* God and makes real our hope for a life in union *with* God. That, I think, describes the essence of Jesus' ministry, and why in him our hope for love is fulfilled. It is as he said: all who enter the sheepfold *through* him will be safe, they will go in and out and find pasture (*John 10:9*).

## The Hopes of the Nations

We have seen how the hopes expressed in the antiphons bring together our personal hopes and our public hopes, and as this last antiphon is sung just a day before the celebration of God-with-us at Christmas, we acknowledge that if God is *not* with us, none of these hopes will be fulfilled. The selfless love that we see in Jesus has its place in the affairs of the nations just as much as in our personal lives, and in the exploration of the hopes for truth, justice, freedom, and peace we have seen the truth of this. The seventh antiphon, with its affirmation that Emmanuel is the hope of the nations and their saviour, points to the truth that the disorder we see in the world *can* be overcome in Christ. God, as revealed in Jesus, is the ground of our being, and our hopes will be in vain—public as well as personal—if they are not built on that foundation.

This resonates with the prophecy of Hosea. Both his wives represented Israel; his anger and his warnings of danger were not directed at private individuals, but at the nation and her leaders. He accused them of following the pagan gods of fertility which led them to prize material things above justice and righteousness, and degraded their worship of God into mere lip-service. Their leaders loved shameful ways: in trade they were dishonest and deceitful, too ready to resort to litigation; they measured their worth by their wealth and status, which they believed would enable them to escape detection for their wrongdoing. Israel, said Hosea, was being destroyed because of her lack of knowledge of the God who alone could save them, and who longed to do so—as he says pithily, "a people without understanding will come to ruin. . . . Their deeds do not permit them to return to their God" (*Hosea 4:14b; 5:4a*). In more derisory mood, he describes the nation as half-baked, "a flat loaf not turned over" (*Hosea 7:8*). There are many parallels with the world today, where political initiatives often seem at best "half-baked", where economic models trounce all other considerations, and where the powerful shelter behind their wealth and status. Although it is clear from Hosea's prophecy that this state of affairs is deeply embedded in human society, the hope persists for a new dispensation.

**From fear to trust**

I believe that at the public level the hope for love is about working towards this new dispensation. Too often it is fear that gets in the way and leads us to worship the false gods of fertility and materialism. "There is nothing love cannot face," declared Paul, and echoing him Bishop Peter Selby said, "Love's most significant effect is to provide an environment of security in which the unknown future of society can be faced."[11] Fear is often the dominant motive in both private and public life, particularly fear of the unknown, fear of the stranger, fear of missing out, and of getting left behind. Love has an open quality that overcomes fear, and in which we are known and valued as we truly are. On one of his journeys Jesus said that in the kingdom (the time of God's coming in its fullness), there is nothing hidden that will not be disclosed, nothing under cover that will not be made known and brought into the open (*Luke 8:17*). Too much of human life is about keeping things covered up, about preserving image and keeping up appearances; about not facing the dark side of our nature. It is as though we fear that if God knows all he will not forgive all. The contrary is the truth. Real forgiveness is only possible when there is complete openness. Only when all is known can all be forgiven. If God is love, there is nothing to fear; forgiveness is where we experience in our hearts that he is with us. In our personal lives, if we want God to be with us, we need to be open and honest about our actions, motivations, and feelings, refusing "to see, think of, or deal with, one's neighbour except in the light of what Christ has done for him, as the brother for whom Christ died".[12]

If, in public life, love is about taking everybody's interests seriously, hope requires us to acknowledge the factors that make this hard to achieve, and among them is the deep and disabling limitation of representative democracy, namely that it is founded on a competition for votes. The need for politicians to please their supporters in order to gain power means that, however high their personal ideals, they will promote the interests of their supporters over the interests of others; and the need to secure campaign funds means that the interests of the wealthy generally take precedence over the interests of the poor. In the commercial world the maximization of financial gain as the dominant corporate objective has the same effect, exalting the interests of shareholders over both the interests of other stakeholders and environmental considerations. This disconnection between ideal and reality was precisely the failure that Hosea condemned in Israel. Although it is far from perfect, there is no acceptable alternative to representative democracy—as Winston Churchill said, it is "the worst form of Government except for all those other forms that have been tried from time to time"—and we have, nevertheless, to acknowledge its failings and work to improve its operation, particularly in the face of existential crises, like climate change and global pandemics, that depend on co-operation rather than competition for their solution. This indeed is one of the possibilities of good that motivates hope.

### Rejecting the wrong path

The need for democratic reform is evident, given the challenges the world faces from *ressentiment* to climate change; and the need is made all the more urgent by the worldwide movement towards populism, where national interests, narrowly conceived, take precedence over the common good. As Hosea understood more than two-and-a-half millennia ago, God is with us, but he is with us in judgement. If we hope for love, we need to turn away from the temptation to take control and to do without God. This is the essence of the temptations that Jesus experienced at the beginning of his ministry (*Matthew 4:1–11*). "Turn these stones into bread," the Tempter said. "Throw yourself down from the Temple, and let God's angels bear you up." "Worship me, and gain the world." It was Henri Nouwen, I believe, who pointed out that these are the temptations of the powerful in every age. *Be relevant!*—give the people what they want. *Be spectacular!*—put on a good show. *Be powerful!*—let people see who is in charge. These are seductive temptations, even for a leader who is well-motivated and wants to do the best for the people; they are especially attractive to those who want to reshape the world after their own designs. These temptations resonate with desires deep within us: "Take control! It's your life. You want to achieve your aims; do it your way!" The temptation is to put ourselves at the centre of concern and to displace God. "Take control!" the Tempter whispers in the ear of Jesus, but he will have none of it; it is God alone whose ways are true, and whom we must worship. John the Elder put it simply: "What love means is to live according to the commands of God" (*2 John 6*). Giving people what they want may fulfil their material needs, but at the cost of their spiritual needs; putting on a good show may bring popularity, but it substitutes spectacle for substance; power may satisfy the leader's ego, and enable him or her to do what he or she wishes, but justice is what the people need.

The hope of the nations is for a world in which these short-term temptations are overcome, and justice and reconciliation are pursued simply because they are right, instead of prioritizing commercial and political expedients or party advantage; love is taking everyone's interests seriously. Maybe the COVID-19 pandemic will move us towards fulfilling this hope. Time and again we hear it said that things cannot go on as before. "The virus is, as it were, revealing humanity to itself."[13] A mirror is being held up to the world, and in it we see the reflections of a different world where self-sacrifice and solidarity are the norm. As Pope Francis said, we see "how our lives are woven together and sustained by ordinary people—often forgotten people—who do not appear in newspaper or magazine headlines nor on the grand catwalks of the latest show, but who without doubt are in these very days writing the decisive events of our time . . . " Commenting on these words, *The Tablet* instanced the example of a nurse who, asked on her way to work why she was putting herself in danger, replied quite simply: "Because I'm a nurse. It's who I am." We see in her words the response of love: a commitment to the common good, come what may; a lesson in the meaning of vocation which prompted the comment: "A self-obsessed society needs such lessons. Those called may not know that it is God who is doing the calling, but they realise it is something that transcends their own interests."[14]

It is God who is holding up the mirror, enabling us to see that being *with* others is basic to our nature. Our links go deeper than our social, economic, and political relations to shared humanitarian concerns about injustice, wellbeing, and survival. Amartya Sen puts it well: "There are few non-neighbours left in the world today."[15]

Acknowledging that God is with us in judgement, and allowing him to be with us in salvation, is the key to a hopeful future. This is the picture with which the Bible ends. After the disturbing visions and warnings of tribulation and conflict, there comes to John of Patmos a vision of peace and harmony. He sees a new heaven and a new earth:

> I saw the Holy City, new Jerusalem, coming down out of heaven from God, made ready as a bride adorned for her husband. I heard a loud voice proclaiming from the throne: "Now God has his dwelling with mankind! He will dwell among them and they shall be his people, and God himself will be with them. He will wipe every tear from their eyes. There will be an end to death, and to mourning and crying and pain, for the old order has passed away."
>
> *Revelation 21:1–4*

The hope for a more moral politics will, I think, always lie in the future, but it cannot be abandoned. It stands constantly before us as an appeal to our better nature; without it we surrender ourselves to the forces of oppression, meanness, and barbarism. And there are enough examples of leaders whose appeal has been moral, and whose love for their people has the quality of *agape*—for example, Gandhi and Mandela—for us to be encouraged in our hope. Christians also take encouragement from the belief that in Christ a new world *has* come into being and awaits its fulfilment. In the love of God nothing is impossible (cf. *Matthew 19:26*). Tom Wright points out that, despite the efforts of the Roman Empire to stamp out the early Christians, this conviction motivated them "to live lives of generosity, caring for the poor, and tending the sick, including people with whom they had no connection either through family or through work. They realized, as they worshipped the God they saw in Jesus and celebrated his good news, that a new way of being human had been launched."[16] A modern equivalent would be the advent of leaders who were prepared to present the moral case for change and not simply the economic case; who aimed not simply to please their supporters or appease the extremists; and who enthroned in their policies God's special concern for the poor. If, as Paul declares, all that stands in the way of justice and peace—all the selfish concerns and ambitions, all the powers of evil—was overcome on the cross (*Colossians 2:14–15*), then we may be assured that our hope is not in vain, but it has to be worked for.

## The God who saves

The most moving aspect of Hosea's prophecy is his portrait of the God who longs to bring his people back to him, that they may enjoy true peace:

> How can I hand you over, Ephraim,
> How can I surrender you, Israel?
> . . . I am not going to let loose my fury,
> I shall not turn and destroy Ephraim,
> for I am God, not a mortal;
> I am the Holy One in your midst . . .
>
> *Hosea 11:8–9*

God longs to redeem them: "I will deliver this people from the power of the grave; I will redeem them from death" (*Hosea 7:13; 13:14*). God offers salvation, that is, the way in which we can live in a right relationship with God, with our neighbour, and with creation. To put it another way: to be saved is to experience as "the source and goal of [my] own being and living" the one who is "the source and the goal of all things".[17] Salvation is popularly thought of as getting to heaven, or being among the "elect", but that is too restricted a meaning, and much narrower than the salvation celebrated by the antiphons. The hopes I have explored reflect the threefold nature of salvation: *from* what we are saved, *for* what we are saved, and the means *by* which we are saved. Salvation is not simply being saved *from* evil, sin, and death, it is also being saved *for* fullness of life, to enjoy here and now the good things God gives, and it is *by* his grace that we are saved. "Because it is all these things, what Christians experience as salvation always overlaps with experiences of liberation and greater fulfilment and enhancement of life . . . "[18] To be saved is to share in the wisdom of God, to seek justice, to live in freedom and peace, to find inner light, and to be reconciled with our neighbour and with

God. This is heaven on earth, the reign of love, that Jesus taught us to pray for: *Your kingdom come, . . . on earth, as in heaven.* The prayers of the antiphons are about making that petition real. As the Christian Aid slogan affirmed, "We believe in life before death."

### The resurrection and the life

Salvation is not something we achieve by our own efforts; it is the gift of God, who is the resurrection and the life. This is the greatest of the I AM sayings, perhaps the greatest and the most hopeful statement in the whole Bible, and like the final antiphon, it sums up all the others. *I am the resurrection and the life.* It is an astonishing claim. Jesus is not speaking of his own resurrection, but of resurrection as a gift of God held out to all, an existential reality. He says he *is* that reality; he *is* the resurrection and the life, not the sign but the reality itself. In him what was a future hope has become a present reality: "Jesus is saying that far from . . . having to wait until some distant and undefined *last day* for a general resurrection to take place, the real resurrection takes place in and through himself, as men hear him and give themselves to him in trustful obedience."[19] It is a profound statement that in Jesus we see the Father, not just his likeness, but his very being, the eternal source of life and love, the means of grace and the hope of glory. God is with us now; nothing is beyond the power of God; the authority of Christ reaches beyond this life. It is a promise that faith will never be disappointed.

When Jesus spoke these words, he was addressing Martha, whose brother Lazarus had died (*John 11:1–44*). She had sent word to Jesus when Lazarus fell ill, asking him to come, but Jesus had deliberately delayed for two days before he went. When he arrived, Martha upbraided him: "Lord, if you had been here my brother would not have died." She knew that Jesus had saved others from death, like the daughter of Jairus (*Luke 8:40–56*), and the son of the Widow of Nain (*Luke 7:11–17*), and she desired with all her heart that he would save her brother also. But he had not come. When Martha in her grief upbraided him, she added, perhaps to soften her criticism, "Even now I know that God will grant whatever you ask of him." Jesus responded by assuring her that her brother would rise again. "I know that he will rise again", Martha replied, "at the resurrection on the last day." But Jesus intends a restoration of life that will be a sign in time of that eternal reality. When his disciples first told him about Lazarus, he had said, "This illness is not to end in death; through it God's glory is to be revealed and the Son of God glorified." In his teaching about the Good Shepherd, which preceded his visit to Bethany, Jesus affirmed that he had the right to lay down his life and to receive it back again, a clear claim that he had authority over life and death. Jesus had delayed going to Bethany because he intended a greater demonstration of the power of God than even his other miracles of restoring life had shown, and in so doing he demonstrated the truth of his claim.

He invited Martha to trust in him: "I am the resurrection and the life. Whoever has faith in me shall live, even though he dies; and no one who lives and has faith in me will ever die. Do you believe this?" "I do", Martha replied, and fetched her sister Mary. Jesus, moved by their grief, wept, and proceeded literally to call forth Lazarus from his tomb. John says that "he raised his voice in a great cry: 'Lazarus, come out.'" And Lazarus came out! I once saw the actor Paul Alexander recite this scene. When he reached the point where Jesus calls out to Lazarus, he paused, and then, walking backwards, he moved slowly and deliberately to the back of the stage, building up the tension, and building up his strength, before uttering the great cry. It was more than a shout; it had depth as well as volume. I have never heard a cry like it; it was as though it penetrated beyond this life. That power and more must have been in Jesus' own cry. There is no region, in heaven or on earth, in which the voice of God cannot be heard; there is nothing in life or in death that God cannot overcome. As Paul said, in ringing tones:

> [T]here is nothing in death or life, in the realm of spirits or superhuman powers, in the world as it is or the world as it shall be, in the forces of the universe, in heights or depths—nothing in all creation that can separate us from the love of God in Christ Jesus our Lord.
>
> *Romans 8:38–9*

The raising of Lazarus was the greatest of Jesus' miracles. To restore to life someone who had been dead for four days shows that there is no limit to God's power; there is no place where God is not with us; hope placed in him is not misplaced. Life is the gift of love, and in restoring life Jesus shows the power of love. As the resurrection and the life he is the sign in time of what shall be in eternity, the source and the means of our salvation. His own resurrection is itself the sign that points to this truth.

### Atonement

In praising Jesus as the Saviour, the seventh antiphon points us forward to Easter, the true source of all Christian hope. Christians have always understood the death of Jesus as effecting a release from sin and a reconciliation with God. Through it we are made one with God (the literal meaning of atonement), thereby regaining our freedom as the children of God. The Jewish way of atonement was through the offering of sacrifice, a practice which Hosea and others had denounced in the name of God:

> For loyalty is my desire and not sacrifice,
> acknowledgement of God rather than burnt offerings.
>
> *Hosea 6:6*

Christians believe that the sacrificial system was brought to an end by Jesus' self-offering. At the Last Supper he took a cup of wine and, having said the traditional blessing, added the words, "This is my blood, the blood of the covenant, shed for many for the forgiveness of sins" (*Matthew 26:28*). Beyond this, the Bible offers no explanation as to how the atonement works. Down the centuries, theologians and others have sought to fill this biblical lacuna; various theories have been put forward, but all have their problems. One theory takes the idea of a ransom literally: Jesus' death was the price paid for our freedom. But to whom was it paid? If to God, then he cannot be a God of love; if to the devil, as some ancients maintained, how is it that he was in a position to exact a price from God? And if he could, then he is placed on a par with God, who thus ceases to be the only God. Another theory maintains that God allowed Jesus to be a substitute, a stand-in, for us; he bore the punishment that was ours, like a scapegoat. But what does this say about the moral character of God? A God who wills that the sinless must bear the punishment due to the sinful is as capricious as the Greek gods of antiquity, and entirely unworthy of worship.[20] As Edward Schillebeeckx said, "God . . . did not bring Jesus to the cross. Human beings did that. Although God always comes in power, divine power does not use force, not even against people who crucify God's Christ."[21] Alan Richardson argued that these and other theories are time-conditioned, reflecting the outlook and morality of the age in which they were conceived,[22] a view that I find convincing.

The truth of the atonement is apprehended through intuition and experience rather than through the intellect; no theory is adequate to the reality, which lies within the unknowable depths of God. The atonement is a mystery, like love, that we may intuit, approach, and experience, but never fully comprehend.[23] Letting the mystery lead us, we know that sin is not invincible, and that God's love will eventually triumph over all that is opposed to it. Against those who argue that only the elect shall be saved, Alan Richardson (following Gustav Aulén) asserts that Christ's victory was complete: God's purpose must succeed in respect of every created soul; if it does not, then he is not God. He continues:

> And what God's purpose of love has eternally secured, Christ's victory on the human level has in the world of time permanently assured. Christ's victory in time is the sign and symbol of God's eternal victory, just as his wooden cross on Calvary is the symbol in time of God's eternal nature of love.[24]

## Image of the God of hope

The final antiphon, like the others, ends with a prayer for salvation, but it adds the affirmation of faith that is implicit in all the antiphons, that Jesus is our Lord and our God. When we call Jesus the Son of God, we are not, of course, talking about a procreative relationship; we are saying that he is the one who makes the Father known, as in the phrase, "Like father, like son". The finite Jesus cannot be equated literally with the infinite God; rather we must say that Jesus is the eternal God expressed in human form, the visible expression of the invisible God. In Jesus the love of God took flesh, the love that brought forth life and sustains it in being, a belief expressed in one of the first Christian hymns:

> He is the image of the invisible God.
> His is the primacy over all creation.
> In him everything in heaven and earth was created . . .
> He exists before all things
> and all things are held together in him.
>
> *Colossians 1:15–17*

The foundation of Jesus' life and ministry was his relationship with the Father. His whole life and being were characterized, in Henri Nouwen's words, by "a total, fearless listening to his loving Father".[25] Between them there is only love:

> Everything that belongs to the Father, he entrusts to the Son, and everything the Son has received he returns to the Father. The Father opens himself totally to the Son and puts everything in his hands: all knowledge, all glory, all power. And the Son opens himself totally to the Father and thus returns everything into his Father's hands. "I came from the Father and have come into the world and now I leave the world to go to the Father."
>
> *Henri Nouwen, quoting John 16:28*

So we say that Jesus is Lord; he is not just a good and holy man, he is LORD—as he himself said: "[T]o see me, is to see him who sent me" (*John 12:45*). But this belief takes time to grow. As Jesus taught and healed the question on many minds was: Who is this? The disciples, too, were unclear. After Jesus had calmed the storm, they asked, "Who can this be? Even the wind and the sea obey him" (*Mark 4:41*). Faith does not grow like a plant, in a continuous, orderly process; it comes in moments of insight, and then only partially, requiring time for the full meaning to dawn. Peter's own journey of faith illustrates the point. As Jesus and the disciples travelled to Caesarea Philippi, he asked them, "Who do people say that I am?" They replied, "Some say John the Baptist, others Elijah, others one of the prophets." He responded, "And you, who do you say that I am?" According to Mark, Peter replied, "You are the Messiah" (*Mark 8:27–9*). In his account, Matthew adds to Peter's response the words, "the Son of the living God" (*Matthew 16:16*). This looks like a later addition, making plain the implications of Peter's reply, because it is clear from the subsequent dialogue in both Gospels that Peter has not properly understood the full meaning of his answer. When Jesus began to make plain that he would undergo suffering and death at the hands of the chief priests, Peter protested, "Heaven forbid! No, Lord, this shall never happen to you." Jesus rounded on him: "Out of my sight, Satan; you are a stumbling block to me. You think as men think, not as God thinks" (*Mark 8:32–3; Matthew 16:21–3*).

Many people today, like Peter at Caesarea Philippi, find the cross and the appalling suffering Jesus endured an obstacle to faith, but it is in the death of Jesus and his resurrection that we find the grounds of our hope. Many people just focus on his teaching, but his life and his death are a single entity. What we see in his self-sacrificial death is a final affirmation of his teaching and the values by which he lived, an understanding of life that could not be surrendered. It was only after the resurrection that the full truth dawned, and the Church could affirm that Jesus was in truth "the Son of the living God". When Peter and John were brought before the Sanhedrin to explain their conduct in curing a crippled man, Peter declared that it was in the name of Jesus that they had acted: "There is no salvation through anyone else; in all the world no other name has been granted to mankind by which we can be saved" (*Acts 4:12*). Some years later, Peter's conviction that Jesus is both Lord and Saviour shines through the pastoral letter he wrote to the churches in Asia Minor. He begins by giving praise to God, "the Father of our Lord Jesus Christ", who "in his great mercy by the resurrection of Jesus Christ from the dead, gave us new birth into a living hope . . . which nothing can destroy or spoil or wither" (*1 Peter 1:3–4*).

It is that living hope which Christians celebrate, and we pray that we too, like Peter, may grow in our faith in Jesus in whom our hope for love is fulfilled. At Christmas, when we look at the child resting on Mary's breast, we see the sign by which God assures us of his love. "The deepest meaning of the virgin birth of Jesus," said Geoffrey Preston, "is that he is not just the product of human evolution but is a new beginning."[26] And in his love God makes that new beginning available to us. In Christ we become a new creation, the old order passes, and all things are made new. John describes Jesus' miracles as *signs*, acts of power that point beyond themselves to an eternal reality. Who is this? Jesus is none other than the human face of God; his miracles are signs that he shares the creative power of God; his teaching is the truth of God; in him we see the gift of life; he carries our hopes for he is love, Emmanuel, God-with-us. This is where we began with the theme of the first antiphon, where we thought about Jesus as the embodiment of the creative power of God, and so this exploration is brought full circle. In the magisterial prologue to his Gospel, John unfolds the mystery at the heart of the Christian faith, and upon which the Christian hope rests:

> In the beginning the Word already was. The Word was in God's presence, and what God was, the Word was. He was with God at the beginning, and through him all things came to be; without him no created thing came into being. In him was life, and that life was the light of mankind . . . So the Word became flesh; he made his home among us, and we saw his glory, such glory as befits the Father's only Son, full of grace and truth.
>
> *John 1:1–4,14*

# Epilogue

*The hope set before us*
*. . . we have as an anchor for the soul,*
*both sure and stedfast.*
*— Hebrews 6:18–19 (King James Version) —*

Václav Havel, the Czech poet and first president of post-Soviet Czechoslovakia, said that "Hope is not the conviction that something will turn out well, but the certainty that something makes sense, regardless of how it turns out." This is the quality of Christian hope. Our hope is not a refusal to face the facts of the world, dreaming of an ideal society, but a belief—in the face of those facts—that a better world is possible and worth striving for. "Those who hope in Christ can no longer put up with reality as it is," wrote Jürgen Moltmann,[1] and the rational response of faith to the state of the world, and the confusions about the essence of human nature, is to work for something better. We are more than "isolated choosing machines in a market-shaped wilderness", as Rowan Williams pithily observes.[2] We know that there is something about women and men that cannot be explained in terms of economics, nor by where we have come from, nor by our genetic inheritance, but can be explained only in terms of where we are going—in other words, by our spiritual inheritance; the potential in us is more important than the actual.

Hope seeks this potential and is driven by it. As said in the Prologue, hope arises from a profound longing, a longing expressed in the "*O*" with which each of the antiphons begins. "*O*", we cry out to God from the world as it is, longing for the world for which we hope. Geoffrey Preston described the *O* as an echo from our emptiness; the cry "*O come!*" is about making space for God alone, a space that he can and does fill with his love, and praying these seven prayers of hope we ask that he will enlarge our capacity for love:

> After all, our *O* is only the echo in time of the eternal *O* of God. It is because God longs for us that we thirst for him . . . The history of all God's dealings with us can be read as a history of those repeated calls backwards and forwards between man and God. We can fairly expect, then, that God will start to fill and expand the emptiness of our *O* as soon as we create it. We do not only have the future to look forward to. We have the present to rejoice in, the present that is already big with the future of the world. That present future of all things is the Christ to whom we cry out in these antiphons.[3]

Preston echoes Moltmann, who believed that God "promises a new world of all-embracing life, of righteousness and truth, and with this promise he constantly calls this world in question—not because to the eye of hope it is as nothing, but because to the eye of hope, it is not yet what it has the prospect of being."[4] The potential is where God already is.

## Love is all you need

This exploration has brought together the public and personal aspects of hope in the conviction that our personal hope for truth, light and a new beginning cannot be separated from the public hopes for justice, freedom and peace; the personal and the political are two sides of the same coin. Personal faith and political action need each other, the one to avoid sentimentality, the other to avoid barbarism, and they are united in the hope for love. In each of these seven hopes the Christian faith offers a deeper understanding than that which generally prevails, challenging the world and its peoples—and indeed the Church itself—to reject the partial solutions of the political fix and our personal desires. It is, I think, in its understanding of love that Christianity has most to offer in the fulfilment of hope. Again, Moltmann puts it well when he argues that only in the perspective of the God disclosed in Christ can there possibly be a love that is more than *philia* (love to the known, the existent, and the like), namely *agape*—love to the unknown, the non-existent, the unlike, the unworthy, the worthless, the lost, the transient, and the dead; a love that can take upon itself the annihilating effects of pain and renunciation because it receives its power from the hope of the resurrection.[5] Christian hope draws on the belief that love is the power on which life is founded, and that ultimately love will overcome all that opposes it. If hope has been truly described in this exploration, then love is the only thing upon which it can rest. It may seem an act of foolishness to found all our hope on love—so much of our experience seems to show the powerlessness of love—but even so, I would argue that the great moves forward in human life have come through love, not force, from spiritual and artistic insights to the great scientific discoveries and political settlements. Above all, it is through the love of God that we understand truth as a person, and justice and freedom as *shalom*; it is the love of God which offers a truly new beginning, guides us to the light, and brings about the reconciliation upon which true peace is based. Love is not as foolish as it seems; Paul was right when he wrote that "the foolishness of God is wiser than human wisdom, and the weakness of God stronger than human strength" (*1 Corinthians 1:25*).

One of the hit songs sung by the Beatles in the 1960s echoed this truth (perhaps unknowingly) with its repeated refrain "All you need is love", but the world has still to heed the message. The Christian hope, seen through the seven hopes I have explored, is a total hope; in other words, it addresses the three basic levels of life: personal, communal, and global; hope for ourselves, for our neighbours, and for the world. In the Prologue I described the context of hope today in terms of a reaction to the working out of the ideas of the Enlightenment, drawing attention in particular to the growing sense of anger at the injustice of our globalized society—economically unified, but not morally united—which is taking increasingly violent forms. In today's world we see *ressentiment* writ large, and I argued that a hopeful response must take seriously the spiritual dimension of men and women, countering the materialistic spirituality of the age. I said, "We focus on the wrong task if we talk of the need to *regain* our spirituality; what we need to do is to *transform* it. The prevailing materialistic, human-centred spirituality needs to be transformed into one that is shaped by other values and motivations, one above all that reflects the wholeness of life and rejects its compartmentalization."

As with much of life, our spirituality tends to be compartmentalized. Some will show a deep and committed religious devotion, but act according to secular values at work and in the world; others will be active in addressing the injustices of the world or the local community, but without relating their work to a transcendent source of meaning. Yet others will be so concerned with the big picture that they overlook the needs of individuals and communities, including those closest to them. If hope takes the world as it is, and yet affirms that a better world is possible and worth striving for, that striving, to be effective, requires a balanced spirituality, which holds together our relationship to the three levels of life, personal, communal, and global. In *Spirituality and Justice* Donal Dorr describes such a balanced spirituality,[6] which he bases on the well-known words of the prophet Micah:

> The LORD has told you mortals what is good,
> and what it is that the LORD requires of you:
> only to act justly, to love loyalty,
> and to walk humbly with your God.
>
> *Micah 6:8*

Micah speaks of the three essential elements of spirituality: religious, moral, and political. At the religious level, a hopeful spirituality acknowledges a reality beyond ourselves, beyond human ambitions and schemes; a reality, as Paul said, in which we live and move and have our being (*Acts 17:28*). Micah speaks of this as walking humbly with God, and this means aligning ourselves with his will and his values. Loving loyalty implies a moral conversion which Dorr describes as being "other-centred", that is, open to the situation and needs of others, willing to love them as we love ourselves, and to be faithful to them. Acting justly is to work towards a society that is just at its heart, whose structures work for the common good, and where God's special concern for the poor is not just recognized but prioritized. The political conversion that this implies is clear.

Dorr's balanced spirituality taps into the kind of energy required if our hopes are to be realized. But it is important to realize that the personal spiritual transformation Dorr describes—essentially a conversion of heart—is, at its deepest level, a gift. We can want to align ourselves with the will of God, and to be more loving to our neighbour, and to pursue justice in our politics, but we cannot achieve our wants simply by an effort of will (though that is necessary); something more is required, namely an openness to the Spirit that allows our own spirit to be touched and changed—which is what Jesus urged on Nicodemus. As Dorr says, hope is a primordial gift from God, and we have to be open to receive it. The same is true about laying hold on the promises of God upon which our hopes are founded. A promise is not a guarantee, and—as John Macquarrie pointed out—there can be no easy optimism about the fulfilment of hope; it requires our co-operation: "God's kingdom cannot come until men have prepared the way for it, and therefore it cannot be something assured and guaranteed, come what may, but must remain an object of hope."[7] We get only fragmentary glimpses of what the fulfilment of hope will be like, but they are enough to keep us moving forward, motivated by Paul's conviction that eye has not seen, nor ear heard, nor have we imagined in our hearts, the things that God has prepared for those that love him (cf. *1 Corinthians 2:9*).

## An anchor for the soul

Hope leads us forward into the discovery of God's new world. "[H]ere we have no continuing city, but we seek a city that is to come" (*Hebrews 13:14*). Hope looks to the future, but it does not forget what has gone before. The city that is to come is built upon the faith and work of those who before us trusted in God and lived in his love. Hope is the confidence that past, present, and future exist in a single continuity where the future is related to the same truth and living reality as the past and the present.[8] Thus the prayers of the antiphons echo the yearning of those of every age and every culture who have longed for justice and peace, for freedom and forgiveness, for truth and inner strength, and for love. For Christians this yearning is renewed each year as we prepare in Advent to celebrate the birth of the Saviour at Christmas. Advent is the season of hope, a liminal season in which we stand at the threshold of God's new dawn; it is a time to draw on his truth, and to ask questions that busyness drives out: Who are we? Where are we going? What is God calling us to become? Like all liminal times, Advent is a time of waiting, a time of trust and longing: "You can invite a new beginning, but you cannot force its arrival."[9] Times of waiting are particularly disturbing in modern life, where we expect certainty, where the waiting has been taken out of wanting, and where trust is in short supply. But waiting and trusting are basic to the journey of faith because apprehending new truths cannot be accomplished in an instant, nor without longing. There may be a flash of light, a moment of insight, but it takes time to assimilate the full meaning of what we have glimpsed and to let it become part of us. Depth of understanding cannot be hurried; like the balanced spirituality described above, we have to be open to receive it.

I return to Eliot's poem "East Coker", in which he explores the search for wisdom. He notes the wisdom of the ages and its deceptions, the wisdom of old men and their folly, and concludes, as we have seen, that "there is at best only a limited value in the knowledge derived from experience", because the patterns we use to interpret our experience are not the same as God's patterns. By contrast, the divine pattern is "new in every moment, and every moment is a new and shocking valuation of all that we have been".[10] Placing our hope in Christ is about learning the pattern of God and the valuation that he places on all that we are and all that we can become. We need to be humble before God's self-revelation in Jesus, open to receive from him the wisdom of humility. So, says Eliot, "the darkness shall be light, and the stillness the dancing."

This is the promise God holds out to us. We catch a glimpse of its fulfilment at Christmas when, after all the preparations, the busyness of the world is hushed, and we know a moment of peace—a moment, perhaps, when, in the stillness, our soul dances. It is in these moments that we are given a glimpse of eternity, and know that we do not hope in vain, that our waiting and longing will have their fulfilment. These are moments to return to when hope grows faint. And if these moments of stillness elude us, it probably has something to do with the quality of our waiting. For those who hope, waiting is not passive; it is an attentive waiting in anticipation of all that God will share with us through his Son. Praying the antiphons prepares us for the fullness of God's revelation in Jesus; we joyfully celebrate his birth because hope in him makes a new world possible. The angels' cry becomes our cry: "Glory to God in highest heaven, and on earth peace to all in whom he delights" (*Luke 2:14*). Jesus is none other than our origin and our destiny, the Alpha and the Omega, who is, who was, and who is to come, the sovereign LORD of all (*Revelation 1:8*). The antiphons, if we catch their mood, will teach us to wait and trust, and to discover for ourselves that the hope he sets before us is "an anchor of the soul, both sure and stedfast" (*Hebrews 6:19, King James Version*).

The door that Jesus holds open can only be entered by a path that, in the modern world, generally remains unused: the way of unknowing, where trust replaces certainty, and faith replaces knowledge. A path unfrequented, but perhaps not entirely forgotten; and in liminal moments, when we reach out to our hopes, our spirit suggests that there is another path that we could take:

> Footfalls echo in the memory
> Down the passage which we did not take
> Towards the door we never opened
> Into the rose garden.[11]

What we seek is a special place of delight, like a rose garden, or a place of safety, like the sheepfold and its pasture which Jesus guards with his life, where we shall find refreshment for our souls and the fulfilment of our hopes. It is there that we discover for ourselves that Jesus' authority does extend over all that separates us from God. The way of hope gives us the opportunity to retrace our steps, to go down the passage which we did not take, through the door we never opened, and discover that it is the gateway to delight, to a new beginning; the path that leads us to God. In the darkness there is light.

# Books referred to

*The Oxford Study Bible: Revised English Bible with the Apocrypha*, ed. M. Jack Suggs, Katharine Doob Sakenfeld, and James R. Mueller (New York: Oxford University Press, 1992).

*The New Interpreter's Bible* (Nashville: Abingdon Press, 2002).

Aulén, Gustaf, *Christus Victor: An Historical Study of the Three Main Types of the Idea of the Atonement*, tr. A. G. Hebert (London: SPCK, 1970).

Beaumont, Susan, *Embracing Liminal Space* (Troy, MI: Susan Beaumont & Associates LLC, 2014; see also <http://www.susanbeaumont.com/embracing-liminal-space/>).

Benedict of Nursia (St), *The Rule of Saint Benedict*, tr. David Parry OSB (London: Darton, Longman & Todd, 1984).

Brookner, Anita, *Hotel du Lac* (London: Jonathan Cape, 1984).

Brown, Malcolm (ed.), *Anglican Social Theology: Renewing the Vision Today* (London: Church House Publishing, 2014).

Bryant, Christopher, *Depth Psychology and Religious Belief* (Mirfield: Mirfield Publications, 1972).

Burnaby, John, *Amor Dei: A Study of the Religion of St Augustine* (London: Hodder & Stoughton, 1947).

Caird, G. B., *The Gospel of St Luke*, Pelican New Testament Commentaries (London: Penguin Books, 1963).

Chang, Ha-Joon, *Economics: The User's Guide* (London: Penguin Books, 2014).

Doctrine Commission of the Church of England, *The Mystery of Salvation: The Story of God's Gift* (London: Church House Publishing, 1995).

Dodd, C. H., *The Epistle of Paul to the Romans*, Moffatt New Testament Commentary (London: Hodder & Stoughton, 1934).

Dorr, Donal, *Spirituality and Justice* (Dublin: Gill & Macmillan, 1984).

Eichrodt, Walther, *Theology of the Old Testament*, two volumes, tr. John A. Baker (London: SCM Press, 1961).

Eliot, T. S., *Four Quartets* (London: Faber & Faber, 1944. The edition referred to is that published in 1959).

Forster, E. M., *Howards End* (London: Folio Society, 1973, published by permission of Edward Arnold Publishers Ltd, London).

Francis (Pope), *Evangelii Gaudium*, Apostolic Exhortation on the Proclamation of the Gospel in Today's World (London: Catholic Truth Society, 2013).

Francis (Pope), *Laudato si'*, Encyclical Letter on Care for Our Common Home (London: Catholic Truth Society, 2015).

Gray, John, *Enlightenment's Wake: Politics and Culture at the Close of the Modern Age* (London & New York: Routledge, 1995).

Harries, Richard, *Being a Christian* (London: Mowbray, 1981).

Harrington, Brooke, *Capital without Borders: Wealth Managers and the One Percent* (Harvard: Harvard University Press, 2016).

Harvey, David, *Marx, Capital and the Madness of Economic Reason* (London: Profile Books, 2017).

Holland, Tom, *Dominion: The Making of the Western Mind* (London: Little Brown, 2019).

Hunter, A. M., *The Gospel According to John*, Cambridge New Testament Commentary (Cambridge: Cambridge University Press, 1965).

Inge, Denise (ed.), *Happiness and Holiness: Thomas Traherne and his Writings* (Norwich: Canterbury Press, 2008).

Jamison, Christopher OSB, *Finding Sanctuary: Monastic Steps for Everyday Life* (London: Weidenfeld & Nicolson, 2006).

Jeremias, Joachim, *The Prayers of Jesus* (London: SCM Press, 1967).

John of the Cross (St), *The Ascent of Mount Carmel* (Tunbridge Wells: Burns & Oates, 1983).

John Paul II (Pope), *Centesimus Annus*, Encyclical Letter on the Hundredth Anniversary of *Rerum Novarum* (London: Catholic Truth Society, 1991).

Kaiser, Otto, *Isaiah 1–12: A Commentary*, tr. R. A. Wilson, Old Testament Library (London: SCM Press, 1972).

Kaiser, Otto, *Isaiah 13–39: A Commentary*, tr. R. A. Wilson, Old Testament Library (London: SCM Press, 1980).

Kidd, Sue Monk, *The Invention of Wings* (London: Tinder Press, 2014).

Klein, Naomi, *This Changes Everything: Capitalism vs. the Climate* (London: Penguin Random House UK, 2015).

Lamb, Christopher, *The Outsider: Pope Francis and his Battle to Reform the Church* (New York: Orbis Books, 2020).

Leo XIII (Pope), *Rerum Novarum*, Encyclical Letter on the Rights and Duties of Capital and Labour (London: Catholic Truth Society, 1891).

Lightbown, Andrew and Sills, Peter (eds), *Theonomics: Reconnecting Economics with Virtue and Integrity* (Durham: Sacristy Press, 2014).

Longley, Clifford, *Just Money: How Catholic Social Teaching Can Redeem Capitalism* (London: Theos, 2014; available to download from <https://www.theosthinktank.co.uk>).

Lunn, Pete, *Basic Instincts: Human Nature and the New Economics* (London: Marshall Cavendish, 2008).

Macquarrie, John, *The Faith of the People of God: A Lay Theology* (London: SCM Press, 1972).

Macquarrie, John, *Christian Hope* (London and Oxford: Mowbray, 1978).

Madeley, John, *Hungry for Trade: How the Poor Pay for Free Trade* (London and New York: Zed Books, 2000).

Mandela, Nelson, *Long Walk to Freedom: The Autobiography of Nelson Mandela* (London: Little, Brown, 1994).

Manson, T. W., *Ethics and the Gospel* (New York: Scribner, 1961).

Marquand, David, *The End of the West: The Once and Future Europe* (Princeton, NJ: Princeton University Press, 2011).

Marsh, John, *The Gospel of Saint John*, Pelican New Testament Commentaries (London: Penguin Books, 1968).

Mishra, Pankaj, *Age of Anger: A History of the Present* (London: Penguin Random House UK, 2017).

Moltmann, Jürgen, *Theology of Hope: On the Ground and the Implications of a Christian Eschatology*, tr. James W. Leitch (London: SCM Press, 1967).

Montefiore, Hugh (ed.), *The Gospel and Contemporary Culture* (London: Mowbray, 1992).

Montesquieu, Charles-Louis de Secondat (Baron de), *The Spirit of Laws* (published in France in 1748, and in England in 1750; the edition referred to in the text is that published by the online library of the Liberty Fund: <https://oll.libertyfund.org/about-liberty-fund-titles>).

Nankivell, Owen, *Economics, Society and Values* (Aldershot: Ashgate, 1995).

Nicholl, Donald, *The Testing of Hearts: A Pilgrim's Journal* (London: Marshall, Morgan & Scott, Lamp Press, 1989).

Nouwen, Henri J. M., *Making All Things New: An Invitation to the Spiritual Life* (Dublin: Gill & Macmillan, 1982).

Novak, Michael, *The Catholic Ethic and the Spirit of Democratic Capitalism* (New York: The Free Press, 1993).

O'Donovan, Oliver, *The Desire of the Nations: Rediscovering the Roots of Political Theology* (Cambridge: Cambridge University Press, 1996).

Oppenheimer, Helen, *Looking Before and After* (London: Collins Fount, 1988).

Panikkar, Raimon, *The Rhythm of Being* (Maryknoll, NY: Orbis Books, 2010).

Paul VI (Pope), *Populorum Progressio*, Encyclical Letter on the Development of Peoples (London: Catholic Truth Society, 1967).

Paul VI (Pope), *Octagesimo Adveniens*, Apostolic Letter on the Occasion of the Eightieth Anniversary of the Encyclical *Rerum Novarum* (London: Catholic Truth Society, 1971).

Pius XI (Pope), *Quadragesimo Anno*, Encyclical Letter on Reconstruction of the Social Order (London: Catholic Truth Society, 1931).

Preston, Geoffrey OP, *God's Way to be Man: Meditations on Following Christ through Scripture and Sacrament* (London: Darton, Longman & Todd, 1978).

Preston, Geoffrey OP, *Hallowing the Time: Meditations on the Cycle of the Christian Liturgy* (London: Darton, Longman & Todd, 1980).

Rad, Gerhard von, *Wisdom in Israel*, tr. James D. Martin (London: SCM Press, 1972).

Rawls, John, *A Theory of Justice* (Cambridge, MA: Harvard University Press, 1971).

Richardson, Alan, *Creeds in the Making: A Short Introduction to the History of Christian Doctrine* (London: SCM Press, 1935).

Richardson, Alan (ed.), *A Theological Wordbook of the Bible* (London: SCM Press, 1957).

Sahlins, Marshall, *Stone Age Economics* (London: Routledge, 2003).

Sandel, Michael J., *Justice: What's the Right Thing to Do?* (London: Allen Lane Penguin, 2009).

Schillebeeckx, Edward, *Jesus in our Western Culture: Mysticism, Ethics and Politics*, tr. John Bowden (London: SCM Press, 1987).

Schreiter, Robert J., *Reconciliation: Mission and Ministry in a Changing Social Order* (Maryknoll, NY: Orbis Books, 1992).

Schumacher, E. F., *Small is Beautiful: A Study of Economics as if People Mattered* (London: Abacus, 1974).

Selby, Peter, *Grace and Mortgage* (London: Darton, Longman & Todd, 1997).

Sen, Amartya, *The Idea of Justice* (London: Allen Lane/Penguin Books, 2009).

Sennett, Richard, *The Corrosion of Character: The Personal Consequences of Work in the New Capitalism* (New York: Norton, 1998).

Sills, Peter, *A Word in Season: A Journey Through the Christian Year* (Ely: Ely Cathedral Publications, 2001).

Sills, Peter, *Your Kingdom Come: Reflections on Faith, Justice and Hope* (Ely: Ely Cathedral Publications, 2006).

Sills, Peter, *Deep Calls to Deep: Seeking the Changeless in Times of Change* (<http://www.peter-sills.co.uk/books>, 2015).

Spragens, Jr, Thomas, *The Irony of Liberal Reason* (Chicago: University of Chicago Press, 1981).

Srubas, Rachel M., *Oblation: Meditations on St Benedict's Rule* (Brewster, MA: Paraclete Press, 2006).

Stevick, Daniel B., *Jesus and His Own: A Commentary on John 13–17* (Grand Rapids, MI and Cambridge, UK: Eerdmans, 2011).

Stourton, Edward, *Absolute Truth: The Catholic Church in the World Today* (London: Viking/Penguin Books, 1998).

Taylor, John V., *Enough is Enough* (London: SCM Press, 1975).

Temple, William, *Readings in St John's Gospel* (London: Macmillan, 1968).

Vanstone, W. H., *Love's Endeavour, Love's Expense: The Response of Being to the Love of God* (London: Darton, Longman & Todd, 1977).

Weiser, Artur, *The Psalms: A Commentary*, tr. Herbert Hartwell (London: SCM Press, 1962).

Welby, Justin, *Dethroning Mammon: Making Money Serve Grace—The Archbishop of Canterbury's Lent Book 2017* (London: Bloomsbury Continuum, 2016).

Westermann, Claus. *Isaiah 40–66: A Commentary*, tr. David M. G. Stalker, Old Testament Library (London: SCM Press, 1969).

Wilkinson, Richard and Pickett, Kate, *The Spirit Level: Why Equality is Better for Everyone* (London: Penguin Books, 2010).

Williams, Rowan, *Faith in the Public Square* (London: Bloomsbury Continuum, 2012).

Williams, Rowan, *Holy Living: The Christian Tradition for Today* (London: Bloomsbury Continuum, 2017).

Williams, Rowan, *Being Human: Bodies, Minds, Persons* (London: SPCK, 2018).

Wink, Walter, *Naming the Powers: The Language of Power in the New Testament* (Philadelphia: Fortress Press, 1984).

Wink, Walter, *Unmasking the Powers: The Invisible Forces That Determine Human Existence* (Philadelphia: Fortress Press, 1986).

Wink, Walter, *Engaging the Powers: Discernment and Resistance in an Age of Domination* (Minneapolis: Fortress Press, 1992).

Wright, N. T., *Simply Good News: Why the Gospel is News and What Makes it Good* (London: SPCK, 2015).

Zuboff, Shoshana, *The Age of Surveillance Capitalism: The Fight for a Human Future at the New Frontier of Power* (New York: Public Affairs, 2019).

# Permissions

Biblical quotations, except where indicated otherwise, are taken from *The Revised English Bible*, copyright © Cambridge University Press and Oxford University Press, 1989, reproduced with permission of Cambridge University Press.

Excerpts from the *New Jerusalem Bible*, copyright © 1985 by Darton, Longman and Todd, Ltd. and Doubleday, a division of Penguin Random House, Inc. Reprinted by permission.

Psalm 85 from *The Psalms* (1966), copyright © The Grail 1963, is reprinted by permission of Harper Collins Publishers Ltd.

Excerpts from *Four Quartets*, by T. S. Eliot, are used by permission of Faber & Faber, Ltd.

The excerpt from the Hugh Kay Memorial Lecture, 2001, © The Christian Association of Business Executives, is used with permission of the Association.

The prayer *Timeless, yet ever in time* is used by permission of Mother Mary David, OSB, Abbess of St Mary's Abbey, West Malling, Kent.

The poem *Gathering God* is from *Oblation: Meditations on St Benedict's Rule*, by Rachel Srubas, copyright © Rachel Srubas 2006, and used by permission of Paraclete Press: <https://paracletepress.com/>.

The excerpt from *The Magnificat,*copyright © 1998 English Language Liturgical Consultation (ELLC), is used by permission. <http://www.englishtexts.org>.

The prayer *O God Father*, © Lord Harries of Pentregarth, is used with his permission.

# Notes

## Prologue

1 The earliest part, chapters 1 to 39, dates from the eighth century BC, and is based on the oracles of Isaiah of Jerusalem, an eloquent prophet after whom the book is named, and who was much concerned with the threat to Israel from Assyria. The second part, chapters 40 to 55, dates from the Exile to Babylon in the sixth century BC and is based on the work of an unknown prophet, generally referred to as Second Isaiah, but whom I prefer to call Isaiah of Babylon. The final part, chapters 56 to 66, dates from later in the sixth century, when the Exile had ended. Scholars identify several authors, the major section being ascribed to a disciple of Isaiah of Babylon, known as Third Isaiah.

2 Rowan Williams, *Faith in the Public Square* (London: Bloomsbury Continuum, 2012), p. 5.

3 Historically, the opposition has come from across the political and religious spectrum; today it comes mainly from the religious right. In the USA, for example, the visceral opposition to Pope Francis among wealthy catholics is motivated by a world view based on the tenets of neo-liberal economics rather than the gospel. Theologians of similar mind offer support, among them Michael Novak (who describes himself as a "neo-conservative"), who has reinterpreted the concept of social justice in a way that is consistent with his political stance, reducing it to no more than social activism: Michael Novak, *The Catholic Ethic and the Spirit of Democratic Capitalism* (New York: The Free Press, 1993), p. 77. On the opposition to Pope Francis, see Christopher Lamb, *The Outsider: Pope Francis and his Battle to Reform the Church* (New York: Orbis Books, 2020).

4 Pankaj Mishra, *Age of Anger: A History of the Present* (London: Penguin Random House UK, 2017), pp. 16 and 21.

5 Rowan Williams, "Ethics and Globalisation", The Hugh Kay Memorial Lecture 2001, pp. 16–17.

6 Mishra, *Age of Anger*, p. 18.

7 Donal Dorr, whom I quote later, discusses the disconnection between uniformity and unity in *Spirituality and Justice* (Dublin: Gill & Macmillan, 1984), p. 105.

8 John Gray, *Enlightenment's Wake: Politics and Culture at the Close of the Modern Age* (London & New York: Routledge, 1995).

9 Mishra, *Age of Anger*, p. 289.

10 The quotation was used in a seminar I attended at Douai Abbey some years ago; alas, I did not note the reference.

11 Mishra, *Age of Anger*, p. 346.

12 Edward Schillebeeckx, tr. John Bowden, *Jesus in our Western Culture: Mysticism, Ethics and Politics* (London: SCM Press, 1987), p. 19.

13 Schillebeeckx, *Jesus in our Western Culture*, p. 21.

14 My use occasionally of the male personal pronoun to refer to God should not be understood as implying that God is of the male gender; God is beyond gender, and generally I avoid gendered pronouns. However, some alternative formulations are clumsy, and terms like "Godself" strike me as inelegant, so sometimes I use the traditional formulation.

15 John Macquarrie, *Christian Hope* (London & Oxford: Mowbray, 1978), p. 13.

16 Jürgen Moltmann, tr. James W. Leitch, *Theology of Hope: On the Ground and the Implications of a Christian Eschatology* (London: SCM Press, 1967), p. 26. The biblical reference is *Revelation 21:5*.

17 Cf. Moltmann, *Theology of Hope*, p. 20.

18 *Exodus 32*.

19 Moltmann, *Theology of Hope*, p. 102.

20 This quotation, a reworking of the words of *1 John 1:5*, is generally ascribed to Michael Ramsey, although some say it originated with John V. Taylor. It can be found in Michael Ramsey, *God, Christ and the World: A Study in Contemporary Theology* (London: SCM Press, 1969), pp. 37 and 41, while John V. Taylor took up the phrase in his book *The Christlike God* (London: SCM Press, 1992).

21 The reply can also be translated, "I will be who I will be," adding a further layer of meaning. Donal Dorr suggested that it is best translated, "I am the

one who will be with you" —implying that God is the one who will be leading them out of slavery into freedom (*Spirituality and Justice*, p. 87).

22 *John 6:35; 8:12; 10:7; 10:11; 11:25; 14:6; 15:1; Revelation 1:8; 21:6; 22:13,16.* Although ascribed to Jesus, the general scholarly opinion is that these sayings were not actually spoken by him, rather that they express the belief of the Church, guided by the Holy Spirit, about the nature of God's self-disclosure in Christ.

23 Daniel B. Stevick, *Jesus and His Own: A Commentary on John 13–17* (Grand Rapids, MI & Cambridge: Eerdmans, 2011), pp. 124–5.

24 Rowan Williams, *Being Disciples* (London: SPCK, 2016), pp. 29–30.

25 T. S. Eliot, "East Coker", *Four Quartets* (London: Faber and Faber, 1959 [1944]), p. 24.

26 Ibid.

27 Rowan Williams, *Being Human: Bodies, Minds, Persons* (London: SPCK, 2018), p. 56.

28 T. S. Eliot, "East Coker", *Four Quartets*, p. 25.

29 Macquarrie, *Christian Hope*, p. 20.

30 From a sermon given by Bishop David Conner in Ely Cathedral, 25 November 2007.

## Chapter 1

1 Stevick, *Jesus and His Own*, p. 352. Cf. *1 John 2:4*: "Whoever says, 'I have come to know him,' but does not obey his commandments, is a liar, and in such a person *the truth does not exist* . . . ". Emphasis added.

2 From *The Psalms: A New Translation* © 1963 The Grail (England) published by HarperCollins and used with permission.

3 *Isaiah 45:23*: "It is truth that goes forth from my mouth, a word beyond recall" (Douai Rheims). Other translations are slightly different, but with the same sense, e.g. " . . . what comes forth from my mouth is saving justice, it is an irrevocable word" (*New Jerusalem Bible*). For Isaiah of Babylon, see Prologue note 1.

4 Stevick, *Jesus and His Own*, p. 124.

5 Richard Gaillardetz, "Is the Pope a Catholic?", *The Tablet*, 7 October 2017.

6 Gerhard von Rad, tr. James D. Martin, *Wisdom in Israel* (London: SCM Press, 1972), p. 289.

7 T. S. Eliot, "East Coker", *Four Quartets*, p. 23.

8 Ibid.

9 *Signs of the Spirit: Official Report, Seventh Assembly of the World Council of Churches, 1991* (Grand Rapids, MI: Eerdmans, 1991).

10 The Hebrew word *ruach* has both senses: breath and spirit.

11 C. H. Dodd, *The Epistle of Paul to the Romans*, Moffatt New Testament Commentary (London: Hodder & Stoughton, 1934), p. 134.

12 N. T. Wright, "The Letter to the Romans: Introduction, Commentary, and Reflections", in *The New Interpreter's Bible: A Commentary in Twelve Volumes*, Vol. 10 (Nashville: Abingdon 2002), p. 596.

13 *Laudato si'*, Encyclical Letter of the Holy Father Francis on Care for Our Common Home (London: Catholic Truth Society, 2015), 190.

14 Williams, *Faith in the Public Square*, chapter 16.

15 *Laudato si'*, 194.

16 *Laudato si'*, 49.

17 This and the preceding quotations: Wright, "The Letter to the Romans", pp. 605, 606.

18 Rad, *Wisdom in Israel*, pp. 296–7.

19 Rad, *Wisdom in Israel*, p. 297. The quotation is from H. Brunner, *Altägyptische Erziehung* (1975), pp. 111f.

20 *The Rule of Saint Benedict*, from the opening words of the Prologue.

21 E. F. Schumacher, *Small is Beautiful: A Study of Economics as if People Mattered* (London: Abacus, 1974), p. 30.

22 Raimon Panikkar, *The Rhythm of Being* (Maryknoll, NY: Orbis Books, 2010), p. 22.

23 I describe this way of prayer in my booklet *Deep Calls to Deep: Seeking the Changeless in Times of Change*, pp. 43–4 (<www.peter-sills.co.uk/books>).

24 In the *Revised English Bible* the passage reads: "He was in the form of God; yet he laid no claim to equality with God, but made himself nothing, assuming the form of a slave." It is part of an early Christian hymn, and reflects the Greek concept of *kenosis*, or self-emptying.

25 Translations of the first Beatitude vary. The more usual rendering is "Blessed are the poor in spirit . . . " The note in the *Revised English Bible* text explains that *poor in spirit* "expresses the religious dimension of a form of Jewish piety

for which 'poverty' and 'utter dependence on God' were synonymous". The translation used (*New English Bible*, 2nd edition, 1970) expresses this sense well.

26 The lines are featured on a prayer card designed by Sister Mary Simon, OSB of Malling Abbey; they are taken from "A Cosmic Outlook" by Frederick William Henry Myers (1843–1901).

27 John Marsh, *The Gospel of Saint John*, Pelican New Testament Commentaries (London: Penguin, 1968), p. 506.

28 Marsh, *Saint John*, pp. 506, 504.

29 The prayer was written by a former abbess, Mother Osyth Lucie-Smith, OSB.

## Chapter 2

1 Walther Eichrodt, tr. John A. Baker, *Theology of the Old Testament*, Vol. 1 (London: SCM Press, 1961), p. 39.

2 The story is told in the books of *Samuel* and *Kings*. There were, in fact, two periods of exile, the first to Assyria in the eighth century BC, and the second to Babylon in the sixth century BC. It is during the Babylonian Exile that new ideas about God and his nature come to the fore.

3 The author of the middle part of *Isaiah*: see Prologue note 1.

4 The four Servant Songs are at *Isaiah 42:1–4*; *49:1–6*; *50:4–9*; *52:13–53:12*.

5 Justin Welby, *Dethroning Mammon: Making Money Serve Grace—The Archbishop of Canterbury's Lent Book 2017* (London: Bloomsbury Continuum, 2016), p. 90.

6 Saint Benedict's approach is garnered from the Rule that he wrote to order the life of his monks. The main chapters are those concerning the Abbot and the Cellarer (chapters 2, 31, and 64), but the way authority is to be exercised is referred to throughout the Rule. For details about the Rule, see the list of books referred to, above.

7 For a fuller treatment, see my essay "Leadership, Ethics and Virtue: Using the Rule of St Benedict as a Model for Leadership", in Andrew Lightbown and Peter Sills (eds), *Theonomics: Reconnecting Economics with Virtue and Integrity* (Durham: Sacristy Press, 2014). I have also developed this in a more specifically Christian context: *Insights from the Benedictine Tradition for Christian Leaders*, a course given at the Anglican Centre in

Rome in 2012, and available on my website: <http://peter-sills.co.uk/leadership-in-the-benedictine-tradition>.

8 Slightly different versions are given in *Matthew* (*26:28*) and *Luke* (*22:17*); the words used in contemporary liturgy come from Paul, who makes explicit that Jesus was inaugurating a new covenant: "This cup is the new covenant sealed by my blood" (*1 Corinthians 11:25*).

9 In this belief Jesus and the Church reach back to another prophecy of Isaiah of Babylon: "Listen to me you coasts and islands, pay heed you peoples far distant . . . the Lord has said to me: 'It is too slight a task for you, as my servant, to restore the tribes of Jacob, to bring back the survivors of Israel: I shall appoint you a light to the nations so that my salvation may reach earth's farthest bounds.'" (*Isaiah 49:1–6*).

10 Charles Louis de Secondat, Baron de Montesquieu, *L'Esprit des Lois*, Book III, chapters 2 and 3.

11 The erosion of norms is the subject of Steven Levitsky and Daniel Ziblatt, *How Democracies Die: What History Reveals About Our Future* (London: Viking, 2018). The two primary norms they think underpin democracy are "mutual toleration" and "institutional forbearance", variations on the same theme. On the abuse of power by authoritarian rulers, they give many examples of the way today lip-service is paid to the constitution while behaving as though it did not exist; for example, the way in which Vladimir Putin swapped the roles of president and prime minister in order to avoid the limit on the number of terms the Russian president can serve.

12 *Matthew 23:1–33*. Jesus pronounced seven "woes", so called because, in older translations, they begin with the words, "Woe to you, scribes and Pharisees . . . ". The same concern for substance over form is seen in the Sermon on the Mount in *Matthew 5–7*.

13 This point is developed by Schillebeeckx in *Jesus in our Western Culture*, pp. 52ff.

14 Oliver O'Donovan, *The Desire of the Nations: Rediscovering the Roots of Political Theology* (Cambridge: Cambridge University Press, 1996), p. 23.

15 John V. Taylor, *Enough is Enough* (London: SCM Press, 1975), p. 41.

16 The "Five Marks of Mission" were developed by the Anglican Consultative Council, 1984–90, and adopted by the General Synod of the Church of England in 1996. They are mirrored in the teaching of other churches. The five marks are: 1. To proclaim the Good News of the Kingdom, 2. To teach,

baptize, and nurture new believers, 3. To respond to human need by loving service, 4. To seek to transform unjust structures of society, and 5. To strive to safeguard the integrity of creation and sustain and renew the life of the earth.

17 The title of the encyclical—*Rerum Novarum*, "About New Things"—comes from the opening words of the letter, and refers to the "revolutionary change" brought about by the Industrial Revolution. Despite its restrained and diplomatic language, its criticisms are hard-hitting and still relevant today. It has been followed by a series of social encyclicals, often on the ten-yearly anniversaries of *Rerum Novarum*; Pope St John Paul II marked the centenary with *Centesimus Annus* in 1991.

18 It has to be acknowledged that the concern for social justice has not always been honoured by the Church, which in the twentieth century often identified with authoritarian and oppressive regimes for whom social justice was anathema.

19 Pope Paul VI, *Populorum Progressio*, Encyclical on the Development of Peoples (London: Catholic Truth Society, 1967), 22. For a collection of extracts from Catholic Social Teaching, see *The Social Agenda of the Catholic Church* (London: Burns & Oates, 2000).

20 Pope Francis, *Evangelii Gaudium*, Apostolic Exhortation on the Proclamation of the Gospel in Today's World (London: Catholic Truth Society, 2013), 189. The universal destination of material goods has a long pedigree. In the same document the Pope quotes John Chrysostom; writing in the fourth century he said, "Not to share one's wealth with the poor is to steal from them and to take away their livelihood. It is not our own goods that we hold, but theirs." *De Lazaro Concio*, II, 6: *Patrologia Graeca* 48: 992D'.

21 Jane Collier, "Contemporary culture and the role of economics", in Hugh Montefiore (ed.), *The Gospel and Contemporary Culture* (London: Mowbray, 1992), p. 103.

22 John Maynard Keynes (1883–1946) was the most influential economist of the early twentieth century. Among other things, he played a major role in the reconstruction negotiations following both the world wars. His major work was *The General Theory of Employment, Interest and Money* (London: Macmillan, 1936).

23 Milton Friedman (1912–2006). His essay "The Effects of a Full-Employment Policy on Economic Stability", in *Essays in Positive Economics* (Chicago:

Chicago University Press, 1953), pp. 117–32, was described by Edmund Phelps as "the veritable *magna carta* of monetarism": Edmund S. Phelps, *Seven Schools of Macroeconomic Thought: The Arne Ryde Lectures* (Oxford: Clarendon Press, 1990), p. 30.

24 Interview for *The Sunday Times*, 3 May 1981. The quotation comes at the very end of the interview (<www.margaretthatcher.org/document/104475>).

25 Owen Nankivell, *Economics, Society and Values* (Aldershot: Ashgate, 1995), p. 75.

26 Quoted by Michael J. Sandel in *Justice: What's the Right Thing to Do?* (London: Allen Lane Penguin, 2009), p. 262. The quotation is from a speech of Senator Robert Kennedy, the brother of US President John Kennedy, during his campaign to become the Democratic Party candidate for president in 1968. On the point made in the text, cf. Alan M. Suggate, "The Temple Tradition", in Malcolm Brown (ed.), *Anglican Social Theology: Renewing the Vision Today* (London: Church House Publishing, 2014), pp. 33 and 71.

27 See Jonathan Chaplin's essay in Brown (ed.), *Anglican Social Theology*, p. 131.

28 John Rawls, *A Theory of Justice* (Cambridge, MA: Harvard University Press, 1971).

29 Amartya Sen, *The Idea of Justice* (London: Allen Lane/Penguin Books, 2009), p. 86.

30 Ludwig von Mises, *Human Action* (London: Hodge, 1949), p. 190, quoted in Collier, "Contemporary culture and the role of economics", p. 106.

31 Collier, "Contemporary culture and the role of economics", p. 106.

32 Ibid.

33 China is a good example. When it opened agriculture and other parts of its economy to market forces after the Cultural Revolution, famine became a thing of the past for many millions, and almost half a billion people were lifted out of poverty.

34 Larry Elliott reporting from the World Economic Forum: *The Guardian*, 18 January 2016.

35 Pope Pius XI, *Quadragesimo Anno*, Encyclical Letter on Reconstruction of the Social Order (London: Catholic Truth Society, 1931).

36 O'Donovan, *Desire of the Nations*, p. 49.

37 Stephen Metcalf, "Neoliberalism: the idea that swallowed the world", *The Guardian*, 18 August 2017 (<www.theguardian.com/news/2017/aug/18/neoliberalism-the-idea-that-changed-the-world>)?]

38 Smith's idea of the invisible hand is a pertinent example of the way he is used by neo-classical economists. Smith noted that individual effort necessarily increases the annual revenue of society, what today is called GDP, and pointed out that although the individual "intends only his own gain, . . . he is in this . . . led by an invisible hand to promote an end that was no part of his intention." (*The Wealth of Nations*, 1776, Book IV, chapter II, paragraph IX). This is a marginal aspect of Smith's theory, mentioned only twice (and briefly) in his writings, and which he did not relate to the working of the market, but this has not stopped neo-classical economists using it to justify their faith in the rightness of unregulated market outcomes.

39 Adam Smith is best known for *The Wealth of Nations*, and his earlier book, *The Theory of Moral Sentiments* (1759), tends not to receive the same attention. Taken together, they support the point made in the text. Cf. Malcolm Brown, "The Case for Anglican Social Theology Today", in Brown (ed.), *Anglican Social Theology*, p. 15.

40 Keynes, *General Theory*, Preface.

41 Structural adjustment programmes aim to reform the economies of the poorer nations so that they become more efficient economically. They are part of the recognition that, while giving aid to poor countries is essential, it is basically a palliative. What is needed is a global trade system that enables them to develop their own economies, so that they can compete effectively with those of the developed world, but structural adjustment programmes do not do this. Typically they require the opening up of emerging economies to world markets through the reduction of tariffs. With tariff protection removed, local producers—above all, farmers—find themselves undercut by cheap products from the rich countries (often subsidized, e.g. by the EU's common agricultural policy), forcing workers off the land with a consequent rise in unemployment. Emerging economies require protection, in the same way that new technologies in richer countries are protected or subsidized during development. Taking the interests of the poor seriously requires similar market protection.

42 Requiring tax to be paid in the country where profits are earned, rather than in the country where the company is registered, would end the scandal of multinationals like Starbucks, Google, Facebook, and Apple paying a minimal amount of UK tax compared with their UK earnings. Abolishing the tax relief on corporate debt would end the bonanza of debt-funded buy-outs by private

equity firms, which also result in significant reductions in tax revenue. Robert Peston shines the light on the private equity world in *Who Runs Britain? How the Super-Rich are Changing our Lives* (London: Hodder & Stoughton, 2008). And Prem Sikka, in an article dated 12 March 2018, describes how Caffè Nero has avoided paying any tax at all through debt financing: <https://leftfootforward.org/2018/03/heres-how-caffe-nero-made-2bn-in-sales-but-did-not-pay-a-penny-in-corporation-tax/>.

43 <https://www.weforum.org/agenda/2019/12/davos-manifesto-2020-the-universal-purpose-of-a-company-in-the-fourth-industrial-revolution>.

44 The World Economic Forum meets annually at Davos in Switzerland. In 2020 the Forum endorsed "The Purpose of a Corporation", a statement issued in 2019 by nearly two hundred chief executive officers of large US corporations, calling for all companies to serve *all* their stakeholders by delivering value to customers, investing in employees, dealing fairly with suppliers, paying their taxes, supporting the communities in which they operate, and protecting the environment. This represents a profound move away from the orthodoxy propounded by Milton Friedman, that the sole purpose of a business was to maximize its profits within the law and ethical custom. See further Charles Wookey, "Business beyond profit", *The Tablet*, 6 February 2020.

45 Pope Francis, *Evangelii Gaudium*, 203.

46 This has become a major concern. Among recent studies see Lightbown and Sills (eds), *Theonomics*, and Clifford Longley, *Just Money: How Catholic Social Teaching can Redeem Capitalism* (London: Theos, 2014).

47 Pope Francis, *Evangelii Gaudium*, 203.

48 Pete Lunn, *Basic Instincts: Human Nature and the New Economics* (London: Marshall Cavendish, 2008), p. 268. See also Ha-Joon Chang, *Economics: The User's Guide* (London: Pelican, 2014).

49 Taylor, *Enough is Enough*, p. 61.

50 Taylor, *Enough is Enough*, pp. 45–6. Taylor points out that the Bible brackets together promiscuity and profiteering, as Paul said: "Put to death those parts of you which belong to the earth—fornication, indecency, lust, foul cravings and the ruthless greed which is nothing less than idolatry" (*Colossians 3:5*).

51 John Madeley, *Hungry for Trade: How the Poor Pay for Free Trade* (London & New York: Zed Books, 2000). This is also one of the main themes of Christian Aid's campaigning: see, for example, their report *Trade Justice: A Christian Response to Global Poverty* (London: Church House Publishing, 2004).

52 The economics of generosity would remove one of the glaring scandals of our time, namely that the rich pay a smaller proportion of their income in tax than the poor. In 2014, research by the Equality Trust showed that the poorest tenth of the British population pay eight per cent more of their income in tax than the richest tenth—forty-three per cent compared to thirty-five per cent (*The Guardian*, 16 June 2014.) This is the precise opposite of the biblical principle.

## Chapter 3

1 Nelson Mandela, *Long Walk to Freedom: The Autobiography of Nelson Mandela* (London: Little, Brown, 1994).

2 The opening words of *The Social Contract*: Jean Jacques Rousseau, *Du Contrat Social, ou Principes du Droit Politique (On the Social Contract, or Principles of Political Rights)*, first published in 1762.

3 Shoshana Zuboff, *The Age of Surveillance Capitalism: The Fight for a Human Future at the New Frontier of Power* (New York: Public Affairs, 2019).

4 As is evident from the Cambridge Analytica scandal and the continuing controversy over the activities of Leave.EU in the 2016 referendum campaign.

5 Christian art reflects the belief that Jesse is the root of true kingship in the device of the "Jesse Tree". In this image Saul, the historical first king of Israel, whom Yahweh rejected, is passed over, and the royal dynasty is traced back to Jesse instead.

6 The Latin version of the antiphon begins *O Radix Jesse*, commonly translated "O Root of Jesse", but this is apt to mislead. The sense of the Hebrew is descendant, branch of the family, or stock, so the *Revised English Bible* more accurately uses the term "scion". The same image is used in an earlier oracle, familiar from the Christmas liturgy: "A branch will grow from the stock of Jesse, /and a shoot shall spring from his roots. /On him the spirit of the LORD will rest, /a spirit of wisdom and understanding, /a spirit of counsel and power, /a spirit of knowledge and the fear of the Lord; /and in the fear of the Lord will be his delight" (*Isaiah 11:1–3*).

7 See the earlier note about Isaiah (Prologue note 1).

8 See page 115 below where the meaning of "prisoner" and "captive" is considered further.

9 Schillebeeckx, *Jesus in our Western Culture*, p. 53.

10 *Evangelii Gaudium*, 192. Similarly, Rowan Williams stresses that language about rights needs to be "grounded in a clear sense of the dignity of the other, not simply of the claims of the self". Williams, *Faith in the Public Square*, p. 268.

11 A conservative estimate of the amount of wine produced is 120 gallons, i.e. sixty-four cases or 768 bottles. And these were just the reserve supplies!

12 *The Rule of Saint Benedict*, Prologue.

13 The translation of this passage is problematic. I have used the *Jerusalem Bible* version because it shows clearly the inspiration for the antiphon. The *New Revised Standard Version* and *New International Version* have the same sense, but the *Revised English Bible* differs: " . . . so now many nations recoil at the sight of him, and kings curl their lips in disgust. His form, disfigured, lost all human likeness; his appearance so changed he no longer looked like a man. They see what they had never been told and their minds are full of things unheard of before."

14 Pope Paul VI, *Octagesimo Adveniens*, sections 45 and 46.

15 Richard Wilkinson and Kate Pickett, *The Spirit Level: Why Equality is Better for Everyone* (London: Penguin Books, 2010), pp. 5–6.

16 David Marquand, *The End of the West: The Once and Future Europe* (Princeton, NJ: Princeton University Press, 2011), p. 129.

17 Sen, *The Idea of Justice*, pp. 179 & 184.

18 Jane Robinson, *Economic Philosophy* (Harmondsworth: Penguin, 1964), p. 47, quoted in Collier, "Contemporary culture and the role of economics", p. 114. It has to be said that this is a very *economic* view of utilitarianism. Historically, utilitarianism has insisted that moral principles be justified by reference to the promotion of human happiness, and the diminution of human suffering. Even so, the individualist ethic has always been central; utilitarians have placed the moral emphasis on the individual and his/her needs and have been hostile to the prescriptions of traditional authority.

19 Kahlil Gibran, *The Prophet* (Wordsworth Editions, 1996), p. 14.

20 Pete Lunn, *Basic Instincts: Human Nature and the New Economics* (London: Marshall Cavendish, 2008), p. 188. These conclusions are powerfully supported by the evidence presented in *The Spirit Level* (see note 15 above).

21 Alan Greenspan, chairman of the US Federal Reserve from 1987 to 2006, admitted this at a Congressional hearing: Edmund L. Andrews, "Greenspan Concedes Error on Regulation", *New York Times* (23 October 2008),

22 Marquand, *The End of the West*, p. 18, quoting Niall Ferguson, *The Ascent of Money: A Financial History of the World* (London: Penguin Books, 2009), p. 230, and Andrew Gamble, *The Spectre at the Feast: Capitalist Crisis and the Politics of Recession* (Basingstoke: Palgrave Macmillan, 2009), p. 17.

23 David Harvey, *Marx, Capital and the Madness of Economic Reason* (London: Profile Books, 2017), p. 198.

24 Improving equality is also the key to reducing expenditure in relation to health and social problems, e.g. obesity, depression, domestic violence, crime, rates of imprisonment, teenage pregnancy, and poor educational attainment. Everyone benefits.

25 O'Donovan, *The Desire of the Nations*, p. 227.

26 See, for example, Madeley, *Hungry for Trade*.

27 The phrase is from *Evangelii Gaudium*, 54.

28 The Holiness Code comprises the second half of the book, chapters 17 to 27.

29 Schillebeeckx, *Jesus in our Western Culture*, p. 52.

30 Residents had voiced concerns about the safety of the tower in the event of fire, but their concerns were ignored. Had they been listened to, the fire could probably have been avoided. The Church has long demanded that the voice of the poor be really heard, as Anna Rowlands has pointed out. In the 1930s, Pope Pius XI (in *Quadragesimo Anno*) called on states to find creative ways of placing the needs and voices of the poorest at the forefront of social policy. Cf. Anna Rowlands, "Fraternal Traditions: Anglican Social Theology and Catholic Social Teaching in a British Context", in Brown (ed.), *Anglican Social Theology*, p. 153.

31 Jon Sobrino was speaking after the Conference of Latin American Bishops in Medellín, Colombia, in 1968: quoted in Edward Stourton, *Absolute Truth: The Catholic Church in the World Today* (London: Viking/Penguin, 1998), p. 116.

32 Dorr, *Spirituality and Justice*, p. 39.

33 Williams, *Ethics and Globalisation*.

34 Williams, *Faith in the Public Square*, p. 229.

35 Rowan Williams makes a related point when he says that Christians cannot "settle down" with the notion that what is lastingly and truly good for one

person or group is different from what is lastingly and truly good for any other. "There are no classes or sub-groups of humanity who are entitled to less of God's love; and so there are no classes entitled to lower levels of human respect or compassion or service." *Faith in the Public Square*, p. 307.

36 Marshall Sahlins, *Stone Age Economics* (London: Routledge, 2003).

37 Otto Kaiser, *Isaiah 1–12: A Commentary*, tr. R. A. Wilson, Old Testament Library (London: SCM Press, 1972), p. 62.

38 Stevick, *Jesus and His Own*, pp. 187–8.

39 Rachel M. Srubas, *Oblation: Meditations on Saint Benedict's Rule* (Brewster, MA: Paraclete Press, 2006), pp. 2–3.

40 From an interview by Peter Stanford, "Jordan B. Peterson: Old Testament Prophet", *The Tablet*, 3 February 2018, pp. 8–9.

41 *Marriage: A teaching document from the House of Bishops of the Church of England* (London: Church House Publishing, 1999), p. 10.

42 Sue Monk Kidd, *The Invention of Wings* (London: Tinder Press, 2014), p. 130.

43 *Centesimus Annus*, 19.

## Chapter 4

1 The precise translation of this verse is uncertain. In the Knox version the first two lines read, "Juda shall not want a branch from his stem, a prince drawn from his stock," explaining in a note (1) that "branch" is literally a rod, which may be a reference to a royal sceptre, (2) that the meaning of the word rendered "who is to be sent to us" is very uncertain, and (3) that for "he, the hope of the nations" the Hebrew text reads, "he shall have the obedience of the nations". The *Revised English Bible* reads, "The sceptre will not pass from Judah, nor the staff from between his feet, until he receives what is his due and the obedience of the nations is his." However it is translated, it is generally believed to be messianic in intent. The next verse confirms this, saying that the One who is to come will tether his donkey and his colt to a vine, to the choicest branch. John describes Jesus as the true vine, and when he entered Jerusalem he chose to ride on a donkey (*Mark 11:1–10*, cf. *Matthew 21:1–9*).

2 Irenaeus, *Against Heresies*, Book 4, chapter 20, section 7—often mistranslated as "The glory of God is man fully alive." Irenaeus (c.130–c.202 AD) was

Bishop of Lugdunum, now Lyon in France, noted for his contribution to the development of Christian theology.

3 This and the following quotation are from Rowan Williams, "Living life to the full", <https://www.catholicsocialteaching.org.uk/themes/community-participation/reflection/living-life-full> (with slight adaptations).

4 Williams, "Living life to the full". Also in Annabel Shilson-Thomas (ed.), *Livesimply: A CAFOD resource* (Norwich: Canterbury Press, 2008), p. 53. Eternal life as a quality of life that can be experienced here and now is explored by Christopher R. Bryant in *Depth Psychology and Religious Belief* (Mirfield, Yorkshire: Mirfield Publications, 1972).

5 E. M. Forster, *Howards End*, chapter 19 (pp. 172–3 in the Folio Society edition).

6 Joachim Jeremias, *The Prayers of Jesus* (London: SCM Press, 1967), p. 103.

7 See, for example, Richard Rohr OFM, *Falling Upward: A Spirituality for the Two Halves of Life* (San Francisco, CA: Wiley, 2011).

8 There are other texts in which Jesus bestows power both to bind and to loose, suggesting that the door can be closed (*Matthew 16:19; John 20:23*). There is a measure of agreement among scholars that this is to be understood as indicating the result of either accepting or rejecting the gospel that Jesus proclaimed (e.g. Marsh, *Saint John*, p. 638). Each person determines whether for him- or herself the door is open or closed. As the old saying has it, the doors of hell are bolted on the inside.

9 Anita Brookner, *Hotel du Lac* (London: Jonathan Cape, 1984), p. 96. The character, Philip Neville, cast as the devil's advocate, extols selfishness on the basis that it leads to healthier decisions, and tempts the heroine, Edith Hope, to exploit her unused capacity for bad behaviour.

10 I use here the simpler version of the baptismal promises of the Church of England *Alternative Service Book 1980*. The current Anglican liturgy, *Common Worship*, contains a more extensive set of vows.

11 Walter Wink, *Unmasking the Powers: The Invisible Forces that Determine Human Existence* (Philadelphia: Fortress Press, 1986), p. 34. (N.B. I have substituted the word "evil" for a longer phrase used by Wink, "autonomous complexes in the psyche or idolatrous institutions in the world".)

12 This development is traced by Wink in *Unmasking the Powers*, chapter 1.

13 Walter Wink, *Naming the Powers: The Language of Power in the New Testament* (Philadelphia: Fortress Press, 1984), p. 105. For the preceding remark see Wink, *Unmasking the Powers*, p. 25.

14 W. H. Vanstone, *Love's Endeavour, Love's Expense* (London: Darton, Longman & Todd, 1977), p. 63.

15 Wink, *Naming the Powers*, p. 107.

16 Wink, *Unmasking the Powers*, p. 69.

17 See Claus Westermann, *Isaiah 40–66: A Commentary*, tr. David M. G. Stalker, Old Testament Library (London: SCM Press, 1969), pp. 100, 337, 367.

18 See page 79. Jesus quoted a prophecy of Third Isaiah (*Isaiah 61:1–2*).

19 Stephen Lea, Paul Webley and Catherine Walker, "Psychological factors in consumer debt: money management, economic socialisation, and credit use", *Journal of Economic Psychology* 16 (1995), p. 700.

20 *Deuteronomy 23:19*; *Leviticus 25:35–6*. Jesus was also uncompromising in his teaching about the virtue of giving generously and without expecting anything in return: "If you lend only where you expect to be repaid, what credit is there in that? Even sinners lend to each other to be repaid in full. But you must . . . lend without expecting any return" (*Luke 6:34–5*). Although the law restricted the prohibition of interest to the community of Israel and allowed the charging of interest to foreigners, this distinction has not been maintained in Christian teaching, which teaches the unity and equality of all peoples in the sight of God.

21 Eichrodt, *Theology of the Old Testament*, Vol. 1, p. 97.

22 Brooke Harrington, *Capital without Borders: Wealth Managers and the One Percent* (Harvard: Harvard University Press, 2016), p. 229. The Society of Trust and Estate Practitioners is a particularly glaring example of the way the concept of a profession, one of the marks of which is high ethical standards, has been progressively devalued in the modern economy.

23 Forster, *Howards End*, pp. 298, 278.

24 See, for example, T. W. Manson, *Ethics and the Gospel* (New York: Scribner, 1961), pp. 15–17, 35. This solidarity is evidenced in *Hosea* chapters 1 and 2. Manson describes the practical outworking of this principle as "the imparting of kindness", where the strict demands of justice are surpassed by the need to show mercy to a fellow Israelite (pp. 37–9). Jesus, of course, extended this moral duty to all, irrespective of race or creed, as in (e.g.) the parable of the

Good Samaritan (*Luke 10:25–37*), which teaches that it is the fact of need alone that puts a claim on our love, not kinship or creed or status.

## Chapter 5

1 Tom Holland, *Dominion: The Making of the Western Mind* (London: Little Brown, 2019), pp. 385–6. I would argue also that the remarkable growth in scientific knowledge is an example of the Holy Spirit leading us into all truth, as Jesus promised (*John 16:13*). It is significant that Christian ministers were prominent among the early scientists, notably the Unitarian Joseph Priestley, one of the pioneers of modern chemistry.

2 Salman Rushdie, *Is Nothing Sacred?*, The Herbert Read Memorial Lecture, February 1990.

3 Richard Harries, *Being a Christian* (London: Mowbray, 1981), p. 23.

4 This translation draws on both the *Revised English Bible* and *New Jerusalem Bible*.

5 The parables of judgement recorded by Matthew include the Wheat and the Tares (*13:24–30*), the Dragnet (*13:47–50*), the Wedding Banquet (*22:1–14*), the Wise and Foolish Maidens (*25:1–13*), the Talents (*25:14–30*), and the Sheep and the Goats (*25:31–46*). In these last two parables Jesus sets out the standard of judgement, first for believers, and then for the world: believers will be judged by the way they have used the gifts God has given them, others by the extent of their compassion for those in need.

6 This view persists today, for example in the hymn "In Christ alone my hope is found", by Stuart Townend and Keith Getty, which contains the lines, "till on that cross as Jesus died,/the wrath of God was satisfied", an error spoiling an otherwise beautiful devotional hymn. A better wording would be: " . . . the love of God was magnified".

7 See, for example, Philip Cushman, "Why the Self Is Empty: toward a historically situated psychology", *American Psychologist* 45:5 (1990), p. 600, and the survey of recent psychological writing to which he refers.

8 Cushman, "Why the Self Is Empty", p. 600.

9 Williams, *Being Human*, p. 33. In chapter 2 Williams explores very helpfully what it means to be a person. See also his Theos Lecture, "The Person

and the Individual", 1 October 2012, <https://www.theosthinktank.co.uk/comment/2012/10/09/theos-lecture-transcript>, accessed 4 April 2020.

10 The phrase is that of Malcolm Brown in "Anglican Social Theology Tomorrow", in Brown (ed.), *Anglican Social Theology*, p. 184, referring to Jessica Martin's Prologue to *The Report of the House of Bishops' Working Group on Human Sexuality* (London: Church House Publishing, 2013). See further Thomas Spragens, Jr, *The Irony of Liberal Reason* (Chicago: University of Chicago Press, 1981).

11 Moltmann, *Theology of Hope*, pp. 285–6.

12 The phrase comes from Williams, *Being Human*, p. 74.

13 The Doctrine Commission of the Church of England, *The Mystery of Salvation: The Story of God's Gift* (London: Church House Publishing, 1995), pp. 38 & 34 respectively.

14 Richard Sennett, *The Corrosion of Character: The Personal Consequences of Work in the New Capitalism* (New York: Norton, 1998), p. 10.

15 Sennett, *The Corrosion of Character*, pp. 15–21.

16 Cushman, "Why the Self Is Empty", p. 602.

17 Christopher Jamison OSB, *Finding Sanctuary: Monastic Steps for Everyday Life* (London: Weidenfeld & Nicolson, 2006), p. 78.

18 Jamison, *Finding Sanctuary*, p. 27.

19 Alan M. Suggate, "The Temple Tradition", in Brown (ed.), *Anglican Social Theology*, p. 39 (referring to the work of Thomas Spragens, Jr mentioned in note 10 above).

20 The discussion was reported by Christopher Lamb in *The Tablet*, 4 April 2009, pp. 4–5, "Beyond Capitalism".

21 Christopher Jamison is quoted from the 2005 BBC TV series *The Monastery*. He explores the meaning of humility in *Finding Sanctuary*, p. 91.

22 Widely attributed to Charles Dubois (1804–67), the Belgian naturalist, but the correct attribution seems to be to Charles Du Bos (1882–1939), the French literary critic.

23 Macquarrie, *Christian Hope*, p. 20.

24 The change was prompted by questions about the fate of those, especially the young, who died in the Maccabean rebellion against Israel's oppressors. The answer was that "the King of the universe will raise us up to a life everlastingly made new, since it is for his laws that we are dying" (*2 Maccabees 7:9*). The

change is rooted in the simple demand for justice that is characteristic of Hebrew religion.

25 Tom Baker, "' . . . and the Life Everlasting'? Some Personal Reflections", *Theology* 86/10 (1983), pp. 425–33.

26 Baker, "' . . . and the Life Everlasting'?", p. 430. Baker's argument is rooted in the same demand for justice that first gave rise to the belief in resurrection—see note 24 above.

27 Baker, "' . . . and the Life Everlasting'?", p. 427. Baker was taking issue with Don Cupitt, *Taking Leave of God* (London: SCM Press, 1980).

28 Resurrection speaks of the survival of the whole person, as we see in Jesus, not the survival of some supposed immortal element, nor survival in a different bodily form. The biblical image is of an en-souled body, or an embodied soul; the two are inseparable aspects of the person.

29 He says the seed has to die before it can come to life as the plant. Seeds do not die; they are transformed and grow.

30 Two approachable philosophical discussions I have found helpful are John Macquarrie, *Christian Hope*, pp. 112ff., and Helen Oppenheimer, *Looking Before and After* (London: Collins Fount, 1988).

31 T. S. Eliot, "East Coker", *Four Quartets*, p. 27.

32 T. S. Eliot, "Little Gidding", *Four Quartets*, p. 48.

33 St John of the Cross, *The Ascent of Mount Carmel*, 2:22.

## Chapter 6

1 See, for example, in the reply of the Chief Priest and scribes to King Herod when he enquired where the Messiah was to be born: "At Bethlehem in Judea, for this is what the prophet wrote: 'Bethlehem in the land of Judah, you are by no means least among the rulers of Judah: for out of you shall come a *ruler* to be the *shepherd* of my people Israel" (*Matthew 2:4–6*, quoting *Micah 5:2*, emphasis added).

2 In the Bible a *charism* is a gift of the Holy Spirit, and a charismatic person is one possessed by the Spirit. The modern use of the term to describe a powerful, attractive, and winning personality is a derogation from the biblical understanding, seeing the gift as originating with the individual, rather than with God.

3 Eichrodt, *Theology of the Old Testament*, Vol. 1, p. 437.

4 Marsh, *Saint John*, p. 394.

5 "This word of the Lord came to me: 'Prophesy, O man, against the rulers of Israel. Prophesy and say to them: You shepherds, these are the words of the Lord God: Woe betide Israel's shepherds who care only for themselves! . . . I am against the shepherds and shall demand from them an account of my sheep. I shall dismiss those shepherds from tending my flock . . . Now I myself shall take thought for my sheep and search for them . . . and rescue them'" (*Ezekiel 34:1, 2, 10–12*).

6 The sheepfold was almost certainly an enclosed courtyard of a house, used as a fold for the sheep, which makes sense of the idea that thieves and robbers might climb in some other way. It is also likely that more than one flock was kept there, which explains the existence of the gatekeeper, and the way that the sheep knew their own shepherd, and he knew them.

7 Marsh, *Saint John*, pp. 396–7.

8 William Temple, *Readings in St John's Gospel* (London: Macmillan, 1968), p. 203.

9 This verse is variously translated. I have used the *King James Version* as it reflects the words of the antiphon. The *New International Version* similarly talks of "what is desired by all nations". The *Douai-Rheims Bible* is emphatically messianic: "the desired of all nations shall come." Other modern translations offer quite a different meaning, e.g. "the treasure of all nations will come" (*Revised English Bible/New Revised Standard Version*), and "the treasures of all the nations shall flow in" (*Jerusalem Bible*).

10 This meaning is reflected in some versions of the antiphon, e.g. "O King of the nations, and their desire . . . " (*Common Worship*).

11 <https://www.un.org/en/charter-united-nations/>.

12 Thomas Traherne, *Centuries of Meditations I*.

13 Thomas Traherne is quoted from Denise Inge (ed.), *Happiness and Holiness: Thomas Traherne and his Writings* (Norwich: Canterbury Press, 2008), pp. 128–9.

14 Inge (ed.), *Happiness and Holiness*, p. 108. The idea that God *wants* imports the notion of feeling that runs counter to conceptions of God as unmoved or, to use the theological term, impassible. The difficulty is lessened, if not removed (Inge suggests), if we follow Helen Oppenheimer's view that impassibility should be thought of as being "unshaken" rather than "unmoved".

15 Walter Wink, *Engaging the Powers: Discernment and Resistance in an Age of Domination* (Minneapolis: Fortress Press, 1992), p. 13.

16 All the main religions have resorted to violence. In Christianity the Crusades and the Inquisition are obvious examples. Islam was spread through battle, a violent legacy that is seen in Islamist militants today. Similarly, Hindus in India and Buddhists in Myanmar resort to violence against those of different faiths who are perceived as a threat.

17 Otto Kaiser, *Isaiah 13–39: A Commentary*, tr. R. A. Wilson, Old Testament Library (London: SCM Press, 1980), pp. 248ff. Kaiser suggests that of the whole prophecy, *Isaiah 28:14–22, vv. 14–16aα and 17b–18* are the words of Isaiah himself, while *16aβ–17a* (the cornerstone prophecy) and *17b–22* are the work of the redactor.

18 For example: the Law, the Temple, Jerusalem, the Messiah, and the remnant of believers (Kaiser, *Isaiah 13–39*, p. 253).

19 Robert J. Schreiter, *Reconciliation: Mission and Ministry in a Changing Social Order* (Maryknoll, NY: Orbis Books, 1992), pp. 55–6.

20 Schreiter, *Reconciliation*, p. 26.

21 Schreiter, *Reconciliation*, p. 58.

22 Wink, *Engaging the Powers*, p. 323.

23 Donald Nicholl, *The Testing of Hearts: A Pilgrim's Journal* (London: Marshall, Morgan & Scott, Lamp Press, 1989), p. 178.

24 Rowan Williams, *Holy Living: The Christian Tradition for Today* (London: Bloomsbury Continuum, 2017), p. 66. Also in Rowan Williams, *The Way of St Benedict* (London: Bloomsbury Continuum, 2020), p. 23.

25 Thus Pope Francis has said that peace is not about a negotiated settlement, but about creating "a new and promising synthesis", which is the work of the Spirit (*Evangelii Gaudium*, 230).

26 *Ezra 10:3* records the decision of the Israelites to put away their foreign wives and their children. This decision and other religious reforms amounted to a complete repudiation of the universal vision of Isaiah of Babylon, which had come to him during the Exile.

27 There is much scholarly support for the view that neither *Ephesians* nor *Colossians* was written by Paul. However, these letters clearly bear the imprint of his theology, and—in line with common practice—I ascribe them to him.

28 See also *Colossians 1:21–2*: "Formerly you yourselves were alienated from God, his enemies in heart and mind, as your evil deeds showed. But now

by Christ's death in his body of flesh and blood God has reconciled you to himself, so that he may bring you into his own presence, holy and without blame or blemish."

29 John Macquarrie, *The Faith of the People of God* (London: SCM Press, 1972), p. 10, quoting *Colossians 3:11*.

## Chapter 7

1 Macquarrie, *Christian Hope*, p. 68.

2 Some of Matthew's texts are appropriate, e.g. the reference to Bethlehem as Jesus' birthplace (*Matthew 2:6*), but others are not, like the Emmanuel prophecy and his concluding reference, "He shall be called a Nazarene" (*Matthew 2:23*). There is no such text; it is probably a reference to *Isaiah 11:1*, where the Hebrew word *nezer*, meaning "branch", seems to have been seized on by Matthew because of its similarity to Nazareth, but it does not support his meaning.

3 The meaning of the Emmanuel prophecy in *Isaiah 7:14* is hotly disputed: who were the woman and her child? However, a precise identity is not necessary for the prophecy to have meaning; any young woman about to have a child would serve the purpose, because Isaiah is using the child primarily as a measure of time: by the time a child soon to be born has reached maturity, the threat will be over. God is with Israel, and Ahaz should trust him! In the background to Isaiah's warning to King Ahaz was the threat to Judah from Syria and Ephraim, and in the longer term from Assyria, from whom Ahaz was seeking protection. For a succinct discussion of the prophecy, see Kaiser, *Isaiah 1–12*, pp. 96ff.

4 Quoted by C. E. B. Cranfield, in his article "Love" in Richardson (ed.), *Theological Wordbook of the Bible*, pp. 131–6, at p. 135, referring to Karl Barth's *Church Dogmatics*, 1/2, p. 417.

5 The phrase comes from Dorr, *Spirituality and Justice*, p. 88.

6 Cranfield, "Love", p. 132.

7 "Hark! the herald angels sing", verse 2: "Pleased as man with us to dwell,/ Jesus, our Emmanuel".

8 Schillebeeckx, *Jesus in our Western Culture*, p. 18.

9 These are the four basic meanings conveyed by seven different terms: *storge*—the natural affection between parents and children; *philia*—loving friendship; *ludus*—playful affection; *eros*—romantic love; *pragma*—mature love, including patience, tolerance, and compromise; *philautia*—self-love; and *agape*—selfless, unconditional love.

10 Schillebeeckx, *Jesus in our Western Culture*, pp. 5–6.

11 Peter Selby, *Grace and Mortgage* (London: Darton, Longman & Todd, 1997), p. 63.

12 Cranfield, "Love", p. 136.

13 *The Tablet*, 4 April 2020, p. 2.

14 Ibid. Pope Francis is quoted from his sermon on 29 March 2020.

15 Sen, *The Idea of Justice*, p. 173.

16 Wright, *Simply Good News*, pp. 97–8 (online version).

17 Doctrine Commission, *The Mystery of Salvation*, p. 35.

18 Doctrine Commission, *The Mystery of Salvation*, p. 31.

19 Marsh, *Saint John*, p. 428.

20 In *Christus Victor* (1931) Gustaf Aulén presents "an historical study of the three main types of the idea of the atonement" and their deficiencies. Although written many years ago, it remains one of the most approachable and cogent accounts. The title refers to the belief that on the cross, Christ achieved the victory over sin.

21 Schillebeeckx, *Jesus in our Western Culture*, p. 23.

22 Alan Richardson, *Creeds in the Making: A Short Introduction to the History of Christian Doctrine* (London: SCM Press, 1935), chapter 5.

23 The same is true concerning Jesus' cry of dereliction from the cross, "My God, my God, why have you forsaken me?" I reflect on this in my Good Friday meditation, "The Hidden Depths of God", in Peter Sills, *A Word in Season* (Ely: Ely Cathedral Publications, 2001), p. 15.

24 Richardson, *Creeds in the Making*, pp. 109–10. Richardson's understanding follows that of the Swedish bishop Gustaf Aulén (see note 20). What they assert is a hope rather than a dogmatic certainty. Cf. John Burnaby, who argues that the freedom granted by love must include the possibility that some will finally reject God, and the eternal life that he offers. "Love cannot, because it will not compel the surrender of a single heart that holds out against it . . . Love never forces, and therefore there can be no certainty that it will overcome. But there may, and there must, be an unconquerable hope."

John Burnaby, *Amor Dei: A Study of the Religion of St Augustine* (London: Hodder & Stoughton, 1947), p. 318.

25 This and the following quotation are from: Henri J. M. Nouwen, *Making All Things New: An Introduction to the Spiritual Life* (Dublin: Gill & Macmillan, 1982), pp. 47–8.

26 Geoffrey Preston OP, *God's Way to be Man: Meditations on Following Christ through Scripture and Sacrament* (London: Darton, Longman & Todd, 1978), p. 23.

## Epilogue

1 Moltmann, *Theology of Hope*, p. 21.

2 Williams, *Faith in the Public Square*, p. 74.

3 Geoffrey Preston OP, *Hallowing the Time: Meditations on the Cycle of the Christian Liturgy* (London: Darton, Longman & Todd, 1980), p. 16.

4 Moltmann, *Theology of Hope*, p. 164.

5 Moltmann, *Theology of Hope*, p. 32.

6 Dorr, *Spirituality and Justice*, chapter 1.

7 Macquarrie, *Christian Hope*, pp. 111, 103.

8 Rowan Williams, *Being Disciples: Essentials of the Christian Life* (London: SPCK, 2016), p. 27.

9 Susan Beaumont, *Embracing Liminal Space* (Troy, MI: Susan Beaumont & Associates LLC, 2014; see also <http://www.susanbeaumont.com/embracing-liminal-space/>).

10 See page 30.

11 T. S. Eliot, "Burnt Norton", *Four Quartets*, p. 13.

Lightning Source UK Ltd.
Milton Keynes UK
UKHW021326010920
369163UK00011B/2405